ANTONIO
CARLUCCIO

A RECIPE FOR LIFE

hardie grant books

A Recipe for Life by Antonio Carluccio

First published in 2012 by Hardie Grant Books

Hardie Grant Books (UK)
Dudley House, North Suite
34–35 Southampton Street
London WC2E 7HF
www.hardiegrant.co.uk

Hardie Grant Books (Australia)
Ground Floor, Building 1
658 Church Street
Melbourne, VIC 3121
www.hardiegrant.com.au

British Library Cataloguing-in-Publication Data. A catalogue record
for this book is available from the British Library.

ISBN 978-1-74270-392-3

Commissioning Editor: Kate Pollard

Cover and internal design by Two Associates
Front cover photograph by John Davis
Typeset by SX Composing DTP, Rayleigh, Essex SS6 7XF
Colour reproduction by P2 Digital

Printed and bound China by 1010 Printing International Limited

10 9 8 7 6 5 4 3 2 1

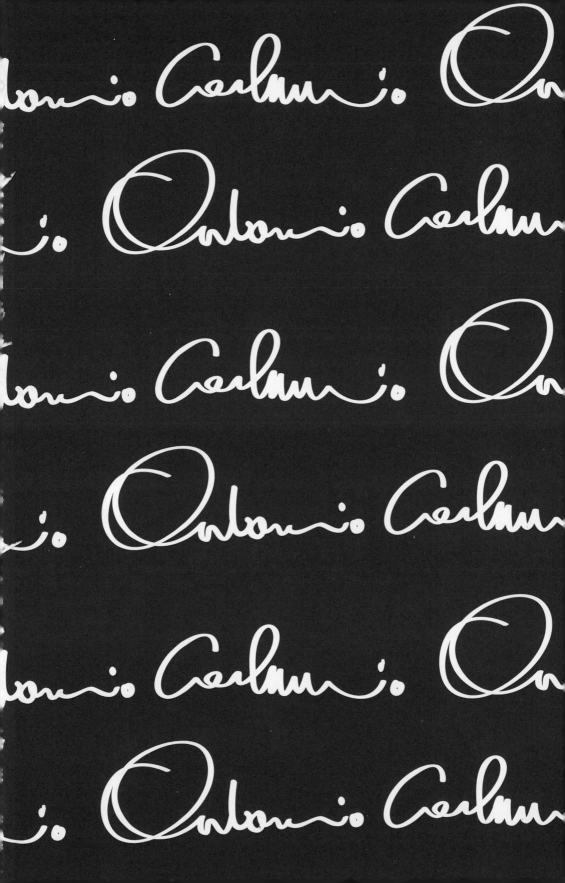

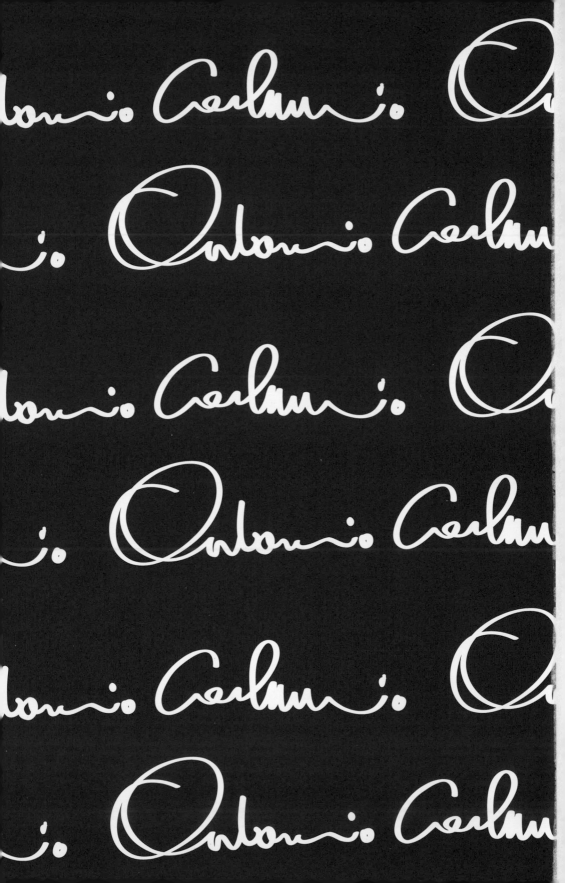

A RECIPE FOR LIFE

CONTENTS

Foreword

This is the real deal. In these memoirs Antonio Carluccio is as frank and honest about himself and his sometimes painful emotional life as he is direct about his sensual appreciation of food, wine and life's other pleasures.

This ebullient Italian cook and writer has been my friend for a long time, and I knew a good deal about his passion for mushrooms, about his success as a restaurateur in Neal Street, Covent Garden, about the chain of Carluccio Caffè (*trattorie*-cum-delicatessens) he built up, and about his many delightful and always instructive television series. But until reading his book I did not know about the melancholy and terrible depressions my jovial friend has suffered, about the attempts on his own life, or the failed relationships. Antonio has always contrived, until now, to show us his sunny side.

This, though, shines so brilliantly, and the story of his life is so rich and full of interest that his autobiography is compulsive reading – and a very good and elegant read it is too! I first read it in one sitting, before going back to reread and relish some of the passages about menus he has cooked and eaten, the places he has been to and lived in, and the people he has met and loved – especially the women. Antonio is a man who genuinely likes women, as much as he adores fresh, silky tagliatelle or beautiful, aromatic *porcini*.

This Italian has such a keen appreciation of the good things of life that he could almost be French. I fondly remember the time when a journalist invited Antonio and me to a competitive lunch – French culture versus Italian culture, Raymond Blanc versus Antonio Carluccio. To the journalist's dismay, we complimented each other on our respective nation's cultural and gastronomic achievements. Her frustration showed as she wrote that we kept patting each other's cheeks and kissing each other, and laughing and chatting, both in our broken English accents, throughout the entire meal.

Intelligent, erudite and analytical – all desirable, even necessary qualities in a memoirist – Antonio is also entertaining. Born in Southern Italy, he is now seventy-five, so can remember World War II, and has a good deal to say about it, as he does about regional differences in his native land. Those who think Britain is the only country where accents matter to one's social position will be startled by this book, almost as much as anyone (if there is any such person) who still thinks that Italian food consists of pizza and spaghetti Bolognese. His take on pre-War local politics in Italy is eye-opening, and he examines his (and my own) much-beloved British hosts with a nonetheless beady eye. His reflections are as full of interest as they are amusing.

Antonio's odyssey has been as unusual as his hobbies (mushroom-hunting and whittling). He has lived not only in Italy and Britain, but also in Austria and Germany. Like me, he is a self-taught cook, yet he deserves a great deal of the credit for persuading us in Britain that the merits of Italian food can be summed up in his own watchwords: minimum of fuss, maximum of flavour.

Above all, Antonio and I share a set of values, in both cases learned from our parents. We cherish and celebrate seasonality, freshness and sustainably produced ingredients. Antonio's attitude to food is as sincere, open and loving, as he is candid about his feelings. Bravo, Antonio!

You will love this book.

Raymond Blanc

Introduction

hy does anyone write their memoirs? It was a question I have asked myself several times while working on mine, as I thought long and hard about my life over the last seventy-five years. I have sometimes found it quite hard, revisiting sad times and making sense of difficult ones, even while it has also given me pleasure to remember old friends and happy times. What I did want to do was to look at what made me the man I am today, and those experiences that shaped my life and allowed me to take my place in the world. Many will know me as Carluccio the Italian cook, from my books and television shows and the Carluccio's Caffès that bear my name, but long before that I was Antonio the boy, coming of age in 1950's Italy, and Antonio the young man, leaving his family to live in Germany and finally, in the mid 1970s, arriving in England with my dog to make my home in London.

There are some things I know. I know that although I was raised in the north of Italy, my heart and soul are rooted in southern Italy where I was born. I also know that I am a traveller and an explorer at heart, both emotionally and physically, and that journey has taken me far.

Even as a teenager I knew I wasn't conformist, but would always make my own way, living and learning and always true to myself. I know, too that my basic character is built mostly on my sensitivity to my surroundings and emotional response to life in all its sensual beauty, whether that comes from enjoying the sun on my face, preparing food with my hands, smelling the earth on a freshly picked mushroom, painting a picture on canvas, savouring a slice of cheese or whittling a hazel walking stick. First and foremost I live through my senses, without artifice or education – *in natura veritas* – and this I discover in retrospect has served me well.

And, looking back, I can see that it is always around food that my professional life has both evolved and revolved as I left my homeland and became, over time, an ambassador for Italian food abroad. It is hard to remember now that there was a time when the BBC could broadcast a television documentary about the harvesting of spaghetti grown on trees, as they did for an April Fool's joke in 1957, and people believed them! Italian food, in all its regional and seasonal simplicity, was unknown here then. By the time I arrived in England eighteen years later, dried spaghetti was still only found in the Italian delicatessens of Soho and other areas of the UK where the Italian diaspora had made its home.

For me, cooking the food of my Italian heritage was a natural thing to do, it was what I had learnt in my mother's kitchen and it was the food I enjoyed: it was a pleasure to share it with friends and family, long before it became my passport to a professional life. The same with my passion for mushrooms, and I was delighted to discover when I came to England that the same abundance found in Italy could be found here, and I could happily forage for them even while they were not yet as prized by others as by myself.

My philosophy of food is much like my philosophy of life, to look for and make the best of beautiful ingredients: minimum of fuss, maximum of flavour. There is no need for artifice or glamorising if the basics are right. Perfection already exists in what is there, to be celebrated and enjoyed in its own right and there is no need to mess unnecessarily with this. On one occasion I was served fresh oysters embellished with a sweet chocolate sauce by a two-star Michelin chef in Turin. Why? It was disgusting and did no favours to either the oyster or the chocolate.

This simple perfection in food is what I sought to achieve first at home, and then at the Neal Street Restaurant in London's Covent Garden that I ran for twenty-six years, affording me a wonderful platform to develop my ideas and expertise. And then I took this further with the Carluccio Caffès. It has been an amazing journey to watch the evolution of a real appreciation for Italian food worldwide, to which I have been proud to contribute. This appreciation is not limited to the UK either, but also extends to Australia where I have enjoyed the warmest of welcomes on numerous occasions, and in India.

Years ago, while I still owned the Neal Street Restaurant, I got to know Camellia Panjabi, a visionary woman with a great taste for food. Born in Mumbai she studied economics at Cambridge before working as marketing director at the Taj Mahal group of hotels in India, for whom I provided consultancy on Italian food. Whenever she came to England, Camellia would bring her own chillies from home, claiming that she could never find ones hot enough for her taste outside India. At the time, I had sourced a collection of red, yellow and green chillies from the flower market for use as decoration at the restaurant. I took a handful and prepared a paste of these with garlic, salt and vinegar in an emulsion of olive oil, for her to taste. As her eyes pricked with tears she agreed, yes, this was hot enough even for her! In the same way that I wanted to introduce regional Italian food to a discerning clientele, she sought to do the same with regional Indian food, first opening the Bombay Brasserie restaurant in London's fashionable Kensington with her sister Namita in 1982, and then Chutney Mary in

Chelsea in 1990, before Veeraswamy, Amaya and then the Masala Zone restaurants so popular today.

The Taj Hotel group was not the only group of hotels to which I provided consultancy in India. Another was the Park Hotel group, with hotels in Delhi, Bangalore, Mumbai, Chennai and Kolkata. In 2005, I was asked by Prya Paul, entrepreneur and hotelier responsible for the group, to train their chefs and, in Bangalore, we collaborated on an Italian restaurant, Italia and the chef, Mandahar, came to train with me in London. For three years running it was voted Best Italian Restaurant in India. This was followed by another collaboration, and the opening of Mist, the acclaimed Italian restaurant in the Conran designed Park Hotel in Delhi.

The same appreciation for good, fresh ingredients and simple preparation exists in India, so there was a natural synergy between us. Through working with Prya I also met the very successful Indian-English novelist Anita Nair, who had been creative director at an advertising agency in Bangalore before her first book was published, and we enjoyed many long conversations about the complexity and mentality of the appreciative Indian palate, which helped me in my exploration of how Italian cuisine might work best in India. Getting to know India, and many Indians both there and at home, through an appreciation of food, has been a delight.

I had the same experience when I did a stint at the Mandarin Oriental hotel in Hong Kong, where my recipes were cooked for a ten-day promotion, as Italian food is very much appreciated there, too. The additional pleasure of this trip, for me, was the chance to eat wonderful Chinese food – my second favourite cuisine after Italian!

Food was also my passport to exploring the excellence of food in Australia and New Zealand, where there is a large contingent of expatriate Italians, all very successful with vineyards, restaurants, agricultural products and also industry. I always feel at home when

I visit, not least because of the warm welcome given me. I had one memorable meal when I visited the Zema family near Adelaide, who invited me to their home for a feast of Calabrese specialities. They had managed to source wild quails, almost unheard of now as most are commercially reared for the culinary market, a delicacy I had almost forgotten. Here in Adelaide I discovered Italians growing prickly pears, chestnuts, walnuts and olives, and cultivating excellent wines, in order to reproduce authentic Italian food.

I also met Vince, who was from Perth and to my mind possibly the best butcher in Australia, because of his commitment to butchering his own meat and producing homemade sausages, salamis, prosciutto and lardons in the Italian way. The devotion from ex-pat Italians to this sort of authenticity, thousands of miles from 'home' in Australia and New Zealand, is another reason why I feel so at home there, and seeing first hand at the food festivals, to which I am often invited, what is possible. I have been welcomed there by the likes of gastronome Simon Johnson, with whom I concur that: 'Quality is my obsession, uniqueness my passion, flavour my primary objective'. Also, the excellent and redoubtable Stephanie Alexander and Maggie Beer, who have done so much to promote excellence in food in Australia, plus the legendary Peter Clemenger and the very mad but delightful restaurateur, vigneron and patron of arts and architecture, Ronnie (Rinaldo) Di Stasio – known as the godfather of Melbourne restaurateurs! There are many others, of course, who are all part of what makes any visit to the antipodes such a pleasure for me.

As well as all the pleasure and success my love for food and Italian food in particular has brought me in life, I have also known great sadness. The death of my younger brother when he was thirteen and I was twenty-three, was the greatest of lifelong losses. I am sad, too that I wasn't able to have children of my own, marrying as I did a woman who had already completed her family, although I still very much enjoy seeing my step-daughter Lucy and her children. I am so glad, though, that after fifty-five years I still have the friendship of my first love Inge, who went on to marry happily and now has two beautiful daughters of her own. But I cannot pretend that it is a happiness not a little tinged with envy.

My sadness has often played out in self-destructive ways, as it's not in my nature to inflict how I am feeling on others. Indeed, I would go to great lengths, often at my most distressed, to keep how I was feeling from those around me, telling jokes and playing the convivial host when I felt quite desperate inside. This evoked great anxiety and depression in me and, although I am not alone in this, I felt quite isolated and alone even when I was amongst company or in my marriage. Luckily, with time, I now have more insight and am better able to manage how I feel. For example, I realised that drinking whisky exacerbated the feelings of euphoria and the depressive slide that followed. This sea-sawing of mood is terribly destabilising and destructive and now, in order to prevent it happening, I no longer drink. Luckily because I had no addiction to alcohol, it was as simple as that to stop, to avoid this effect on my mood.

In writing this book I have been true to the events that happened in my life and also my feelings about them, so inevitably there have been occasions when I have had to reflect on times when all was not entirely rosy. On balance however, even though it might have made life less painful to have lived it less emotionally, approaching life in this way also creates the potential for moments of great happiness and joy. My motto could easily be that it is better to 'Live one day as a lion, than a hundred days as a sheep'.

Overall, in spite of leaving my parental home without any strategy of what to become or what to achieve, I feel relatively content now that my life has followed a good path. Looking back I see now that there were moments when I could have taken a more hard-nosed route, taken advantage of someone or other in order to improve my own position in some material way, or even sell my soul, putting financial gain before principle. I was never motivated by a desire for great material wealth or celebrity, but to achieve what I could in a way that my temperament, inner belief and integrity allowed, and now I am very glad for that.

There is an Italian saying, *l'arte di arrangiarsi* – the art of getting by – without cheating or doing someone else down, but by making the best of things. Of course when I was twenty years old, I thought I knew everything and was arrogant enough, as all young men are, to think no one could teach me anything. But life taught me differently and I now know that by being open to ideas, people and opportunities, I was able to forge a life that was true to me, in spite of its ups and downs. And with my hand on my heart I can say, this is my story and I am happy with it.

CHAPTER ONE

A Cook is Born

 was born on Monday 19 April 1937, in the town of Vietri sul Mare on the south-west coast of Italy, son of Giovanni, the town's stationmaster, and Maria Carluccio. 'Monday's child is fair of face', the saying goes, and I was the baby of the family until my brother Enrico was born ten years later. At first it was my brother Carlo, five years older than me, who became my closest ally, playmate and carer, and I did the same later for Enrico, my mother already having more than enough to keep her busy. Keeping us all fed, clothed, washed and cared for, without the labour-saving devices of today, was a full-time job and, with no other help, we children soon learnt to take care of each other and ourselves. The Carluccio family now numbered seven, living in the stationmaster's house in this beautiful seaside town.

Today it is a UNESCO World Heritage site, and with good reason. Vietri sul Mare is not called one of the pearls of the Amalfi coast for nothing. It's a spectacular spot, south of Naples and Mount Vesuvius – quiet since its last eruption in 1944 – overlooking the Gulf of Salerno. The first of thirteen beautiful seaside villages along this spectacular stretch of coastline, it sits below the majestic San Liberatore and Falerio mountains. Their steep, terraced hillsides overlook a natural harbour with a busy marina on the Tyrrhenian Sea. Today Vietri sul Mare has around 8500 inhabitants and a thriving tourist trade, although at heart it is little changed from the place where I was born.

The village was then, and remains now, a delightful spot. Vines, olive and citrus trees grow on the well-tended terraces that step down to the white walls and terracotta-tiled roofs of the houses, set against the backdrop of the deep blue sea; the summers here are hot, the winters mild. In 1937, Vietri was home to around 2000 people who benefited then, as now, from its wonderful climate and excess of delicious foodstuffs that were taken for granted – tomatoes, aubergines, olives, lemons, the famous mozzarella cheese from this area, and a plethora of fresh Mediterranean fish.

The dome of the seventeenth-century Church of San Giovanni Battista, built in late-Neapolitan Renaissance style on the site of its tenth-century predecessor, is covered with blue and yellow tin-glazed majolica tiles, which glitter in the sun in celebration of the town's ceramic tile industry. Production of these wonderful, internationally famous tiles has contributed to the village's prosperity since the fifteenth century – they come in bright, deep shades of blue, red, yellow and green, colours that are typical of the area. The local museum has many outstanding antique examples. On 24 June, the town's feast day, the bells of San Giovanni Battista's adjoining *campanile* ring loud enough to wake the dead.

The marina is full of boats, many of them fishing vessels from which the daily catch is brought ashore. However, if you want to take a ferry to Olbia in Sardinia, Messina in Sicily, or even further afield to Valletta in Malta, you have to go from Salerno. Ferries have always been a feature of this busy seaside place, but back in 1937 it was the railways that ruled in Italy. After the creation of the Ferrovie dello Stato (State Railway) in 1905, and from 1922 to the beginning of the war in 1939, investment in an ambitious modernisation programme ensured that Italian railways were the envy of the world. In the year of my birth, the new electrified mainline from Milan to Naples (via Bologna, Florence and Rome) meant that specially designed trains reached speeds of 201 km/h for the first time. So proud was Benito Mussolini of this new model, the Elettrotreno 200, with its sleek steel superstructure and aerodynamic lines designed in the wind tunnels of the Politecnico di Torino's engineering department, that he sent one to the Universal Exposition in New York in 1939, and a new world record for a train speed of 203 km/h. was recorded. The rumour was that Mussolini himself was at the controls at the time of this record-breaking event, but this story probably comes from the same source as the one that claims he made the Italian trains run on time. The truth is that the Italian railways and their punctuality became something of a propaganda tool for the fascists, probably due to Mussolini's attempts at the time to drum up popular support.

There is no doubt though that in the year I was born the railways of Italy were in their heyday, and being a stationmaster was a prestigious and well-respected job, on a par with being the town's doctor or mayor. Today, even though the railway station still exists in Vietri, it is a small local stop with most mainline trains running via its close neighbour, the larger Salerno.

It is, however, testament both to my clever father's desire to provide for his family and his love for my mother that he joined the *Ferrovie dello Stato*. Papa had done his obligatory service after school in the military department of the railways, and through this connection had met and fallen in love with Maria Annunziatina, daughter of a *prefetto,* or state representative, of the railways. She was very young when they met, and just sixteen when they married. There had been no previous association with the railway on Papa's side – his family had a successful book-binding business in Benevento. Although those in the bookbinding trade were considered artisans, they were highly regarded, working as they did with fine leather, embossing and tooling and binding important books, and his family had an excellent reputation and its own successful shop. But Papa left the book-binding in the care of his two elder sisters, turned his back on the business and joined the railway as a *capo stazione* for the love of my mother and probably out of courtesy to his new father-in-law. It might have been a bit of a wrench for him, but I think he felt that working for the state railway would offer him a better chance of creating a secure future for his family, which explains why I and my five brothers and sisters were born in so many different places, the factor common to all of them being a railway station.

At first Papa remained in his hometown of Benevento, fifty kilometres inland and north-east of Naples, famous for its Roman antiquities and complete with a busy mainline station. Here my eldest sister Grazia was born in 1927. Giuseppe, always called Peppino, was born in Pignataro Maggiore in 1929, Papa having been posted there. The family then moved to yet another *stazione* at Prata, near Avellino, also home to my legendary maternal grandmother Nonna Giuseppina, managing to stay posted there long enough for both my sister Anna and my brother Carlo to be born in 1930 and 1932 respectively. Then the family moved to Vietri, where I was born. So far, even though there had been four moves, these had all been around the same area of southern Italy.

None of this meant anything to me, of course, and I have no memories of my early life in Vietri sul Mare because I was no more than seven months old when my father was posted to a new station. We upped sticks once more and left the mild Mediterranean winters of the south to travel to northern Italy, finding ourselves in the region of Piedmont, about sixty kilometres south-east of its capital Turin. Papa had accepted this new post believing that it might lead to better opportunities, although it also meant leaving behind the support of our family and friends, not to mention the benign climate of the south. We arrived at the stationmaster's house in Castelnuovo Belbo in November, to find snow on the ground and temperatures in the winter regularly reaching -20°C. It must have been quite a shock for my mamma with a babe-in-arms and four other children under the age of ten to care for.

Castelnuovo Belbo was a small town of around 1500 people when my father arrived to take up his position as stationmaster there. Historically it had been a Roman encampment on the banks of the river – *Castrum novum ad Belbum* – and a few ancient castle ruins still exist today in the via Romita. The fine town hall and the parish church of San Biagio, with its curious Baroque tower, are still there although the population of Castelnuovo today has shrunk to around 900 people.

In 1937, the station was a short distance from the town centre, on the line between Alessandria in the north and Nizza Monferrato to the south. Here we lived in an apartment on the first floor of the station house, the ticket office and waiting room below, overlooking the railway itself. It was not large: my parents had a room, my two sisters another, and we three boys shared. With only one bathroom, there was always a queue! But Papa's journey to work was a short one: just one flight down the stone staircase with its iron handrail. It also meant that lunchtime remained a family meal. My mother cooked every day for my father and my sisters and brothers, and we all sat down together, at least until we children were old enough for school.

One of my earliest memories of life at home – apart from the time I pulled a jug of boiling coffee off the stove; I still have a scar on my left arm from the burn – was of when my mother cooked pasta for my father's lunch. She would ask me to go down to the station platform to see if the train was running on time. When I saw it coming down the track I would run back upstairs to the kitchen to tell her and she would know to put the pasta on. Then, in exactly five minutes, my father would walk up the stairs and, by the time he had washed his hands and taken his seat at the table, the pasta was perfect. Freshly cooked, but al dente.

It was in these subtle ways that I began to learn about good food: that pasta, for instance, must not be left to stand but eaten straight away. Although my father didn't cook he knew about and appreciated good food, and especially my mother's cooking. Sometimes she would ask him to taste a *ragù* (pasta sauce) or something else she was making, and he would taste it then pause, purse his lips in concentration and say, 'A little more salt maybe?' or, 'A little more of this . . . or that . . . perhaps?' And she would nod and do as he suggested. Sometimes when we ate, she would say, 'Oh, this is not so good, I'm sorry, it's not turned out very well' – even when it was perfect, just to check our appreciation. And we would all chorus, 'No, no, Mamma – it's good, it's wonderful, don't worry!' to reassure her. Mealtimes were always family affairs where we caught up with each other and the news of the day, things were discussed, jokes enjoyed and arguments settled. You can share your differences and your reasons for being happy when you eat together. I still believe that's very important.

If the climate was tougher in the north than in the south, it didn't bother us as children although it must have been hard for my mother, who was originally from the town of Pescara, on the beautiful Adriatic coast of Abruzzi, halfway down the left side of the 'leg' of Italy. It was she who had to manage all the domestic arrangements – shopping, cooking, cleaning, clothing, school – while my father was earning the money to support us. We lived surrounded by the farms and vineyards and woods that covered the rolling hills around us. Soon these became both our playground and hunting ground; with the war approaching, we would soon have to learn to barter and forage for food there like everyone else. But I never felt we were poor, underprivileged or malnourished in any way – Mamma was a genius at managing the family income, and she and my father made a good team. Although I knew that we children came first in her heart, she was a good and loving wife. Family, for both my parents, lay at the heart of everything.

When the Germans invaded Poland on 1 September 1939, the war took off although it took a little longer to reach Castelnuovo. Rumblings had been heard for some time in Europe and it was probably these that had prompted my father to make his move north when he did. Although Italy was one of the Axis powers allied to Germany, it remained neutral for the time being. Believing the country to be ill prepared for war, Mussolini's Under-secretary for War Production, Carlo Favagrossa, had stated that Italy couldn't possibly be ready until October 1942. The huge national debt – 93 billion lire when Mussolini came to power – had increased to 405 billion lire in the ensuing twenty-one years. After the German invasion of France, and in the mistaken belief that the fighting wouldn't take long to be over and would not therefore be too costly, Mussolini declared war on both Britain and France on 10 June 1940. At three years old, this meant nothing to me – and at that point probably meant nothing much to the rest of my family either because my father, as a railway employee responsible for a mainline station, wasn't conscripted.

Piedmont is surrounded on three sides by the Alps, and borders France, Switzerland and the Italian regions of Lombardy, Liguria and the Aosta Valley. Landlocked, unlike much of the rest of Italy, it is the second largest of Italy's regions, after Sicily, and over 40 per cent of the terrain is mountainous, with the rest either hills or river plains. Geographically it is very well disposed to growing not only vines – with over half of its 700-square kilometres given over to vineyards, making it one of the great wine-making areas of Italy – but also rice, and to producing milk and great cheeses. While the south of Italy is celebrated gastronomically for its Mediterranean diet rich in olive oil, tomatoes and fish, the north of Italy has its own delights and specialities –

truffles, chestnuts, rice, cheese – producing typical northern dishes like *risotto ai funghi,* or *Brasato al Barolo,* a beef stew made with the local Barolo wine, or the tiny ravioli stuffed with meat sauce and sage and known as *Agnolotti del Plin,* as well as a diverse range of cheese. These include *Taleggio, Gorgonzola, Toma Piemontese, Murazzano, Grana Padono* – and the traditional *Fonduta,* influenced by the Swiss fondue, made with *Fontina* cheese from the Aosta valley. Small wonder then that I love food, after cutting my first teeth on simpler, domestic versions of such regional delicacies.

My mamma's kitchen, although not large or luxurious in any way, was the heart and soul of our home. Various pots and pans hung on the walls along with drying herbs and onions, but the centrepiece was the cooking stove fuelled by wood or coal, whatever we could get, a bit like an Aga. The heat of this was very variable unlike ovens today with their thermostats, although my mother could judge it well. Attached to one side of the stove was a water container, which was kept constantly filled with around five to six litres of water so that there was a supply for washing and cooking. In winter the kitchen was always warm and cosy.

Even though there were open rings on top of the stove on which you could boil the water for pasta and rice, and cook vegetables, a lot of things were cooked in the oven. One of my earliest memories is of collecting sweet chestnuts from the woods with my brother, bags and bags of them. They'd expand as they cooked, splitting their jackets, and we'd have to prick the shiny outer cases to prevent them from exploding in the heat of the oven. I learnt from my brother how to juggle them from hand to hand to avoid burning my fingers, until they were cool enough to peel and eat. When they were in season we would collect as many as we could, bringing them home to gorge on or else make into *marmellata di castagne* (chestnut jam), to store for the winter months. When the weather was freezing outside, my mother used to give us hot chestnuts to put in our pockets. We'd warm our hands on them as we walked to school, and later we would eat them.

Chestnuts were also a feature of All Saints' Day, 2 November, in the region in which I grew up. On this day it was the custom for every *trattoria* to celebrate the first chestnuts of the season by boiling them with bay leaves and salt, and serving them with a glass of red wine and the compliments of the house.

Although Mamma made all the bread that we ate, this wasn't baked at home. Every couple of days she would take flour and yeast and oil, and mix and knead the dough at home, and then this would be placed in a basket and covered with a warm clean cloth to be taken by my brother Carlo to the local baker's oven on the way to school on his bike. All the local families did this; it was traditional. Rather than baking bread at home, it made sense for everyone to use the bigger baker's oven. Mamma was renowned for her bread, a sort of heavier *ciabatta* (Italian for 'slipper', which is what it looks like) in style – so much so that the baker would always like to keep a small loaf of her bread, just for himself. Then Carlo would pick up our loaves on his way home again, and on the days this happened, I was greedy for that still-warm, first crust of fresh bread.

Mamma also made a wonderful sort of jam, *mostarda*, that we ate on the bread. This is traditional in the Piedmont area, using freshly pressed Barbera grape juice with fruit added to it – plums, pears, peaches, apricots, apples, figs – every possible sort you had to hand, and also walnuts. This would be cooked together with sugar in a huge copper cauldron, capable of holding fifty litres. It was placed over a wooden fire outside for up to twelve hours with everyone taking turns to stir it, to prevent any sticking and burning. The cauldron was so large that it would be positioned between two buffers at the end of the railway track, under which a fire was built. After it was cooked and reduced by about half, you were left with a delicious sweet brown mess of a jam that could be preserved in jars and stored for months. Into this we could dip a spoon or a knife to spread the *mostarda* on our buttered bread, or sometimes my mother would use it to make *crostata* or jam tart. This we would eat for our *merenda*, the teatime snack eaten long before supper when we would first come in ravenous after school or from foraging in the woods.

When I was old enough I started at the local *asilo* (nursery school), taken there each day by my brother Carlo. Here, lunch was never very substantial, usually something like a simple rice and cabbage soup. It was tasty but always the same, making me dream of, and appreciate, my mother's excellent cooking. We were so active, playing outside with each other and our friends, or walking or climbing in the hills, that we were always hungry. Mamma's wonderful jam was always there, to be spread on bread when we came home for tea. We took it for granted when really it was a marvellous treat.

On one occasion during the war, we had the *mostarda* simmering away on the fire when we heard the noise of a German reconnaissance plane flying overhead – we used to call this the *pippo* plane – and because this was during the curfew and after dark, we knew there would be trouble if they saw the fire burning. Anxious to protect our precious jam, instead of hurriedly putting out the fire we rushed to get a big, thick blanket and all stood around, holding it above the flames to hide them, while the jam continued to bubble away underneath and the unsuspecting plane flew by overhead!

Preserving food at the end of the summer, in readiness for use during the long, hard winters, was especially important during the war. So as well as making the jam, my mother would be kept very busy pickling and preserving, sterilising and bottling, the onions, peppers and mushrooms available locally, using vinegar and olive oil sent to us by our relatives in the south. She was always busy in the kitchen and my brothers and sisters and I would have to help, collecting, peeling, chopping and preparing food along with her.

By 1943 Italy had surrendered to the Allies. But in the mountainous north, close to the border with France, German forces combined with Mussolini's new fascist Italian Social Republic, and fighting continued in opposition to the Allies and the *Resistenza* of combined partisan fighters who supported them. Caught between the two – the German Army with their fascist supporters, and the partisans – were local people like my family, just trying to survive. This wasn't easy but, as my mamma always said, the opposing forces were just people like the rest of us. As the stationmaster's wife, she often found herself giving food to both hungry German soldiers (these were the Wehrmacht, not the SS) and partisans alike, although never at the same time. Both my parents realised that, in order to protect their family, it was important to appear supportive of both sides during that difficult time. So the Germans would come for lunch, the partisans for supper, and neither side made trouble for us. As a young boy, I discovered I was something of a mascot to both sides and soon learnt that if I smiled winningly I might be scooped up and fussed over and given chocolate, a rare treat in wartime Italy, or else my mother would be given some butter or other scarce item in appreciation of the meals she cooked for them.

Perhaps because of the war we were very much a community, working together with the local farmers, sharing what we had. Although I don't remember this, I believe that as a toddler I was such a favourite of one farmer's wife that she took little imprints of my feet in fresh plaster as a keepsake. Another farmer, the owner of a vineyard and wine company called Cossetti, thought our family was too large and offered to adopt me – an idea to which my mamma gave short shrift, telling him in no uncertain terms that I was unavailable for adoption! This didn't stop me playing in his wine cellar, where my presence was amiably tolerated. I used to love catching a thin stream of unfermented wine in my mouth as it leaked from the huge woodchip and canvas filter, so sweet and delicious. Inevitably, I once drank too much and it fermented in my stomach – not enough to make me drunk but it caused quite a tummy ache. After that I learnt to sneak rather less of it, and to ration my pleasure or suffer the consequences.

We children did what we could, each having our own role to play and contribution to make. As a very small boy, one of my household jobs, for example, was to collect some surplus fruit from the neighbouring farm every day, which we could eat for our dessert. Depending on the season, this might be grapes, peaches, pears, cherries or apples – sun-ripened and fresh, always excellent. There was also the tradition in the local vineyards of *racimolare* – which literally means 'to glean from the fields' – where the farmers would allow all the local people to come and retrieve the bunches of small grapes left behind at the end of the harvest. And as a community there was one annual event in which we all participated, and which was particularly enjoyable: the stripping of the corn.

Corn, or maize, was an important crop locally, as food for both humans and animals. It wasn't eaten then as you would have it today, boiled or barbecued and bitten off the cob. Instead we used the freshly ground maize to make polenta – an important staple of our diet – slowly simmering it with water until it thickened, and serving it as an accompaniment to *ragùs* of chicken, sausage, pork or rabbit. So the harvesting of maize was important to all of us. Once it was gathered, it needed to be stripped of its dry outside leaves before the husks, or cobs, could be put into a machine to strip them of the kernels, which would then be ground for maize or kept whole for animal feed during the winter. So a mountain of the harvested corn was piled into the courtyard of Marcolina, the local farm, and everyone, young and old, would gather together to strip the husks, piling the dried leaves to one side, the cobs to the other. It was a very social event, with lots of singing and drinking, and lasted all day, everyone working together.

I also learnt from a young age to gather what I could from the land, foraging in the woods in particular. In the summer I would gather the leaves of *rucola*, also known as wild rocket, which grew in abundance in the area where we lived. After I'd picked the peppery young leaves my mother would use them in her cooking, tossing them into salads, pasta or soup, or making a sort of pesto. I soon learnt to select only the bright green ones, discarding any that were yellowing or showing damage, already developing my eye for what was good under Mamma's keen-eyed supervision. Over the years I turned my increasingly discerning eye to wild asparagus and other delicacies, also pointed out to me by my mother.

She was less keen on us foraging for mulberries. The trees grew well in our area and were greatly appreciated because silk worms fed off their leaves and their cocoons were collected and sold on to silk manufacturers. Although not native to Italy but imported originally from Asia, the gnarled old trees grew well on the nearby farms. We were happy to help the farmers collect the cocoons when the time was right, and would then wait impatiently for the spiky fruit to ripen. When it did, we would collect as much as we could of it, eating it as we went along, smearing our fingers, faces and clothes with the lurid, dark purple juice. Afterwards it was impossible to get the stain out of our clothes. However hard I tried not to, I always managed to get some of the juice on my shirt or trousers, much to my mamma's displeasure. When we brought the fruit home it would be used for the *mostarda* but also for tarts, purees, syrups, juices, even a mulberry liqueur, or else bottled and preserved for the winter months.

On late-autumn mornings, thick with fog weaving mysterious shapes through the stark outlines of the leafless trees, I used to go out with Giuanin, a friend of my father, and his dog Fido, a black and white mongrel trained to look for truffles in the woods. Equipped with sturdy boots, for the ground was often rough, a small bag containing an orange for refreshment, and a *vanghetta* (a truffle hunter's hoe-like spade), we would walk through the woods. Fido's nose would snuffle frantically along the ground, able to pick out the scent of a truffle up to a metre below the soil's surface. Like all well-trained dogs, he was invaluable to the *trifolao*, or truffle hunter. When Fido located a precious white truffle, he would become highly excited in anticipation of his reward of a biscuit or piece of salami – *funghi* was of no interest to him – and would start digging up the soil, which was Giuanin's signal painstakingly to unearth the prize with the *vanghetta*, taking care not to bruise it. Then he would lovingly examine it, brush away any soil and place it in his bag. At the end of our day's endeavours, Giuanin would give me a small truffle and I was always very proud to bring it home for my family to share; a slither on some pasta here, or a shaving on some rice there, the flavour wonderfully intense. He also taught me to identify other mushrooms safely, and so began my lifelong passion for the subject.

At the time we also kept a few animals, as was traditional in the area, and for some reason – probably in return for a favour my father had been able to provide – a local farmer had given us two pigs, which we were fattening up on the scraps from our table. Cabbage leaves, beets, old bread and pasta ... nothing went to waste. The pig would provide us with meat to eat and cure, sausages and salamis, and lard to use in cooking. The fact that we had not one, but two pigs, housed in a shed next to the station, was not a problem until the partisans, themselves short of food, issued an order that that anyone with two pigs had to give them one. My father might as well have replied 'Over my dead body', because he was not prepared to give up such an important source of food for his family without a fight. He knew he had to take action before the partisans came for a pig. So, that very night, he sharpened his long knives and organised for the local butcher to come over. They turned the waiting room of the railway station into an improvised slaughter house.

Although this butchery was done in great haste and secrecy, however tightly I rammed my fingers into my ears or burrowed my head under my pillow, there was no disguising the awful squealing I could hear coming from downstairs as that poor pig met its end! Once that was over, they worked through the night to butcher and prepare the meat and clear away the evidence. The next day my mother set to work, producing large amounts of sausages, hams and lard, all preserved in salt. There was also a plateful of precious parts of the pig, like the liver, heart and kidneys, to be given as a gift to the farmer who had given us this valuable gift. Even the blood had been collected and made into a black pudding we would eat with onions – delicious! – or else into a sweet concoction called *sanguinaccio* by mixing it with cocoa powder, sugar, milk and eggs. Suffice to say that by the time the partisans turned up to claim it, Papa was able to deny all ownership or knowledge of a second pig, in spite of the bags under his eyes after his long night's work.

The killing of the pig in our own home didn't leave any bad memory for me, however. I understood the necessity and shared in the spoils. I saw dead bodies too, during the fighting around us, but one event in particular stands out in my mind with stark, horrendous clarity. I was six years old when the local farmer asked me to kill a kitten newly born to the farmyard cat. Usually, he would just bundle up any unwanted offspring in an old sack and drown them in the river. As children we were vaguely aware of this, but had never witnessed it at first hand or else didn't really understand what it meant. This time, however, coming across me playing in the farmyard, the farmer handed me a newborn kitten with the specific instruction that I should go and kill it.

Looking back, it was a cruel and macabre challenge to pose to a small boy. Another child might have refused, run away to his mother, or taken the kitten and let it go. I don't understand to this day why I acted as I did, but I obeyed. I took the kitten away and killed it. I didn't know how to do it, so I put this still-blind, completely white creature, squirming and mewling for its mother, on the sand by the river. Then I picked up a large rock and, closing my eyes, dropped it on the kitten's head. I was very shocked to see the lifeless body afterwards, knowing that I had been completely responsible for its death, a rivulet of blood from its mouth bright red against the white fur. I went back to the farmer and told him 'I've done it', as if pleased to have completed his order when, in my heart, I had wanted to refuse and didn't understand why I hadn't. I still think about it today – that confused small boy, trying to live up to the callous challenge set by a man who should have known better, but too upset and ashamed of his own behaviour to confide what he'd done to anyone in his own family.

The war impinged on our lives but there was no bombardment immediately around us because even though we lived in a railway station, it was in the middle of the countryside and not a big mainline one. I do remember the bombardment of Alessandria by the Allies, in particular the Americans. It was one of the major stations of northern Italy, and further up the line from us. I can recall hearing the bombs and seeing the red glow of burning buildings far away, and being aware without really knowing what it meant that people were being killed and the adults around me were saddened by it. As children we were constantly being warned *never* to pick up anything we found for fear of its being booby-trapped, toys or pens, things like that, because we'd heard that the Germans were throwing booby-trapped objects like this from planes to tempt and maim Italian children, so as to damage morale amongst the population.

Once, towards the end of the war, I saw the German guns in the hills firing on the partisans, and afterwards the bodies of dead men, cut in two by the brutal machine-gun fire. But mostly I remained protected from the worst of the horrors, although things changed when my father was first imprisoned and then sacked from his job in Castelnuovo

Belbo, and we lost our home. As the war ended and I turned eight years old, I was sent away to live with my grandmother and aunt for two years.

Soffritto alla Napoletana

Offal ragu

Because the padrone *(or boss) always used to get the better parts of an animal when it was slaughtered, the offal was usually discarded and given to the poor. Not today, however: heart, liver and lungs are now a delicacy commanding very high prices. This specialty is also cooked, though slightly differently, in Southern Italy, but this is the Umbrian method. The original also includes the spleen and intestines, but for obvious reasons I suggest you use only the liver, heart and lungs. Be brave, as, believe me – this is a very delicate and tasty dish.*

Serves 4
the pluck: lung, liver, heart, lambs
    kidney
50 g (2 oz) lard
3 medium onions, finely chopped
2 x 425 g (15 oz) cans plum tomatoes
6 tbsp tomato puree
8 bay leaves
2 tbsp fresh parsley, chopped
salt and pepper

Prepare the pluck by cutting off all the fat and gristle, then cutting it into chunks.

In a heavy non-stick pan with a lid, melt the lard over a medium heat. When hot, add the onions, stirring occasionally until they begin to soften and colour.

Now add all the pieces of meat, stirring until they are brown all over. Add the tinned tomatoes, puree, bay leaves and season. Give it a good stir, making sure all the pieces are coated in the sauce while bringing it to a simmer. Place the lid on top and gently cook on a medium heat for about an hour, occasionally stirring to ensure the sauce doesn't stick to the bottom of the pan.

You can now serve it, either as pasta sauce with large pieces of pasta such as paccheri, or as a soup diluted with good stock and served with a toasted slice of bread on top.

CHAPTER TWO

Growing Up

y father Giovanni was a naturally enigmatic man, not a great talker, but he had big ideas about travel and about life in general, and would talk to us about these. It was thanks to him that I received some notion of the wider horizons that might one day be open to me. He was also very hard working and took his job as stationmaster seriously. With his thick hair and dark eyes, wearing his smart uniform jacket and stationmaster's red hat trimmed with gold braid, he cut quite an imposing figure. Looking back, it is easy to see how he'd once caught my mother's eye! As a small boy I loved to be with him, spending time in his office, watching him work.

There were many different aspects to his job and Papa was always busy. He was responsible for the signalling, making sure the trains were able to run safely and efficiently and on time, while also managing the ticket office and helping people in the station, giving information and seeing to the customers. The station also had a garden, and he had to manage the gardener. It was important to Papa that his station should look good – the flowerbeds weeded, the platform swept, the paintwork fresh. There was no doubting the fact that he took great pride in his job and in doing it well.

Growing up around steam trains, we took them for granted; to us the station was a playground in the same way as the hills, woods and farmland surrounding it were. If my mother scolded us for staining our clothes with mulberry juice, starting in fright to see our skin stained with what, at first glance, looked like blood, she was equally irritated when we came home covered in coal dust. I would wait on the railway platform until a train hissed and wheezed into the station, smoke belching from its chimney and steam billowing all around as it drew noisily to a halt. Then I would scramble on board, to be welcomed by the driver and the fireman who seemed to enjoy the diversion of entertaining a small boy after the rigours of keeping the fire stoked and the pressure gauges gleaming. For the fireman in particular it was hot, sweaty, physical work and rivulets of sweat ran from beneath his cap, forging white marks down his grimy cheeks, the strong, sinewy muscles of his forearms bulging beneath his rolled-up sleeves.

Once I was aboard the train, he would allow me to load some coal into the roaring belly of the locomotive and inevitably my little hands would struggle with the shovel, so that he would have to help, filthy though he was with coal dust that rubbed off on me. And when the shovel proved too cumbersome, I would pick up what I could by hand to toss into the flames, causing the men much amusement with my feeble efforts. It seemed to me one of the world's greatest excitements to be so near to the workings of a train. Seeing the roaring flames of the engine close up was a wonderful thing for a small boy. Then, once the water tanks were replenished and the fire well stoked, I would scramble down the steps again, my hands and face smeared black. The brakes would be released with another loud hiss and the train would jolt into life, the driver releasing the steam through the whistle, hooting to signal its departure. During the winter months, when the temperature plummeted and the snow and harsh frosts made collecting wood difficult, he would throw us a shovelful of coal on to the platform when the train stopped, providing extra fuel for our stove during the freezing cold months. Once again my hands would be black with dust as I helped to gather up the precious fuel.

Treating the station as part of our personal playground included 'borrowing' the castors from the signal cables: circles of metal that made ideal wheels for the little carts we liked to build. Fortunately for us the cables were not live! They ran along poles, with the castors facilitating their smooth transition whenever Papa operated the signal levers – so it probably wasn't a good thing that we removed them, although they did make excellent wheels instead. Another feature of the station that we imitated in our own games was the crane used for moving heavy goods on and off the trains. Fascinated by its structure and strength, we liked to watch the men hauling the sacks or boxes up and out of the goods trucks, swinging them over the *remblais,* or loading platforms, before lowering them to the ground to be released. We would fashion pulleys and platforms of our own from bits of wood and wire and string, lifting small weights up and down to copy the men at work.

This 'borrowing' of something to facilitate something else, in a spirit of enterprise and making do, is something every Italian learns to appreciate from an early age as *l'arte di arrangiarsi* – the art of getting by, of bending the rules where necessary to get something done. Sometimes it is for the greater good, but more often for the benefit of the individual concerned. This is a philosophy I learnt in childhood and one that has stood me in good stead during times in my life when I have had to be particularly enterprising. The same way of looking at things that means a young child can find an inventive alternative use for cable castors can in adult life become a useful approach to problem-solving, and while *l'arte di arrangiarsi* can sometimes be abused and manipulated, used wisely it can be a powerful tool.

Although holiday for my father was in short supply given the nature of his work, he did make time for the local village tournaments that were held during the summer months. These were usually arranged around some form of sporting competition, in particular a traditional game popular in the Piedmont and Liguria regions called *pallone elastico* – literally, elastic ball. Played between two villages, it involves two teams of four-a-side punching the ball across the field with their bare fists, having to keep it in the air by passing it fast and furiously between the players, keeping possession and the ball from touching the ground, and thereby scoring points. Various versions of the game, which is a bit like a cross between tennis and volley ball but using a hard, white rubber ball of 10.5cm in diameter and weighing about 190g, still exist in Italy to this day, known latterly as *pallapugno* (punch the ball). You can see boys playing it in the streets, although football is increasingly more popular. In one version of the game, *pallone col bracciale*, which dates back to the sixteenth century, a rigid wooden cylinder was worn over the forearm with which the ball was hit, and for an inexperienced player this could be dangerous; an arm could easily be broken. These events were always highly social and a good opportunity for those watching to cheer from the sidelines with a glass of local wine to hand.

The first occasion my father took me to a game in the neighbouring village of Bruno, balancing me precariously on the crossbar of his bike as he pedalled, is a very special memory of time spent with him. Not only did I receive his undivided attention, it was the first time I tasted the local *amaretti* – delicious almond macaroons, crispy on the outside and soft on the inside, from the neighbouring village of Mombaruzzo, handmade and hand-wrapped. We would buy them to take home and share, as a treat for all the family.

The amaretti from Mombaruzzo were different from those I later sourced in Saronno, and sold in my chain of Carluccio's restaurants and delicatessens, in one very important aspect: the paper in which they were wrapped. It is with the *Amaretti di Saronno* papers that I do my lighted wrapper trick for pyrotechnically inclined young friends by taking the thin, tissue-paper wrappers from the macaroons, carefully smoothing them flat and then fashioning each into a cylinder, gently standing it upright and setting light to the top of it. The delicate wrapper then becomes a paper lantern gently ascending skywards, working on the same principle as the Montgolfier hot air balloon.

Generally, because he worked from home as it were, as children we saw a lot of Papa. He was also an enthusiastic, amateur photographer, and his wood-and-brass Gandolfi plate camera was the one extravagance in his otherwise frugal life. A Gandolfi camera is a beautiful thing, with its polished wooden frame, shiny brass fixtures, and concertinaed leather apparatus designed to create the correct focal distance for the lens. But while it produced beautiful results it was quite a palaver setting it up, in comparison to today's phone-camera culture. It involved setting the Gandolfi up on a tripod to keep it steady during the long exposure time, then polishing the glass plate to prevent any smears being reproduced on the photograph – not to mention mixing the chemicals necessary to produce the flash. The highly flammable magnesium and potassium chlorate were combined and lit by hand, exploding with a loud bang while the photographer took the picture – no wonder everyone in early photographs always looks so surprised, having had to sit still for such a long time while the preparations were made, before being subjected to a loud bang and flash of white light as the chemicals ignited! Too heavy a hand with these and the effect was dramatic; too little and the results were poorly lit. The chemicals were stored for safety by my father in the *lampisteria,* a storage cupboard under the stairs, along with petrol and other flammable materials. A cigarette butt carelessly discarded or some childish misuse of matches and the whole station house could have gone off like a rocket, leaving the neighbours to wonder why the Germans had finally targeted the Carluccio family and bombarded such a sleepy village. Luckily this never happened and we continued to sleep safely in our beds at night.

Papa also stored petards, small explosive devices, in the *lampisteria*. These were the shape and size of a pocket watch, and were used to warn the trains when the weather was foggy, which it often was in the area, or visibility was poor for some other reason. Secured to the track with a malleable lead strap bent to hold it in position, when the train wheel went over it the weight would cause the petard to detonate and the loud retort of the explosion would warn the train driver to look out for an imminent railway signal. On one occasion I stole a couple of petards, fixed them to a bit of unused track at the end of the line, and detonated them by dropping a large stone on top. At such close proximity, and without the bulk of the train to contain the explosion, the retort was both extremely loud and effective, but also quite dangerous as it could have caused me an eye injury or worse – I could have been, quite literally 'hoist by my own petard', as the saying goes. My childhood curiosity duly satisfied, even I could see that causing mini-explosions like this might get me into trouble of one form or another, so I never did it again.

There was one occasion during the war when being the child of the stationmaster really paid off. Because of bombing further up the line, and damage to two bridges on either side of Papa's station, a goods wagon full of supplies became temporarily stuck at ours. This meant it came within my father's area of responsibility. He promptly used his authority to requisition the contents – rice, oil, salt, the sort of basics that were hard to come by during the war – for fear of their being stolen. He promptly 'borrowed' them and put them to good use: *l'arte di arrangiarsi* at its best!

At the beginning of yet another hard winter, when it was going to be difficult for us to manage, Papa suddenly had a good supply of desirable items to barter with the local farmers and others in the village. We could swap flour for rice, for example, and my mother could make bread again, or trade olive oil for vegetables or chickens, which we kept for their eggs. Everyone was happy! Papa also requisitioned wine from the goods train and sold it off to a local merchant, using the money he was given in exchange to buy a piano for my sister. My own infant efforts to copy her, and the constant playing of the same simple song over and over again, nearly drove my family mad, but to me the piano was another source of pleasure and amusement.

As members of a railway employee's family, we all benefited from free rail travel. I took this for granted throughout my years of growing up, becoming familiar with train travel from an early age. I think the free travel was, in part, what made it possible for my mother to contemplate living in the north, so far from her family and with such young children to take care of unsupported by them. At least regular free journeys made it possible for her to keep in contact.

At that time, the difference between the north and the south in Italy was seen as quite wide, not just geographically but socially and culturally as well. It's not that there was bad feeling as such, more a sort of competitiveness; whether you came from the north or the south was something that would always be commented on by others. 'Ah,' someone might say knowingly when my parents spoke, 'you're from the south.' This was because of their accent, of course. In fact, my father could speak in Neapolitan dialect to my mother and from time to time would do so, perhaps when he wanted to communicate something he didn't want us children to understand, as parents sometimes do. But the fact that they were from the south would frequently be remarked upon, in the same way that, when I grew up, people would always remark that I was from the north, on the basis of my accent alone. I think this is all rooted in the popular Italian misconception that those from the north are naturally more hard-working than those from the warmer climes of the south; that there is more industry and commerce in the north, and that this confers some sort of superiority on its inhabitants. But I never really understood why the accent with which you speak should be worthy of such inference or even comment – either then or now!

Papa was well-known, liked and trusted by both sides, the partisans and the Wehrmacht, during the war. He was also what the Scots would call 'canny', with a keen eye for opportunity, or *l'arte di arrangiarsi,* should it come his way. For example, one day he saw a group of partisans, having been discovered by the Germans, beating a hasty retreat with their provisions, one of them trying to run while carrying the heavy carcass of a pig. Seeing the man struggling with this large, dead weight over his shoulder, which was hindering his efforts to escape, Papa immediately offered to help him reduce the weight of his cumbersome burden – by cutting off one of its legs to lighten the load. This, of course, he would keep for himself! The man agreed, and my father brought home a large leg of pork, in some triumph. Mamma, with her usual expertise, made numerous meals from this unexpected booty, including one of my all-time favourite dishes, *pasta e fagioli* – a very simple bean and pasta soup, intensely flavoured and enriched by the rind of cured pork. To this day, it is my favourite comfort dish – extremely tasty, warming, filling, and both easy and quick to prepare. Part of its comfort factor for me comes from the memories I associate with it: the sense of taste is closely linked to the sense of smell, and related more strongly to memory than is visual stimulus. Today, inhaling the warm scent of *pasta e fagioli* instantly transports me back to the security and warmth of Mamma's kitchen.

It was this same keen eye for opportunity, however, that eventually got Papa into trouble. Not for what he did exactly, but because of the way it was viewed in a country under occupation. It led unfortunately to his arrest and imprisonment. As the war progressed there were fewer trains and travellers, and less for a stationmaster to do. Never one to rest on his laurels, Papa looked about him for what other opportunities there were and began a sideline in wine brokerage, finding customers for the local vineyards and negotiating the price paid, taking a percentage of the proceeds for doing so. Just next to the station, for example, were the vineyards of Signor Cossetti, the man who had offered to adopt me. These produced a vast quantity of *Barbera* and *Dolcetto* red wines, and a delightful sparkling sweet white called *Moscato* – whose unfermented juice had once given me such a stomach ache. With access to free rail travel, Papa was able to travel to Nizza Monferrato, Alessandria and elsewhere at no expense in order to pursue this sideline.

No surprise then that I too became a wine merchant in later life, having seen at a tender age how it was done! Ominously though, because they couldn't fathom the reason for his constant train travel, the Germans started to suspect my father was engaged in covert activities; they had been watching him and monitoring his movements for some time. Their eventual and mistaken conclusion was that he must be in some way working for the partisans. On the basis of this the Wehrmacht arrived at our door one night, and arrested Papa on a charge of spying. They took him away there and then, and imprisoned him in Nizza.

My father's imprisonment in 1944 was a serious matter for us. Without him we had no income and potentially no home. The next day my mother walked the ten long kilometres to Nizza, with me in tow, to visit him. Seeing my usually smart papa with his tie, belt and shoelaces confiscated made me cry, and I begged the Germans to release him. I don't know whether it was this robust airing of my infant distress, the soldiers' past experience of my mother's excellent cooking, or the realisation that my father had in fact been doing nothing illegal – or all three – but several days later he arrived home, none the worse for his experience, the incident dismissed.

Papa might not have been a spy, but he was a fascist – or, rather, a member of the Fascist Party. Not out of any political conviction, but purely in order to work for a state body like the railway. You had to be a member of the prevailing political party which, before the war, was the PNF or Partito Nazionale Fascista (National Fascist Party), created by Benito Mussolini in 1921. The PNF was dissolved in 1943 and replaced by the PFR or Partito Fascista Repubblicano (Republican Fascist Party). Like Papa, my brothers and I, from no political allegiance but because there was no real choice in the matter, had joined fascist youth organisations – at the time, all good Italians were more or less obliged to join one fascist organisation or another.

My brother Carlo, for example, became a *balilla*, a member of the ONB, the Opera Nazionale Balilla, that was attached to the Italian education system of the time and run by the Ministero Educazione Nazionale. Mussolini had asked one of his education secretaries, Renato Ricci, to organise the ONB and he had based his ideas on those of Lord Baden-Powell, founder of the Boy Scout organisation in Great Britain. And just as the Boy Scouts had an organisation for younger boys, the Cubs, so the ONB had the same: the Figli della Lupa (Children of the She-wolf), named after the myth of Romulus and Remus, twins and founders of the city of Rome, who had been suckled and raised by a she-wolf.

The Figli della Lupa was organised for six- to eight-year-old boys – I can't remember if there was an equivalent for girls, but I don't think my sisters joined anything similar – and I duly became a member, my first and last formal allegiance to any political party. My greatest interest in joining was that on 6 January all good Figli della Lupa received presents from the *Befana Fascista* – a witch who only brought presents to good children, much as *Babbo Natale* (Father Christmas) or *Gesù Bambino* (Baby Jesus) might, and – as was true in this case –

such presents generally involved chocolate, which was a rare treat and something to which I, as a small boy, was extremely partial!

After *Il Duce* was deposed and executed by the partisans in 1945, showing any sort of allegiance to Mussolini, including being a fascist, was no longer a good thing. So Papa's position as stationmaster was threatened because of his past, obligatory membership of the PFR. The next thing he knew he was made redundant 'pending investigations', and without either a job or a home we could no longer live in Castelnuovo Belbo. This was nothing short of a disaster for us. With no home to call our own, the Carluccio family's future hung in the balance. The only option was to return south and take refuge with our extended family there. So we went back to Benevento, my father's original home, but there wasn't room for all of us children at the house of his sister there, and I, being the youngest, was shipped off to live with my maternal grandmother and aunt at Prata near Avellino, fifty kilometres away.

Donna Peppinella, as my granny Giuseppina was affectionately known by the local villagers, lived with my unmarried aunt Dora at Prata di Principato Ultra, to give the small hillside town its full, rather grand name. It lies between the mountains of Irpinia on the banks of the Sabato river, and is famous for its Basilica dell'Annunziata, built over sixth-century catacombs and housing an eighth-century fresco of the Madonna and Saints. My grandfather had died a couple of years previously, and I only really have one memory of him as a sick old man, not long before he died, lying in bed with his naked torso covered with *sanguisughe* – leeches! – sucking his blood in an attempt to lower his blood pressure. Even today the thought of it makes me feel slightly queasy. Poor man, there was no real treatment then for the high blood pressure from which he suffered, apart from this vain attempt to reduce the volume of blood in his arteries through the action of leeches, which I doubt was very effective. But my memories of my grandmother, who lived to the age of ninety-two in full possession of all her faculties, more than make up for the rather macabre last picture of my grandfather that remains etched on my memory to this day.

Fortunately Prata was not too far from the rest of my family in Benevento, and I used to see them quite regularly. Not that I remember minding living separately from them during this time because I was quite spoilt by both my grandmother and my aunt, who doted on me. For the first time in my short life I had the full attention of both the adults with whom I lived – and I was everyone's little mascot. After regularly taking last place behind my elder brothers and sisters, I found I quite liked this new state of affairs and my mother was relieved, not only at having one less mouth to feed but because I seemed happy enough. Although I had had no idea when we left Castelnuovo Belbo that I would never see my old home or friends there again, having been told at the time nothing more than that we were going to visit our relatives, which we had done many times before, in fact I greatly enjoyed this move to the south with its gentler climate and plentiful delicious food.

Avellino lies about forty kilometres north-east of Naples, and if anyone has heard of it today it's probably because it is the ancestral home of the fictional Tony Soprano, lead character in the HBO TV series *The Sopranos*. In the story, Tony's father emigrated from Avellino to America in the early twentieth century. My grandmother's town of Prata was about ten kilometres north of Avellino, and not so far from the town of Benevento, which many years ago had been the capital of the Duchy of Benevento. Avellino is famous for its hazelnuts – one-third of Italy's total production comes from here – and one of my favourite childhood treats was the *croccante di nocciole* that Mamma made with lightly toasted hazelnuts and caramelised sugar, creating a delicious hazelnut crunch. It is also an area renowned for its *Aglianico* and *Taurasi* wines, as well as cherries, cheese (including the *Caciocavallo* of Montella), the sweet chestnuts of Montella and the black truffles of Bagnoli Irpino.

Nonna Giuseppina owned her own farm. Not only was the climate good, the soil was also very rich on account of the property's proximity to Vesuvius. My grandmother ran her farm with great knowledge and skill, like her own small kingdom, and was extremely successful. There was always an abundance of vegetables in her cooking, and I particularly remember the broad beans – *fave* – which I loved. In the south, *fave* were considered good for human consumption and there were many excellent ways to serve this nutritious vegetable, while in the north they were sniffed at, thought suitable only for animals or peasants – another example of those not-so-subtle regional distinctions at work. *Fave* are traditionally sown on November 2, All Souls' Day, and small cakes in the shape of the bean, although not made out of them, known as *fave dei morti* (beans of the dead), are cooked as part of the celebration.

There was also *zuppa di fave* made from fresh or dried fava beans, seasoned with onions, beet leaves and cured bacon fat or *prosciutto*. Freshly picked and podded, *fave* were also eaten raw with pecorino cheese or local salamis, or pureed with wild chicory, a popular dish in the southern area of Puglia. Not only are *fave* delicious, with their buttery texture, slightly nutty flavour, and many culinary uses, they also benefit the soil by increasing its nitrogen content, acting as a natural fertiliser. My grandmother, a highly knowledgeable woman, knew how to rotate and cultivate her crops in such a way as to maximise their yield. Growing *fave* was a recognised part of this traditional process.

While living with my grandmother, I was looked after by a young girl called Lina Fasulo, daughter of Savino Fasulo the *mezzadro* on my grandmother's farm. A *mezzadro* – or sharecropper – has a legal contract to farm an area of land and is entitled to a half-share of its yield, the rest being given to the legal owner. Lina was my nanny, and her name always used to amuse me because a *fasulo* is a bean. So her father was Signor Fasulo, which translates as Mr Bean, a name which used to make us giggle. Lina was no more than twenty years old when she worked for my grandmother, and looked after me with great affection. She is still alive, and when we last met I could see in her even now the young girl who would raise her finger, but seldom her hand or her voice, in admonition to me as a child.

Savino Fasulo also tended a vineyard, so there was wine to be traded too. Between him and my grandmother, the cultivated land produced a huge variety of seasonal crops: potatoes, wheat, maize, onions, broad beans and more, along with hazelnuts and walnuts. And the fruit! Peaches, apricots, *cachi* (persimmons), oranges, lemons, cherries, pomegranates, apples and more ... all picked when ripe. What couldn't be eaten was traded or preserved. Then there were the wild foods that were foraged for – sometimes Savino would arrive with a small basket, lined with fresh leaves, bearing gifts of freshly picked wild strawberries, figs, chestnuts, mulberries or *funghi*. Really, when it came to fresh foods, we were spoilt for choice even during the war.

When I wasn't foraging for mulberries, chestnuts or *funghi*, or playing in the garden with Lina or Signor Fasulo's donkeys, or travelling by horse and cart to market, I started my real education. This was the responsibility of my 'aunt' Linda, a teacher and relative of my grandmother's, who lived next door. Here she taught me my letters and numbers, though I often found it monotonous work, and boring, and lonely. But this one-to-one tuition paid off when I returned to formal education because by then I was a year ahead in my studies.

Most of the people living in this small town were farmers or artisans, along with a few who worked in administration. Often people had more than one job. The local postman Ciccio, for example, had three. First of all he distributed the post, and as a result of this was well known by everyone. That was in the mornings. Then, in the early evening, he was the town crier, standing in the central piazza while those around him promenaded – travelling home from work, meeting friends, running errands – singing out in his loud *basso profondo* voice the day's news. This was seldom very exciting, generally just some details about what was opening in the neighbouring town's cinema or details of some other event or activity, occasionally spiced up by news of a birth, marriage or death.

It was Ciccio's third job, however, that was my favourite because he was the equivalent of today's ice cream man. Back then this was not a case of turning up in a van with a musical chime, but rather of wheeling into a shady spot on the piazza the equipment and ingredients needed to make a fresh lemon sorbet, while we salivated in anticipation nearby. The slightly laborious process tested our patience to the limit. First he would assemble a large wooden container in which there stood a copper cylinder, with a lot of ice packed between the two. Into the copper container he would tip the juice of many freshly squeezed lemons, along with sugar and water, keeping the empty half-lemon shells to one side. Carefully securing its lid, Ciccio would then use the ice cream-maker's handle to rotate the copper cylinder at high speed, the centrifugal force causing the liquid to stick to the sides and freeze. This he would scrape off with a wooden spoon, collecting it at the bottom of the freezing container. Once all the liquid had been transformed into a perfect sorbet, he would take a spoon and fill the half-lemon shells, before handing them out to the queues of children waiting impatiently. Each scoop cost one lira. To this day, I have never been able to replicate the simplicity of this sorbet, but maybe it was more to do with the elements of anticipation and excitement, and the completely fresh, sun-drenched lemons that were used in this traditional method. There is a good reason why Italian ice cream-making is renowned the world over, born as it was from the need to provide refreshment in a frequently fierce heat.

It was not just ice cream that satisfied my sweet tooth. My aunt Dora liked to take me on trips and we used to visit Napoli to see my uncle Gaetano and his family. There my favourite treat was the rum *babà*, a pastry of Borbonic origin, filled with currants soaked in rum, and also the *sfogliatelle ricce*, one of the most famous Neapolitan pastries, filled with semolina, fruit and lemon liqueur, often prepared for the feast day of St Rosa on 30 August. *Pastiera di grano*, a pastry base (often made with *pasta frolla* using egg yolks) with a ricotta, wheat grain and fruit filling, was a traditional Easter dish in this area, while another Neapolitan speciality was *struffoli*, deep-fried pellets of dough, the size of hazelnuts, crisp on the outside and soft inside, traditionally sweetened with honey, a little cinnamon maybe or with orange zest, sometimes served warm and often prepared for the festivities of Christmas or Easter.

With the end of the war, the liberation of Italy and VE Day on 8 May 1945, my father's job with the Ferrovie dello Stato was eventually reinstated but not before a thorough investigation which took several months. He was then declared a 'good fascist' (whatever that now meant), promoted to *Capo Stazione di Prima Classe* and allocated responsibility for the station at Borgofranco d'Ivrea, in the province of Turin. Several months after that the family was finally settled in the stationmaster's house we were reunited after my 18-month idyll in the south with my grandmother, and I returned to live with them in the north where the next stage of my life began.

Pasta e fagioli

Pasta with beans

The best beans to use are fresh borlotti beans, which can occasionally be found outside Italy now. Available around August and September, they are recognisable by the green and red colouring of the pods. If you can't find fresh, you can use canned, but another alternative is white cannellini beans. If you use dried beans, leave them to soak in water the night before you use them. Then boil them in some unsalted water for 2–3 hours until they are tender. If you are using fresh beans boil these for 30–40 minutes until they are cooked. If using canned beans, simply drain and rinse well.

Serves 6

2 celery stalks, finely chopped
115g (4 oz) prosciutto trimmings,
    chopped into small cubes
4 tbsp extra virgin olive oil
2 medium potatoes, cut into cubes
1 fresh red chilli, chopped
2 garlic cloves, finely chopped
3 ripe tomatoes, skinned and chopped,
    or 1 x 425 g (15 oz) can chopped
    plum tomatoes
1 kg (2¼ lb) fresh borlotti beans,
    or 250 g (9 oz) dried borlotti or
    cannellini beans, or 2 x 425 g (15
    oz) cans unsalted borlotti beans
1 litre (1¾ pints) chicken or beef
    stock, or water
115g (4 oz) tubettini or mixed pasta
10 fresh basil leaves, shredded
salt and pepper to taste

Fry the celery and prosciutto in a large saucepan in the olive oil over a medium heat. After a few minutes add the potatoes and chilli, stirring to prevent the prosciutto from browning. After about 10 minutes add the garlic and cook it for a couple of minutes before adding the tomatoes. Wait a further 10 minutes before adding two-thirds of the drained beans, keeping the remainder aside to be mashed and added to thicken the dish. Pour in the stock or water and bring to the boil. Now add the pasta and, after 8 minutes, add the basil leaves and the mashed beans. Season with salt and pepper.

When serving, a trickle of extra virgin olive oil on the top of each dish will enhance the flavour amazingly.

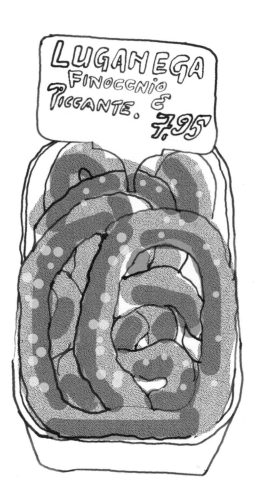

CHAPTER THREE

Back to the North

e now lived in the region of Italy known as Piemonte. According to thirteenth-century scholars, the name Piedmont comes from *ad pedem montium,* which literally means 'at the foot of the mountains' – Borgofranco d'Ivrea certainly was; and not just at the foot of the mountains, but surrounded by them too. Further north this time even than Castelnuovo Belbo, about fifty kilometres from Turin and close to the Aosta valley region, we were also not far from the French and Swiss borders. Today the A5, the great *Autostrada Torino Aosta,* hammers down to Turin from the Mont Blanc tunnel at Courmayeur on the Italian/French border, but in the 1940s the only way to travel long distances was by train. There was no Mont Blanc tunnel then either. That took eight years to construct, with work starting in 1957 and the tunnel finally opening to great acclaim in 1965.

When I lived there as a boy, Borgofranco d'Ivrea was a town of about 2500 inhabitants. It is not much bigger now with only about 1000 more people, and retains the same charm as it did then with its narrow streets, steeply pitched red-roofed houses, and medieval church of Santa Maria. The striking Palazzo Marini flanked by its thirteenth-century tower stands in the centre of the old town, and with its attractive tree-lined courtyard, beautiful staircase and fresco of the myth of Persephone – daughter of Zeus and the harvest goddess Demeter, lured into the underworld and tricked into eating the pomegranate by Hades – is now home to a Scuola di Educazione all'Arte which has an international reputation for music and art.

Perhaps the most striking natural features of the area are the extraordinary *balmetti* – a diminutive of the Ligurian word *balma*, meaning cave – where *cantinas* or cellars were created from naturally occurring recesses in the rocky hillsides, and used for storage for at least the last 300 years. There are literally thousands of these *balmetti* burrowing away into the mountain; from the outside the entrances to them look like a cluster of old farm buildings nestling at the foot of the hills. These extraordinary natural storage facilities have a stable level of humidity and the temperature remains constant at 7/8°C all year round, whatever the temperature outside. They also benefit from a unique, natural air current that gently and constantly circulates within them, providing an excellent environment in which to store wine, cheese, and cured meats like salami, in particular *salame della duja*. (A *duja* is the name of an earthenware pot in which the freshly made salami, covered with liquid lard, is stored to mature for two to three months.) In a region abounding in many delicious foodstuffs and wines, this unique natural storage facility has proved invaluable. This perhaps explains why exceptional cheeses like *Robiola di Roccaverano* and *Gorgonzola*, as well as artisanal salamis like *Filetto al Barolo, Bresaola della Val d'Ossola* and *Bale d'Aso* (which literally means 'donkey balls' but which are in fact round sausages, similar in appearance and size to their namesake, once made of donkey meat and traditionally produced in the commune of Monastero di Vasco but now produced using cured pork or beef), all became widely known as specialities of the area.

So my family settled down once more in the stationmaster's house, my father again donned his red and gold cap and my mother was kept busy organising new schools for us and working in her kitchen while we children got to know this new area in the foothills of the Italian Alps, on the banks of the Dora Baltea river. I was glad to be with my brother Carlo again; it was good to have a playmate of a similar age after receiving the close attention of my grandmother and aunt. Much as I loved them and had enjoyed being spoilt for a time, Carlo and I could go to school together and afterwards explore the woods and hills surrounding the town, two brothers growing into manhood. Despite the usual squabbles between siblings, it felt good to be back with all my brothers and sisters again, and in such beautiful surroundings.

The Aosta valley is glacial in origin, with wonderful mountain lakes – Lago di Montalto, Lago Sirio and Lago San Michele – alpine pastures, the river valley itself and extensive woodlands of beech, ash, hazel, walnut, alder, birch and maple that turn the lower hillsides from vivid green in the spring to the blazing colours of autumn. Since I was now old enough to accompany my brothers, with Carlo in particular keeping a watchful eye on me, we would go on a day's hike to the Colma di Mombarone, or simply Mombarone as it is more generally known, *colma* meaning high place in Piedmontese dialect. And it definitely *was* a high place, rising to almost 3000 metres, though the views of the surrounding peaks, in particular the highest ones of Monte Rosa and Cervino (also known as the Matterhorn), were spectacular and well worth the six-hour climb.

There were only about five months of the year when the summits weren't snow-covered, and it was then that we would leave for the mountains early in the morning, taking with us a picnic of Mamma's bread, salami and cheese, plus maybe some fruit, whatever was in season, carried in cloth bags slung over our shoulders. We didn't bother to carry a drink, satisfying our thirst instead from the clear, cold mountain streams.

It wasn't a particularly difficult climb. The first leg of the journey from the small town of Andrate where the mountain route began was relatively easy, taking us through wooded areas, although higher up there were short stretches where the going was quite steep and dangerous, with precipices to both sides of the path. But for long periods we walked through alpine pastures full of cows, some wearing the traditional bell around the neck, and along the way we would come across *baite*, little dry-stone buildings where the farmers could churn their butter and make cheese from the cow's milk, leaving the produce to mature in the cool mountain climate before transporting it back down as it was needed, either to be consumed, stored in the *balmetti* or sold. At the top, the high place or *colma* of Mombarone, there was a small chapel, built a hundred years or more before by the local Alpine inhabitants, and always a welcome sight to myself, Carlo and Peppino. This was journey's end, where we could stop and wonder at the panoramic views of the surrounding countryside, enjoy our picnic and rest our feet before returning home.

At the beginning of every walk, our first priority was to find a good walking stick. We each selected one from the woodlands at the start of our route before the climb became steeper; we would need the support of a stout stick in its higher, rockier reaches. My elder brothers were allowed to carry knives with which they would cut and trim a suitable branch, providing one for me too. A straight hazelwood stick was easily sourced from one of the many thickets surrounding the path. Since the nuts were prized in Piedmont, hazel trees were often coppiced so that the young shoots grew straight up from ground level, ensuring a plentiful supply of suitable material for us. Once you found a good walking stick, the trick was to hang on to it and so we would carve our initials into the bark so as to avoid arguments over ownership. Initially, when I was too young to be trusted with a knife, my brothers or Papa did the carving of initials for me. But as I grew older I acquired my own knife – essential kit for an outdoor life spent foraging, and always carried in the pocket of my trousers or jacket. So not only could I initial my own stick and then, in time, that of my younger brother Enrico, I could also while away indeterminate lengths of time by whittling a piece of wood – an immensely satisfying pastime for any young boy.

To this day, I like to walk with a stick and still enjoy taking my knife and working on a piece of wood, crafting a unique pattern into its bark by peeling away strips of it. Each stick is completely unique, and I like to make these not only for my own use while out walking or mushroom-hunting, but also as gifts for friends – signing each of them with a small mushroom shape to identify it as one of mine. You need to choose a straight piece of wood, although if there is the occasional offshoot, these can be removed and the knots they leave behind integrated into the pattern. The wood needs to be fresh, so that the bark is still soft and easy to work. The knife needs to be sharp, and the work is best done all in one day, so that the wood dries and hardens uniformly, and mellows into gently muted contrasts between bark and wood, the patterns becoming all the more pleasing as they age.

The task of devising the pattern and fashioning it into the wood is surprisingly relaxing, especially if you are sitting outside in the sun, taking in the air and the scent of the fresh sap, and anticipating a pleasant walk. I still like to use hazelwood when I can. The trick is to find a stick that branches at just the right height, so that you can cut it at the best length for walking and then fashion the dividing branch at the top to create a thumb-hold, a sort of cradle for the thumb that improves your grasp and makes the stick all the more comfortable to use. Other woods can be good, too – ash, alder and beech, for example – but if you want to pattern the bark by peeling away strips, you will need to work with freshly cut wood, not a seasoned piece.

The local practice of coppicing the hazel trees was not just for the benefit of us young walkers; it also meant that a good supply of pliant young hazel sticks could be used for basketwork and, in prehistoric times, to make coracles – small, round boats made of a basket-like frame covered with stretched animal skins.

I always felt privileged when my older siblings allowed me to accompany them, instead of shouting '*Vai a casa!*' – 'Go home!' – when I attempted to join them. Too often as the youngest I had been told I was not wanted and had trailed home in tears, to complain to my mother that they wouldn't let me play with them or join in their games. She would generally laugh, tousle my hair and say, 'Never mind, come and help me pod some peas,' or else provide me with some other absorbing task to take my mind off my hurt feelings. At other times she too would be busy. She'd shoo me out of her kitchen, and then I would have to go and play by myself with her warning that I was to stay out of trouble ringing in my ears.

My four elder siblings, all closer in age to one other than they were to me, hadn't wanted me along at first because they were inevitably charged with my safety, and didn't want their games spoiled by having to remain responsible for someone who couldn't keep up, or who fell over, or who got cold and hungry and then whined and complained about it! Then there had been the occasion when we had been playing by the river's edge and I had fallen in and had to be rescued. To my four-year-old mind the insult of the initial tumble and then being drenched in icy water was only compounded when my brother Carlo took me home. Leaving his game, he slung me over his shoulder – waterlogged, kicking and screaming, and very far from grateful. No wonder they didn't always want me along!

Sometimes my older brother Peppino could be prevailed upon to look after me, and it's true he did sometimes take me fishing with him, and tried to teach me how to do it. He would show me the way to stand very still in the shallows of the river and place my hands in the water, waiting for a fish to swim towards them before deftly scooping it up. But I didn't like plunging my hands into water in this way, never entirely sure what its depths might hide, so a certain lack of conviction hampered my efforts and I wasn't successful. I continued to find fishing frustrating and unsatisfactory as a pastime. Peppino, however, managed to catch something nearly every time, skilfully and patiently waiting for his prey. I, being too young to appreciate what was required, soon grew bored and would whine about wanting to get out of the cold water, disturbing his concentration. Another reason he would want to tell me, *'Antonio, a casa!'* But after we were reunited as a family in Borgofranco d'Ivrea, I was little older and perhaps a little more assertive, and found myself left out of their games and expeditions less frequently.

People still walk along the trails of the now somewhat commercialised Andrate Nordic Walking Park today, or go mountain biking or even paragliding there. Back then we just threw together some simple provisions and set off, with no special shoes or coats, to follow the trails worn smooth by the Alpine cows and cowherds, enjoying the extraordinary vistas as we hiked to the summit. We didn't have unlimited opportunities to do this, of course. In winter the walks were unsafe, and at the height of summer we'd lack the energy for them, and of course we were expected to pull our weight when it came to doing various household chores. But every time we could be we were outside. When it grew too cold for that, we might take our games into a farmer's barn, playing amongst the cattle for warmth.

Mine was quite a robust childhood therefore, with no family car when I was young so no transport apart from the free train travel and the occasional cart ride cadged from a local farmer. Otherwise we walked everywhere as a matter of course. It was freezing cold in the winter and, apart from the oven in the kitchen and a fire in the living room, there was no heating in our house. In winter we often woke to find ice on the inside of the windows and our breath visible in the air.

At night we'd use a warming pan, containing glowing embers from the fire, to take the chill from the icy sheets, being careful not to scorch them. In the mornings we would scurry across the chilly bricks of the floor to the warmth of the kitchen. It was here, too, that we would have our baths, but only once a week, when a huge metal container would be hauled in and laboriously filled with hot water. We would take it in turns, during which time the kitchen was off-limits to the others, and the last to bathe had to make do with tepid, soapy water. The rest of the time, it was a 'lick and a promise' – hands and face only washed briskly in cold water. In the summers, when it was hot, we would swim so often that our bathing was done in the cool, pristine waters of the nearby rivers and lakes, and the metal bath was left to gather dust until the autumn.

When you live like that, outside whatever the weather, playing, or foraging for fruit or nuts or mushrooms, you become very aware of the changing seasons – spring, summer, autumn and winter – all marked by distinct variations in climate and vegetation. That's especially true when you walk to school every day. Spring brought us a welcome relief from the chill of winter, and as the warm air ruffled the blossom on the hillsides we began to anticipate the fresh fruit that was promised by this benediction, bored with the dried and preserved varieties that had been our staple diet throughout the winter months.

Cherries came first, in early June, gleaming a rich sun-ripened red, cascading down the branches. My long-term schoolfriend Carlo Motta and I were charged with locating the first ripening trees and inevitably returned with our lips stained with a surfeit of evidence. Then the peaches would begin to ripen, large, sun-filled, yellow globes flushed with soft pink. Perhaps more delicious to me as an adult, by which time I could appreciate their more subtle flavour, were the smaller, white *pesche di vigna* – the little peaches that grow among the grape vines. Then came plums, apricots and other soft fruits, like wild alpine strawberries and blueberries, followed by the *cachi* or persimmons that nobody much bothered with because of the very hard skins, although when you got at the soft fruit inside it was very sweet with a distinctive flavour. These were followed in turn by apples, quinces and figs, and then of course there were the grapes. Although these were grown mainly for wine, the farmers would often take handfuls of bunches, hang them from the rafters in the barns, and let them dry a little, naturally sweetening as they did so, becoming smaller and more raisin-like, tasting similar to Moscato wine.

A really big event every year was Christmas. The festive season didn't begin weeks in advance like it does now until you are weary of the over-indulgence, but just a week before the day itself, after the school term finished. Mamma's culinary preparations, however, would have been going on for a long time, with many special things already secreted away for a *Buon Natale*. These included treats like *croccante di nocciole,* made with either the wonderful local hazelnuts we collected or, failing that, shop-bought ones, and *torrone* (almond nougat). She would make and store these weeks in advance, in between tackling her other chores. As children we liked to help make *ricciarelli* (almond biscuits).

Mamma would also have preserved wild mushrooms from our autumn foraging, and made some good salami and chicken liver pâté for our antipasti, designed to tease the palate before the main course. On Christmas Day itself these antipasti would be followed by *tortellini in brodo* (little pasta dumplings in clear broth) to fill us up a little more, and then the main course, some roast meat, which could be goose or wild boar or sometimes even venison, maybe a *filetto di capriolo al Barolo* (fillet of venison in Barolo wine) or *lepre in salmi* (jugged hare), depending on with whom Papa had been doing a bit of business lately. A meal like this could go on for several hours, which was sometimes a little boring for a child. We didn't get masses of presents, maybe just one or two from our immediate family, but these were always carefully wrapped and put beneath the tree, and it was a special time of year for all of us.

We'd become quite competitive about the tree with our school friends, boasting about how big it was, or whether we had lights or candles, or what decorations or chocolates we had to hang on it. One Christmas I went off with my friend Carlo to find and cut down a suitable tree. We wanted one one that would be fine and big enough to surpass the trees of all our friends. We found first one then another, but none seemed quite good enough. As we walked further and further up the mountainside in our search it began to get dark and foggy. It was already snowy and cold. I stumbled about, losing my footing, and also lost my bearings. I became separated from Carlo and, in fact, quite lost. I wasn't worried at first, but then as I kept slipping on the snow and falling over concealed rocks I realised that it could become a problem if didn't find my way back home soon as it was very cold, and I definitely wasn't dressed to survive a night in the open. Luckily my parents were alerted and Papa gathered some villagers together to come and look for me. I was soon located and brought home. My fingers and toes were numb with cold but otherwise I was none the worse for wear.

Papa's preparations for Christmas included assembling the *presepio*, the nativity scene that is a staple of Italian Christmas decorations, with its figures of the Virgin Mary, St Joseph and *Gesù Bambino* in his manger, and the lowly animals in attendance. In southern Italy in particular, where my parents originated, this was an important tradition with the figurines lovingly passed on down generations of the same family. Our family *presepio* was in the Neapolitan style, a large configuration taking up a lot of space and quite wonderful to my childish imagination. My task was to gather the soft green moss that Papa would use to fashion the surrounding 'hillsides' on which to position the model sheep and shepherds' figures, with a small pile of rocks stacked nearby to suggest the mountains. A stable was placed in the middle of this landscape in which the holy pair, flanked by donkey and cow, hovered in attendance over the empty crib, ready for the Christ child's arrival on Christmas Eve. An angel clutching a star was wedged on the roof, her mouth perpetually pursed as if ready to utter proclamations of great joy, and the whole scene was illuminated by small lights, operated from a transformer, thanks to Papa's attention to various pieces of wire screwed laboriously into place.

One year he surpassed himself with a decorative waterfall, a little stream trickling through the precarious mossy landscape; this rather dodgy mix of water and electricity threatened to surprise the shepherds long before the archangel ever arrived! Mamma's exhortations to us not to play with the *presepio* – which were generally ignored, hence the chipped nature of the donkey's ears and the Virgin Mary's nose – held rather more emphasis than usual that year since she did not wish to see her children electrocuted before they'd even had time to open their presents.

Christmas Eve meant Midnight Mass. After a light supper of fish the whole family would muffle themselves up against the cold and go off together, returning home to the first of the festive treats and Mamma placing *Gesù Bambino* in the manger. The three kings didn't arrive with their gifts until 6 January, on the twelfth day of Christmas as tradition dictates, with the startling announcement of the Epiphany that *Gesù Bambino* was in fact the King of the Jews and not a Catholic as I had always presumed. Apart from the Virgin Mary, who had been pondering this since the Archangel Gabriel's first visit to her nine months previously, it seemed to come as a surprise to everyone else too, including Herod. As a child I was completely captivated by the Christmas story, with its large cast of characters and complicated plotline. We were a Catholic family. Although my parents were not devout they were believers and I was raised in the faith; but today, in spite of recognising the beauty and the mystery of the Christmas story, I am an atheist and agnostic.

The other key feature of our family Christmases was panettone – the sweet bread loaf originally made in Milan, its traditional cupola shape stuffed with raisins and flavoured with candied orange peel and lemon zest – which Papa received in abundance as a Christmas gift from numerous people. But however much we loved it, there was a surfeit of it at Christmas. We ate it even for breakfast for what seemed like weeks afterwards, sometimes dipping it into steaming mugs of hot chocolate – made with real, melted chocolate whisked into hot, frothy, full-fat milk – for an extra treat, or served with *crema di mascarpone*. Panettone also makes a very fine bread and butter pudding that the English in particular seem to like – a rather prosaic example of fusion cuisine, perhaps, but delicious nonetheless!

Chocolate was also a bit of a seasonal treat although that, too, has a regional history originating in Turin. It was in the sixteenth century that Emanuele Filiberto of the Royal House of Savoy moved his court's capital from Chambéry in France across the Alps to Turin, and chocolate first became fashionable in Italy. A daughter of Philip II of Spain, Catherine Michelle, who had married into the House of Savoy, had a great liking for the chocolate imported from the Spanish colonies in South America, and she introduced the beverage and its source to the court of Emanuele Filiberto and thus Turin. It was some time before the Swiss claimed it as their particular area of expertise. To this day, the annual *CioccolaTo*, Turin's famous chocolate festival, fills the air with the aroma of chocolate and the city becomes a *ciocco-dipendenti* – chocoholic's – paradise, with its local specialities like *Cremino Nocciolato Gianduia* and *Gianduiotto*.

After my father's promotion life settled down for us. Because of the free rail travel we enjoyed as a result of Papa's job, we travelled a lot.

Not just to visit relatives, but also to visit the city of Turin with all its attractions. As I grew older, I was allowed to join my siblings on day trips and then, eventually, to travel alone. Papa believed that we should explore and learn and make full use of our opportunity to travel, which he believed would help develop our characters.

School was in Borgofranco, where I went every day with Carlo. Because of the good start I'd been given while staying with my grandmother, I was ahead of my class and found the work very manageable. But the next big event in my life was to affect me more than any other for a long time and, because of what happened later, still affects me to this day. At the start, though, it was the happiest of events: the birth of my younger brother Enrico, the summer after my tenth birthday.

Mamma was pregnant again at thirty-eight, not old by today's standards. But back then and ten years after the birth of her previous baby, me, I think this pregnancy must have been something of a surprise to her, however welcome. I know that she had nine pregnancies in all, and six live births – the three lost babies were all miscarried in the years before my birth, not after it. I remember nothing of her pregnancy with Enrico and did not notice any alteration in her size; she would not have made any fuss or drawn attention to it in any case, simply continued looking after Papa and us and going about her daily chores as usual. Whether or not my sisters were called upon to give her a bit more help in the house I have no recollection, but the impending arrival of a new baby certainly didn't impact on my life in any way that I remember.

Although at this age I knew more or less how animals mated and produced their young and had probably heard my elder brothers talking about sex, to me the way that babies were made or what two consenting adults shared in the privacy of their bedroom was of no real interest. I suppose I had a rough idea of the difference between girls and boys since I had sisters and several young school friends who were female, but since they were seldom interested in playing football or looking for mushrooms they were hardly my first choice of playmate.

Several years before this, when I was about four years old, my friend Nino and I used to play with another young friend from the *asilo,* Pia, who lived close by. On one occasion the three of us were playing doctors and Pia was our patient. Innocently copying the way we had seen the doctor take a temperature, we tried to insert a straw into her little bottom in the same way. Unfortunately this hurt her and she ran back home crying. It was unintentional on our part. The harm didn't seem too great to us and we thought her distress a little over-dramatised, so later on we told her we were sorry and thought no more of it – until Nino and I were both heavily reprimanded by our respective mothers.

The resulting furore seemed to my young mind out of all proportion to the actual event. I was confused and didn't understand why the adults were concerned about our behaviour although I gathered it had something to do with the exposure of Pia's bottom. I also gathered that this was in some way wrong. It wasn't until I was much older that I understood why, but the trouble this innocent game caused me put me off playing with girls for quite a long while after that!

The day Enrico was born, 2 August 1947, was much like any other during the summer holidays. After my chores were done my day was pretty much my own and I would have spent most of it outside: swimming, walking, picnicking, gathering fruit, playing with my brothers or other friends. But I do remember that on this day I was on the railway embankment under the shade of some trees, not far from the station house which had all its windows but one shuttered against the blinding heat, when I heard the unmistakable sound of a newborn baby's lusty, indignant wail, signalling the midwife's initial slap straight after birth. It was about three o'clock on a sultry afternoon and, on hearing this shocked and offended cry, I immediately sprinted the short distance home to meet my new brother, already proudly cradled in Papa's arms. The midwife and my sisters were caring for my relieved but exhausted mother when, for the first time, I felt that stab of pride that comes from being an elder brother.

This first bond between us remained a lasting one. Although I was his brother, the ten-year age gap between us meant I felt as responsible and tender towards Enrico as a young father. His newborn head looked so small and vulnerable lying in the crook of my arm as I took my turn to cradle him and welcome him into the family. My sisters were quite proprietorial, eager to mother him and fuss with his little napkins and vests; my elder brothers were less so. The only time my mother had her newborn to herself was when she breastfed him. She managed this on her own for the first few months, whereas with me she had needed the help of a wet nurse too. The rest of the time there were five pairs of willing hands anxious to care for Enrico, and none more so than mine. As he grew older, and began to crawl, walk and learn to speak, and the interest of the others waned, I was his constant attendant, so pleased finally to have a younger brother to tend to and teach. It was such a relief to me no longer to be the youngest now that there was a new baby in the family, and the age gap between us was too great to give rise to any jealousy. My own status was elevated to that of adored big brother – and I was! It was to be a relationship of enormous importance to me.

Filetto di capriolo al Barolo

Fillet of venison in Barolo wine

Ever since I first started cooking I have always used wine for the preparation of dishes. I don't understand why some people use cheap wine, as it is the quality of the wine itself that is essential to producing rich flavours. Alternatively, I would always suggest using a good dry white wine over a champagne, as the bubbles only evaporate once it goes into the dish, so there really is no point cooking with it.

Serves 6
800 g (1¾ lb) venison fillet from a
    large deer
flour, for dusting
55 g (1¾ oz) butter
a few slices of white truffle,
    to serve (optional)

For the marinade
1 bottle of good Barolo wine
4 tbsp extra-virgin olive oil
a few juniper berries
a few bay leaves
a small sprig of rosemary
1 onion, thinly sliced
3–4 cloves
a pinch of freshly grated nutmeg
salt and pepper

Mix together all the ingredients for the marinade, trim the meat of gristle and skin, then add it to the marinade, cover and leave to marinate for at least 12 hours.

Remove the meat and pat dry, then cut it into medallions 2 cm (¾ inch) thick. Put the marinade in a pan and bring to the boil, then lower the heat and boil until reduced to a third of its original volume. Pass through a fine sieve and keep warm.

Dust the medallions with flour and fry in the butter for 3 minutes on each side: they should be rare and tender. Serve very hot with the sauce, together with polenta sprinkled with a few slices of white truffle if desired.

CHAPTER FOUR

Leaving Home

In the next few years I passed from boyhood to adolescence. My life continued to expand beyond the immediate confines of my family: through new friendships, the train travel we enjoyed, the summer holidays spent in Prata, and the independence I gained with approaching maturity.

It was during this time that the high-speed diesel train, the Littorina, was introduced by the Ferrovie dello Stato, to replace the old steam trains. This created a problem for me – by this time at senior school in Ivrea some miles away and needing to travel by train from Borgofranco d'Ivrea – because there was no longer a service that stopped at our station at the right time. A word from Papa, however, and it was arranged with the driver that although the early train wouldn't actually stop at Borgofranco, it would slow down enough for me to jump aboard quickly via an open door as it made its way through the station, much to the surprise of other passengers patiently awaiting the scheduled service. This Italian-style solution to a problem – *l'arte di arrangiarsi* once more – worked a treat, ensuring I was at school on time. No one high up in the railway service ever found out about the train rides I hitched!

Although I was not a natural academic I didn't find schoolwork difficult, which left me with lots of time to get involved with the various sports I loved. It was in the physical education class that I really excelled. I became very good both at athletics – running, hurdles, high jump and long jump – and the javelin. As I grew stronger and fitter from time spent on the track, my javelin-throwing became increasingly expert. In my imagination, I was a noble African warrior, hunting my prey. My other great love was art: I loved painting, drawing and sculpting. When I wasn't on the athletics track I was in the art room. I was not much given to solving complicated maths problems or reading great works of literature, although I was competent enough at both. For me, art and athletics remained the highlights of my time at school.

At weekends I liked to spend time with my younger brother Enrico, or Cicci as we called him. He was growing up fast, and I was glad to pass on to him some of the things that Carlo had taught me, whether this was cutting and initialling for him his first walking stick, teaching him how to forage safely for mushrooms or to kill, skin and gut a rabbit, ready for Mamma to cook. I taught him how to fire a pebble at a target, having first helped him find and cut a suitable Y-shaped stick from which to make a catapult. We would spend many happy hours together in the Soave hills of the area, watching the vineyard workers prepare the soil while we foraged between the vines for edible poppy plants or wild lamb's lettuce for salads. There was one occasion when we were very hungry, one cold winter's day, and helped ourselves (*l'arte di arriangiarsi* once again!) to a cabbage from a field. After rubbing off the soil and removing the cabbage's outer leaves, I took out my knife and sliced it very thinly before we doused the shredded leaves with a little vinegar and salt to eat with a chunk of bread as our *merenda*. It was delicious – hunger being the best sauce.

Cicci and I had a happy and easy relationship. Of all my siblings, I found him the most similar in temperament to myself. He was a little quieter than the others, both by nature and by virtue of being the youngest, a little more watchful perhaps, but with a strong imagination and sense of adventure, an urge to fly away and discover new places. Certain things were understood between us without any need for explanation. When someone shouted at him '*Vai a casa!*' it would pierce my heart too; I could feel his indignation as if it were my own. We also shared a love of nature, and I spent many happy hours showing him how to recognise the different varieties of trees in the woods, or types of herbs or plants that would be good to eat. We both appreciated the natural beauty around us. I helped him with his schoolwork, his letters and learning to read; showed him how to manage his shoelaces and buttons; shared with him my *merenda*. And, remembering how much I'd hated being denied involvement in my elder siblings' games, I always tried to include him in mine.

One of the big annual events, when the streets of Ivrea bustled with people and activity, was the town carnival with its Battle of the Oranges. This event has its origins in the Middle Ages, a mixture of fact and fiction confusing the details while providing a great excuse for a lot of feasting and fun. The story dates back to 1149 when the local lord was a despotic ruler called Ranieri di Biandrate, who had declared his own right to sleep with any bride on her wedding night: *jus primae noctis,* or *droit de seigneur* as it came to be known by the French. Legend has it that Biandrate got his comeuppance when one feisty bride, Violetta, the beautiful daughter of the local miller, refused to sleep with him on her wedding night. Not only that, she cut off his head with a dagger and then flaunted it to the people gathered beneath the castle walls, before throwing it in the river. This courageous act liberated them all from his tyrannical ways. She's the heroine of the carnival and known as the *mugnaia,* from the Italian word for miller.

The event was first celebrated by the throwing of beans, to represent the stones the townspeople threw against the castle walls. But around the nineteenth century the custom of throwing oranges was introduced – not a fruit that is native to northern Italy but one cheaply imported from the south. The carnival occurs in February, with mock battles occurring on the Sunday, Monday and Tuesday of the designated week, and the town is reduced to a mess of oranges. Townspeople on foot represent the rebels and throw oranges, rather violently, at those riding in carts, who symbolise the castle. Anyone who doesn't want to get pelted with fruit must wear a red hat or suffer the consequences!

We needed little excuse to become involved in the seasonal revelry – especially as it meant the preparation and enjoyment of special meals to celebrate the area's liberation from the despot. During carnival the streets are lit up and, not surprisingly, filled with the scent of oranges. The *balmetti* are raided for wonderful wines like the white *Erbaluce*, sparkling *Barbera* and sweet *Passito di Caluso*, and regional specialities are served in the streets – particularly *fagioli grassi per Carnevale* (fat beans): enormous pots of beans, cooked with sausages and pork rind, not unlike the French *cassoulet*. Other speciality dishes include *merluzzo con polenta* (salted cod with polenta), and delicious carnival pastries like *bugie, la torta di nocciole del Piemonte, baci di dama, brutti ma buoni* and *canestrelli*.

It was around this time that my own adolescent interest in girls began to emerge. I was about thirteen when I first had sex, courtesy of a local girl who was well known for being free with her favours. She was a few years older than me and had the benefit of experience, so she showed me what to do. It was not without excitement for me, but I had no feelings for the girl. Although I was pleased to be able to boast a little amongst my peers, the experience was not one of which I was particularly proud or something that I equated with love. After a couple of times with this girl, and without much else in the way of a relationship, there seemed to me no point in continuing. She swiftly transferred her affections, without causing any regret to either of us.

There were a couple of other girls for whom I yearned, rather hopelessly, but apart from the village *favorita* there was not much scope for fulfilment. We might have oranges thrown at us but, for the most part, Italian girls from good families remained chaste and inaccessible unless an offer of marriage was on the table. There was a double standard at work here. Those girls who would agree to have sex with boys were considered unworthy of being a love interest, although for us boys it was considered necessary to achieve a degree of manhood, and the only way to do so was by having sex with girls with whom we wouldn't consider having a relationship!

There was one girl I used to see when I was travelling to and from Ivrea on the train to school, who one day told me that I had wonderful eyes. Struck by this, I took myself off to the local photographer and paid him, with what lire I had managed to scrape together, to take a portrait, focusing on my eyes, which I duly gave her as a gift. It was to my mind at the time a very romantic and dramatic gesture, but it makes me smile to think of it now . . . all my idealistic dreams as a young man! I was also in love with my best friend Giorgio's sister Luciana, and he in turn was in love with Maria Christina, but for both of us this was an idealised, inaccessible form of love. There was no way I would lay a finger on my best friend's sister! So, after that initial, youthful experience, making love to a woman was not something to be enjoyed again until years later, providing in the meantime plenty of DIY.

This was, however, a happy and social time for me. I was content enough at school, still enjoying my art and athletics. I had numerous local friends, a good bunch of schoolmates, my family, and one or two special confidants. As relatives of *Capo Stazione di Prima Classe* Signor Carluccio, family members enjoyed a good standing in the town, and while our parents were strong on discipline, we knew they loved and supported us in their own way and they did not interfere too much in our choices of future career.

But things were not the same for my best friend Giorgio, brother of the first girl I loved. Son of the local doctor, he was a handsome, intelligent and thoughtful young man, who loved literature and writing poems for his beloved Maria Christina, but he was placed under relentless pressure from his father to study medicine. I remember how sometimes, when we were hanging out together, Giorgio would take himself off with a sigh, saying, 'I must go and study,' long before the rest of us called it a night. So when he failed his exams, the pressure was too much for him to bear. In a terrible fit of depression, he drowned himself in a local canal. It came as an unbelievable shock to me that he should have felt so desperate while I had remained in ignorance of it. As so often after a suicide, there was a strong feeling of guilt together with the grief I felt – was there something I could have done, something that might have made a difference? With these thoughts clamouring in my head, I sat in vigil beside him the night before his burial, and the next day his father, brothers and I stumbled in tears towards his final resting place, carrying his coffin on our shoulders.

With my schooldays drawing to a close, I now had to make some decisions about my future. I knew I didn't want to go to university in Turin, where my brother Carlo was studying engineering. That was not for me. I wanted to see something of the world beyond the immediate vicinity, and my desire for travel and adventure was piqued by a large, colourful poster Papa had recently put up in the station waiting room. It proclaimed: *Girerai il mondo, imparerai un mestiere* – you will travel the world, you will learn a profession – I would join the Navy! In 1946 the *Marina Militare* was established as the Republican Navy, after the demise of the Regia Marina or Royal Navy, and in 1949 Italy had joined NATO. Given its strategic position between the Soviet and US super powers, the Italian Navy was assigned control of the Adriatic Sea and the Strait of Otranto, as well as the defence of the naval routes through the Tyrrhenian Sea, and they were keen for new recruits.

I knew nothing of this background at the time, but the poster captured my imagination, with its depiction of blue seas and smart white uniforms and the prospect of escape from the confines of rural life. I announced my intention at home. While Cicci naturally supported me, my parents were initially opposed to the idea until finally, worn down by my pleas, Papa slapped me on the back and declared it would make a man of me. After his approval of the idea, Mamma genuflected and resigned herself to my departure. I immediately sent off my application and waited for the Navy's summons.

In 1954 I boarded the train from Turin to La Spezia, travelling first class, courtesy of Papa's position. On the way south from Turin, along the coast via Genoa, I found myself sitting in a carriage opposite a beautiful, elegant woman – in her thirties at least whereas I was just seventeen. We started talking and I found out that she was the wife of a captain in the US Navy, stationed at La Spezia at the time. This glorious Doris Day lookalike was extremely friendly. Sharing chocolate and oranges, we chatted until our arrival in the early hours of the following morning. Upon leaving the train, we went together to drink coffee at the station bar where she was greeted by a number of naval officers with a salute although they couldn't quite figure out who I was, being clearly so friendly with the captain's wife. I was in seventh heaven when she said she'd like to see me again before her return to America, my fantasies escalating in hopeful anticipation, and then we shared a taxi – she bound for the Hotel San Giorgio, where we agreed to meet again.

Feeling over the moon, I took another taxi to the naval school's recruitment offices. When I arrived at the main entrance the guard on duty initially thought that I was something other than a rookie recruit, since they generally arrived on foot, by bus or on the back of a friend's battered Lambretta. It wasn't until the following day when I tried to leave in order to visit the object of my adoration that the guard realised who and what I was. He laughed heartlessly at my desperation and ignored my entreaties to be allowed out. I was required, before formal acceptance into the school, to take and pass a series of exams –

which lasted an agonising three days, all without being able to call the beautiful captain's wife at her hotel. Finally I finished them. On being given leave at last, I rushed immediately by taxi to the hotel – only to find that my beautiful new friend, on whom I had lavished every erotic and romantic hope of which a young man is capable, had left. No one, not even Napoleon after his defeat at Waterloo, could have felt worse than me at that moment. My dream was shattered.

Luckily the next few weeks were demanding and interesting enough to take my mind of this romantic failure. I and a number of other new recruits found ourselves shipped off to the small island of La Maddalena, part of an archipelago in the Strait of Bonifacio, between the southern coast of Corsica and the northern coast of Sardinia. It had been an Italian naval base since 1887; in 1943 Benito Mussolini was briefly held prisoner there. Renowned for its wonderful sandy beaches and crystal-clear waters, the island is a holiday destination these days. Then as now it was accessible only by boat, although connected by a causeway at low tide to the neighbouring island of Caprera, famous for its association with the Italian hero and revolutionary Giuseppe Garibaldi, and nowadays a nature reserve.

On La Maddalena there wasn't much to distract us and the local girls weren't interested in lowly naval cadets, of whom I was just one among about 600. I found the military drill, the early rising, rigid discipline and endless rules and regulations, daunting at first, but as with everything in life you learn to adjust and I soon settled down. My main interest, though, was in learning mechanics, and this I did enjoy. I was fascinated by the huge steam turbines of the engines and studied hard, graduating second in my year with the prospect of further study at the Officers' Academy at Livorno on the Italian mainland.

One of my most vivid memories of this time is of meeting Clelia Garibaldi, daughter of Giuseppe, the great patriot and fighter who was something of a hero of mine and many other Italians. In his seventy-five years Garibaldi managed to fight in, and survive, three Italian Wars of Independence, plus numerous others on both sides of the Atlantic, including both South and North America. He was also exiled numerous times and met many notable historical contemporaries, from US president Abraham Lincoln to the British Prime Minister Lord Palmerston while also finding time to write at least two novels, an autobiography and memoir, marry three times and father seven children. Garibaldi became a central figure in the Italian *Risorgimento*, the move towards the reunification of Italy, and his larger-than-life character has been commemorated in statues all over the world, from La Spezia to Buenos Aires, Taganrog in Russia to Washington Square, New York, the Vatican City to Staten Island, and elsewhere. No wonder Italians loved his adventurous, romantic soul.

Along with eight other cadets, I was given the privilege of taking a birthday cake made by the naval kitchen in La Maddalena to Donna Clelia in the Garibaldi family home on Caprera. I couldn't believe my luck, to have this chance of meeting a blood relative of an amazing historical figure I had read about in my school history books. In 1955 she was celebrating her eighty-eighth birthday. Although I can't now remember what sort of cake it was that we took her on 16 February that year, today I would probably choose to make something celebratory like a *torta di nocciole e cioccolato* – chocolate and hazelnut cake – which is one of my favourites, delicious, and robust enough to survive a journey in the uncertain hands of a naval cadet!

Donna Clelia had lived on the island since 1889, seven years after her father's death, working as a writer and running the Garibaldi home as a museum. There was a family connection with the naval academy of Livorno as her younger brother Manlius, who had died of tuberculosis aged twenty-seven, had been a cadet there. I remember meeting a small, slightly heavy-jowled but sharp-eyed and alert woman. She was afflicted by the arthritis that had troubled her father, but delighted with her cake as well as with the sight of eight young cadets, resplendently attired in glowing naval whites. After her death in 1959, two naval cadets stood vigil over her body before its entombment alongside her father's. The house, still with the pine tree in its central courtyard that was planted by Garibaldi himself to mark Clelia's birth in 1867, is now a state-run museum.

Even though I enjoyed studying mechanics and being able to continue with athletics, loved the spectacular landscape of the coastline and the chance to visit Donna Clelia, I didn't much like the isolation of naval life. Sardinian society was very traditional. You couldn't meet a young woman from one of the local families without a formal introduction. We knew no one who would do so on our behalf, and these good, Catholic girls were not allowed out much in any case. Our only chance to experience the comfort a woman could offer was to visit the local brothel in the hills behind the naval barracks. With only three women working there, their services were rather over-subscribed with around 300 keen customers a week. We didn't get much *libera uscita* – free time – just two afternoons a week, and then many of the cadets would make a beeline for this *casa di piacere* or house of pleasure.

I was not judgemental about the activities of my fellow cadets, but it was not for me. If they were happy to pay 210 lire a time, then good for them, but I had learnt from my earlier experiences that I preferred a little romance, to be able to take the time to talk to and get to know a woman – at least a little! – before enjoying her body. For me, sex has always been as much in my head and heart as elsewhere; an emotional as well as a physical union. On La Maddalena I preferred instead to practise my athletics and spend time in the company of similarly minded friends, rather than drink too much, frequent the brothel, and boast about it afterwards.

Now I found myself at something of a crossroads. Was the Navy in fact the right career prospect for me? I was still only eighteen and, although I had left home, my current occupation hadn't given me as much of the *girerai il mondo, imparerai un mestiere* as I would have liked. And I was lonely in this all-male world. So, having completed the first stages of a naval career, and faced with the prospect of joining a *Condottieri* training cruise ship, the *Raimondo Montecuccoli,* which would be heading off soon for the 1956 Melbourne Olympics, I would shortly have to sign up for another seven years. I didn't want to continue, but my only way out of the Navy now was by deliberately failing the next batch of exams. By that time my superiors knew of my intention to fail. It was a recognised practice that others had chosen to exploit in the past in order to secure their freedom. However ignominious it was to me to fail when previously I had passed second in the class, it had to be done.

My time spent in the *Marina Militare* was not without merit, however, and I am grateful to the Italian Navy for all that it taught me about mechanics, self-discipline, companionship, service and hard work. But ultimately I knew it was not for me. It was with feelings of great happiness that I returned home to Borgofranco, my family and Mamma's *ottima cucina*!

Fagioli grassi con prete

Fat beans with puree

This dish reminds me of meals eaten with my family. With the help of leftovers and some beans, my mother was able to turn a humble dish into a work of art. Next to spaghetti with sauce, this peasant dish – with its countless variations – is the most common meal in all the twenty Italian regions. So you could say that Italy is in fact united by food!

Serves 4
pork skin
4 tbsp parsley, finely chopped
2 garlic cloves, crushed
2 tsp grated nutmeg
olive oil
3 carrots, finely chopped
3 celery sticks, finely chopped
3 medium onions, finely chopped
1 litre of chicken stock or beef stock
400 g (14 oz) borlotti beans
400 g (14 oz) cannelloni beans
400 g (14 oz) flageolet beans
salt and pepper
bread, to serve

To prepare the skin take off most of the fat with a thin sharp knife and roll it out flat with the skin facing down. Now generously salt and pepper your skin also adding the parsley, garlic and grated nutmeg. Roll it up into a sausage and tie it together with string.

Get a deep non-stick pan hot with a lid and add a healthy dollop of oil. Then fry the carrots, celery and onions stirring until they have softened. Add the stock, stir in all the beans and now add your roll.

Place lid on top and simmer gently for about 2 hours. Serve with fresh bread.

CHAPTER FIVE

Return to Borgofranco

Although my brother Cicci lamented the loss of my smart naval uniform he was glad to have me home, and even while Mamma tutted about the weight I'd lost on a naval diet, I was young and fit and now had to find something else to do to earn my keep. In the mid-1950s, Italy's economic situation wasn't good and there was considerable unemployment, although it was worse in the south.

The national television network, Radio Audizioni Italiane or RAI, began broadcasting in Italy in 1954, although it would be some years before the Carluccio family owned a television set. But this was a very important moment in Italian history. For centuries the country had been divided and there were many regional differences from north to south, with local dialects the only spoken language in some areas; social and cultural attitudes varied too. Now, thanks to RAI broadcasting in the official Italian language, the whole country could be unified – linguistically at least – for the first time. This would be effective in creating a sense of Italy as a country, even while many Italians continued to celebrate their regional differences.

With this unifying influence and the end of the fascist regime, the country began to experience a new sense of vitality. During the 1950s many businesses began to flourish as Italy experienced a post-war economic boom. It started to exploit its excellence in industry and design – exporting everything from the Fiat 500, Alfa Romeo and Ferrari cars, to the fashions of Pucci and Gucci. Exports of Piaggio's Vespa scooter (so named as it looks like a wasp) really took off after Audrey Hepburn appeared riding on the back of one behind Gregory Peck in the 1953 movie *Roman Holiday*.

Gaggia espresso machines arrived in Britain, the first one appearing in Soho, London in the same year, in a coffee bar called Moka in Frith Street. It was opened by Gina Lollobrigida. Her saucy short hairstyle, christened the 'artichoke cut', was copied around the world, and the new coffee-bar culture went on to be immortalised in the Cliff Richard movie *Expresso Bongo* in 1959. Italian actors like Sophia Loren and Marcello Mastroianni graced the movie screens, and this was the time of *la dolce vita*, embodied by Fellini's movie of the same name, its appeal quickly spreading abroad. This was particularly the case in America, where many southern Italians had emigrated, and was never more evident than when Dean Martin topped the charts in 1953 with 'That's Amore', while MGM released tenor Mario Lanza's film *Arrivederci Roma* (*Seven Hills of Rome*) to huge acclaim in 1958. Even Walt Disney got in on the Italian act when the two canine stars of the 1955 cartoon film *Lady and the Tramp* made eyes at each other over a plate of spaghetti and meatballs to a soundtrack of Peggy Lee singing 'Bella Notte'.

Back in Borgofranco in 1955, however, *la dolce vita* appeared to be passing me by as I struggled to find a job. I was very keen not to be dependent on my family and urgently needed to find work. Then the husband of a friend of my mother's, who worked in the local aluminium factory, came up with an idea to produce and market perfumed hair oil for men. Western men had used hair products to soften and groom their hair for over a century, from the macassar oils (palm oil allegedly sourced from Makassar in Indonesia, and combined with essential oil of ylang-ylang) of Victorian times, to the Brilliantine produced by French perfumer Edouard Pinaud at the turn of the twentieth century.

In Britain Brylcreem, originally manufactured in Birmingham in 1928, was a popular pomade made from an emulsion of water, mineral oil and beeswax. Hair oil was particularly in vogue in the 1950s as young men everywhere attempted to slick back their hair like the actors and pop stars, Elvis Presley in particular, we all sought to emulate. As the embodiment of the potential market, with my thick dark hair on which I could demonstrate the fashionable product, I put myself forward as a salesman.

The perfumed hair oil was bottled in little square glass jars with a black screw-on top and carefully packed in units of six. These were wrapped again in newspaper for safety, and carried in the basket of my bicycle. I cycled far and wide with my wares, to both shops and barbers, selling the hair oil to retailers and, occasionally, direct to customers. It didn't earn me much, little more than pocket money, but I was at least able to buy my own cigarettes and drinks when I went out. Other work had to be found and for a while I also took a job as a crane operator on a building site.

At the same time, I began to get involved with a social political organisation, the *Movimento Comunità*, founded by industrialist and entrepreneur Adriano Olivetti. During the Fascist regime, Olivetti had lived in exile in Switzerland where he evolved his philosophy of community living, publishing his book *L'Ordine Politico della Comunità* through his own publishing house NEI (Nuove Edizioni Ivrea), which later became Edizioni di Comunità, in 1946. He had some big ideas, which I supported, advocating the creation of new political, social and economic ties between central and local government, while also seeking to turn his philosophy of community ideas into reality through an *Istituto per il Rinnovamento Urbano e Rurale* (IRUR), creating new industrial and agricultural ventures to support urban and rural renewal of the area around Ivrea, ultimately designed to help reduce local unemployment.

He was something of a visionary and worked hard to create fair working conditions within the Olivetti business, which had and still has its headquarters in Ivrea, to support both his workers and the community in which his company was based. The local people recognised his commitment and supported Adriano Olivetti in return by electing him Mayor of Ivrea in 1956 before he went on to stand as a *Movimento Comunità* candidate in the general election and win a seat in 1958. It was an exciting time and I worked for the *Movimento Comunità* in a voluntary capacity since I admired its principles. Because so many of the people in the villages surrounding Ivrea worked for Olivetti, and because there was this commitment to *comunità*, or community, there would also be arts and music events organised for the workers to enjoy in their free time, and I became involved in some of these. They were very social occasions – a concert here, an art competition and exhibition there – in which everyone was welcome to take part.

Through this association, I got the chance to work as a journalist for the *Sentinella del Canavese* – the local newspaper in Ivrea – reporting on some of the events. This was very exciting for me and I still remember the pride I felt when I saw my first article, a concert review, and my name in print. I really enjoyed this new work. It was social, it was varied, it was linked to what I believed in and enjoyed, and it encouraged me to write for the first time, which I still continue to enjoy. Most of the time I was reporting on local news and events but occasionally it could be something quite shocking. One night I was called from my bed to go and report on a car accident on a quiet road in Saint-Vincent d'Aosta, about thirty-five kilometres from Borgofranco, involving ten people. Eight people were travelling in one car and had collided with another at a crossroads on Strada statale 26, driven by a man with his girlfriend who had just left the famous Casino de la Vallee on the via Italo Mus in Saint-Vincent. The woman had died immediately and the man was badly injured, while in the vehicle carrying the eight, one was killed and seven injured. Those hurt were taken to hospital. My reporting of this terrible incident, published the following morning, later received a journalism prize, but that did not diminish my horror at this terrible accident or the sad memories it evoked of another one I had witnessed, which had involved a young man on a Vespa colliding with an articulated lorry. Wearing a crash helmet wasn't obligatory then but I doubt if that would have saved him from his horrific injuries in any case. Afterwards I discovered that the victim had been one of my friends. Reliving that, and remembering the suicide of my dear friend Giorgio, I felt overwhelmed by the sadness and hopelessness of life, and was depressed for days afterwards without realising that this was a feeling that would go on to dog me all my adult life.

The journalistic prize for my reporting of the accident, however, brought me to the attention of another newspaper – this time the Turin-based *Gazzetta del Popolo*. I was approached to work for them, covering a larger area. I was very pleased to accept a job on this rather more prestigious paper, and they paid more – five lira a word! For a while I felt that the world was my oyster once more. Then it became clear to me that there was editorial interference in what was being published in the newspaper. I began to notice that the content of my articles was sometimes changed by the editor. I wasn't happy about this, uneasy that something I didn't necessarily agree with was appearing under my name. It did not reflect well on my integrity. I felt this was something that couldn't continue and, having argued my case on a number of occasions and been given short shrift, I felt my only option was to resign. Which I did, and would do again today for the same reason.

Although I was not quite twenty years old, I was already troubled by the hypocrisy rife in both religion and politics, and the effect this had on the world about me. Now the supposed freedom of the press, which

I had fully espoused, seemed to be similarly affected and I wanted nothing further to do with it. My innate belief is that the human race is capable of great truth, integrity and grace, and that it is possible to hold those principles dear without doing harm or causing pain to others. I believe this is the starting point from which all other choices in life should be made. Although it had initially been a good and formative experience for me to contribute to the newspaper, continuing to work for it would have meant relinquishing something I believed in, and I wasn't prepared to do that. So, full of youthful idealism, I resigned.

Once again, I needed to find a job.

This time, already an admirer of Adriano Olivetti's ideas, I turned my attention to finding a position with his company. Olivetti was much admired at the time for its distinctive corporate style based on technological excellence, innovation, quality and design. Adriano's father Camillo, who had been born in Ivrea and studied engineering at the Politecnico di Torino before going on to study further at Stanford University, had founded the company. He had returned home from America full of ideas, and set up the company in 1908, the first Olivetti typewriter appearing at the Universal Fair in Turin in 1911.

When I joined the company, almost fifty years after that, its international reputation for technological development, innovation and quality, coupled with its commitment to continuous improvement in the welfare of its employees, made it the leader in its field. It manufactured world-class typewriters, and perhaps one of the loveliest things Olivetti ever produced, iconic in design terms, was the first portable typewriter, the Lettera 22. Made in all sorts of different colours, streamlined, light but robust enough to be portable without being damaged, they really were beautiful and put the company on the map in terms of modern design. This was a manual typewriter, however, and by then the firm was already very busy developing its electronic side – not only typewriters but calculators as well, including another innovative product, the Olivetti Divisumma calculator, designed by Natale Capellaro.

In truth, there wasn't a huge amount of choice at this time when seeking employment around Borgofranco, other than seasonal agricultural work, and all I had to offer a future employer at this point was a qualification in naval mechanics and a way with words. By this time Olivetti had more than 24,000 employees, of whom 10,000 worked in the company's seventeen overseas subsidiaries, because around 60 per cent of its production was for export. This was an exciting time for the company, which was branching out into electronics with research teams based in both Connecticut in the US and in Pisa, developing Italy's first electronic computer, the Elea 9003. I very much admired Olivetti, he was such a visionary in so many ways, and before his death – he died of a heart attack while travelling by train from Milan to Lausanne in 1960, aged just 58 – the company really was exceptional.

It was not quite such an exciting time for me personally, however, as I was employed as an *operaio semplice*, literally a simple worker. Every morning I put on my regulation overalls, took the train from Borgofranco to Ivrea and worked in the *officina*, the technical department, where components for the calculators were produced. I worked on an automatic production line, checking the quality of each component, making sure nothing faulty got through that could adversely affect production further down the line. It was that tedious combination of repetitive work where you also had to stay concentrated and focused to be effective. You couldn't afford to drift off into reverie, otherwise a faulty component could really mess things up, so although it was a menial job it was not without responsibility. However, it was mind-numbingly boring most of the time! I decided to work hard in order to be promoted away from this initial task and, in due course, I was. This time to an assembly line where the work, although still repetitive, was a little more skilled, and where precision and attention to detail were important as the component parts had to be fitted together quickly for the production line to continue running smoothly.

The company did take good care of its employees. They recognised that even this menial, repetitive work was important to overall production, and that it could, in turn, be quite stressful. They valued everyone's contribution, however low down the line, and supervisors kept a constant eye on how we were coping, with transfers to other areas of work when necessary, in order to reduce the stress of the continuous monotony. The company would also provide time off at a *casa di riposo* – a rest home – for the worst cases of fatigue. In this way they were unique, years ahead of their time when it came to industrial relations and employee welfare. But it paid off. The workforce was efficient and for the most part content, and I appreciated being part of it.

We also enjoyed a free meal every day, in the *mensa* or canteen. Working hours were from eight in the morning to midday, then from two to six pm. Many who lived locally went home for the two-hour lunch break. Those of us who lived a little further afield ate in the canteen, and each day a meal was prepared for around 2000 of us. For canteen food it was really quite good. Each day there would be various choices, and you could enjoy a four-course meal starting with antipasti, some salami perhaps, then a choice of two or three different pasta dishes, followed by some meat or fish, and finally some sort of dessert – fruit, or crème caramel or something like that. We had wine too, *quartinos*, a glass with your meal, and no one was ever drunk. It seems quite extraordinary now, when so many lunches are just a sandwich taken at a desk without a proper break to recharge the proverbial batteries, but I think Olivetti recognised that a properly fed workforce actually works better. I believe they were right.

After a while I was chosen for additional training, learning how to

1.

2.

1. *My mamma, aged about 17, on the beach in Italy. She was quite a beauty when she was younger.*

2. *Papa always looked smart. Here he is in 1925, around the time when he met my mother.*

3. *Me around age 3.*

4. *Looking well-behaved in my school photo, aged 9.*

3.

4.

1.

Carluccio Antonio

Classe III^a A 51-52

2.

3.

1. *My class photo, 1952. I'm in the back row, second from the left.*

2. *I always love sport at school. Here I am doing high jump.*

3. *This is me in the arms of my Aunt Dora in 1939, who, with my grandmother, looked after me when I was a small child.*

1.

1. *Cicci in 1960. This is the last photo of him taken before the accident.*

2. *This is the only photo I have of me and all of my siblings together, which was taken in 1949. From left: Anna, Giuseppe (Peppino), Grazia, Carlo and me, holding Enrico (Cicci).*

2.

1.

2. 3.

4.

4. *With Inge in around 1960.*

5. *On the day of my wedding to Gerda (centre).*

6. *Working hard at Olivetti. I'm just at the centre in the black tie.*

5.

1. *Taking a drive in my beloved Fiat 500.*

2. *Looking dapper in my Navy uniform in 1958.*

3. *With two friends from school, Luciana and Donatella. I was in love with them both!*

6.

Looking every bit the film star in Hamburg, 1972. This photo was taken by a famous stage photographer.

1.

2.

1. *Eva.*

2. *Christa on holiday in Corsica, around 1972.*

3. *At home with Gerda.*

3.

1.

2.

3.

1. *Playing the around in some passport photos, around 1974.*

2. *My beloved dog Yan, 1978.*

3. *Sculpting clay with my dear friend and talented artist Eduardo Paolozzi at The Royal College of Art, London, in 1993.*

repair and assemble more complex aspects of the calculators that were now being manufactured. Although I'm not particularly technical, I am logical and I enjoyed this and learnt quickly, being promoted to *operaio specializzato*, which meant more interesting work and an increase in salary. This made me very happy. Now I was earning enough not only to pay my way and buy presents for my family, but also to save a little, which I did, eventually having enough to buy myself my first Vespa. I was so proud of this scooter and of being independently mobile, able to offer a friend a lift or to run errands for my family. I drove daily to work, finally forsaking the train whatever the weather conditions, loving the freedom my Vespa afforded me.

Life felt good. I had work, and a decent pay packet. I had a social life, although no specific girlfriend amongst the young women I knew, and I was desperate to fall in love. I joined the *gruppo sportivo* at Olivetti, where I trained hard and achieved a record of 65 metres with the javelin and 15 metres with the triple jump. I hoped one day to be good enough to join the National Athletic Team. Olivetti also ran a workers' cinema, regularly showing films, and although this wasn't a particular interest of mine, I do remember going to see the 1939 Hollywood blockbuster *Gone With the Wind* for the first time when they showed it, complete with Italian subtitles. Personally, I always thought that *'francamente mia cara, non me ne frega niente'* lost a little in translation, in spite of Clark Gable's sardonic intonation when Rhett Butler finally dismisses Scarlett O'Hara for the last time: 'Frankly, my dear, I don't give a damn.' Another promotion at work, this time to *servizio tecnico assistenza clienti* – technical assistant to clients – was good news, but it still saddened me that while my working life was successful, my personal life lacked the fulfilment I sought.

Looking back, I can see now that I was probably slightly depressed. Although my job was stable, without further training and skills I was never going to progress on to the creative side, and I began to understand that this was where my heart lay. I could, however, afford to take a proper holiday, the first in my life, and so I went off to seek some personal *dolce vita* on the Italian Riviera.

Although I knew the Amalfi Coast a little, from staying there with my grandparents, I had grown up in a landlocked area, surrounded by mountains. I had also loved the rugged Sardinian coastline of my naval training, but Laigueglia, on the Ligurian coastline not far from the French/Italian border, approximately 130 kilometres due south of Turin and about eighty south-west of its capital Genoa, was new to me. I took the train, travelling first class as usual courtesy of Papa, the line running down to Genoa and then along the Riviera di Ponente Ligure, following the beautiful Ligurian coastline to Laigueglia. When I arrived, I walked from the station along the via Roma to my hotel in the heart of the Riviera delle Palme, overlooking the Baia del Sole. Laigueglia had once been little more than a fishing village but, post-war and with travel opportunities opening up, the Riviera of the Ligurian coastline attracted many holidaymakers to its handful of beachfront hotels, not only from Italy but also from neighbouring France, and farther afield from Switzerland, Austria and Germany. It had a lovely, hospitable climate all year round, which was another of its attractions. I found and checked into my hotel, with its view of the sea and Gallinara Island in the distance, a green oasis of a nature reserve in the sparkling blue of the Ligurian Sea.

That first evening, as is the custom in Italy, I dressed as smartly for dinner as my limited wardrobe allowed, but before finding a table I joined the other holidaymakers in the custom of *la passeggiata* – walking a little around the piazza or along the beach promenade. It is a social custom, partly for the purpose of *vedere e farsi vedere* which simply means 'to see and be seen', and I certainly wanted to be seen, a slim, handsome twenty year old, but also to see what young women might be around with whom I could possibly strike up a conversation.

After walking for a while, enjoying the ambience, the evening's gentle sunshine and the beautiful view, but without entering into any conversation, I returned to my hotel to eat. It is the custom in Italy, on entering a dining room full of people, to exchange a greeting, a gently murmured *Buonasera,* in friendly acknowledgment of each other. Sitting down to my antipasti, together with a glass of chilled white wine, I noticed two women at an adjoining table and we nodded a greeting to one another. They were a mother and daughter, I judged by looking at them, and probably not Italian, given the angelic blonde hair and blue eyes of the girl. The next morning, at breakfast, they were there again. *Buongiorno,* I said, this time with a little more emphasis, looking directly at the girl, and was rewarded with a captivating smile which made my heart skip a beat. As they finished their breakfast and left, I began to wonder how I might make their acquaintance properly.

Later, walking along the promenade towards the beach, I saw them again, enjoying the sun in their bathing costumes, talking to an Italian boy on the beach. My heart sank a little. Who was he? But I called out a hello, and we finally met formally. Fortunately the lovely young woman from Austria spoke good Italian and the other boy was just someone who worked on the beach. She was called Inge, and she and her mother had arrived the previous day from Vienna. That evening I was invited to join them for dinner at the hotel, and was able get to know Inge and Mutti a little better. As we Italians also say, *l'appetito vien mangiando* – appetite comes from eating – and in their company I could feel my appetite for life returning. From then on, with Mutti's approval, Inge and I spent every day together, sunbathing on the beach, swimming in the sea, walking on the promenade, talking boat trips and cycle rides: two young people in love. And I was, very much so. For the first time in my life I was deeply, happily in love: all my dreams of closeness and romance were answered in every way. Inge had changed my life for ever.

At the end of our ten happy days together, she and Mutti had to return home to Vienna. The idea of being separated from Inge was almost too much for me to bear. Indeed, if it had not been for my conviction of her love for me and mine for her it would have been unbearable, but we felt so sure of each other I knew it would stand the test of time. Cutting my own holiday short, I decided to accompany them by train to the border between Italy and Austria, as I did not have my passport with me to travel further. We sat together on the long train journey across northern Italy, holding each other's hand tightly. As we approached Tarvisio, in the mountains of north-eastern Italy and on the Austrian border, I felt bereft. I knew I would have to leave Inge here. I stood for a long time on the platform after watching her train pull out of the station, feeling both sad and happy at the same time. Sad at our separation, happy to know I would see her again, although not knowing exactly when and how. Then I had to wait overnight at Tarvisio, sleeping on a bench in the waiting room, for the return train and the long trip back to Borgofranco.

We wrote each other long letters every day. My first question when I got in from work was, *'Niente posta oggi?'* Any post today? My siblings, amused by my lovesick behaviour, would occasionally tease me, denying me my post, but to me it was an extremely serious matter. Testament to our love, Inge and I exchanged hundreds of letters over the time we were apart. I was completely besotted by her, and fortunately she felt the same. My devotion was met with some scepticism by my friends. The male ones were jealous, the female ones a bit dismissive. The double standard still prevailed and this time it was worsened by the fact that Inge was from Austria. A foreign girl was considered fair game by many young Italian men at the time, someone to conquer as a boost to the male ego, and a holiday romance was seldom taken seriously. The girls in turn saw Inge as competition, and were suspicious of her liberal attitude. Sex before marriage was still unusual in the close-knit Italian communities where I grew up, where the Catholic edict on contraception was that it was a mortal sin, worthy of excommunication. Taking a risk was more than most girls were prepared to do when an unwanted pregnancy was considered scandalous. Even if it was hushed up, the girl's reputation was tarnished for good. A lot of unhappy marriages began because of a pregnancy or a pregnancy scare, thanks to this punitive and illiberal attitude. But their reaction didn't bother me. My relationship with Inge, complete on every level, was based on genuine love, commitment and consideration, and unrestricted by Catholicism.

That Christmas, Inge – with the full permission of Mutti – invited me to her home in Vienna, to spend the holiday with her and her family. This was my first trip abroad, the first time I would leave Italy and my first Christmas apart from my family. Again I took the train, from Ivrea to Turin, then on via Milan, Verona, Padua, and on again to Travisio to cross the border into Austria. Then I travelled further into this foreign country, via Udine, Klagenfurt and Graz, until finally I reached Vienna for the first time, and was reunited with Inge.

My Christmas was a really joyful one that year, especially as I was so warmly accepted by my girlfriend's immediate and extended family. I loved the snow-capped, steeply roofed houses, with the tall, thin Advent candles in the windows. I loved singing 'Stille Nacht' and 'O Tannenbaum' on Christmas Eve at the local church, and seeing the glittering lights on the frosty, cobbled streets as we walked between the Burggasse and Siebensterngasse, and around the Christkindlmarkt at Neubauguertel. Walking through this winter wonderland, holding hands with Inge, with the scent of freshly cut pine trees in the air, sipping piping hot *glühwein* and nibbling on spiced *lebkuchen* then buying a gingerbread heart for my girlfriend, is one of my abiding memories of this first Christmas away from home.

Here I tasted for the first time *käsespätzle*, little pasta dumplings served with a cheese sauce, and *Wiener eintopf,* a delicious potato stew with boiled sausage, cooked by Mutti. Here I heard Strauss played for the first time by the Vienna Symphony Orchestra, conducted by Herbert von Karajan, at the Wiener Konzerthaus. Inge and I shared so many things that first Christmas together, as we both had a love of art, music, nature – and each other. I felt so welcomed and at home in this new city I was sad to return to Italy, but in the New Year Inge was due to go to London as an au pair and to learn English, while I returned to Borgofranco determined to learn German. While I waited for letters to come from England, I diligently studied at the Berlitz School, glad to be able to practise in my correspondence with my girlfriend.

After she had completed her time in London, Inge decided to come to Italy so that we could be together, and with my connections at Olivetti and her language skills, she started working there as a foreign language secretary. Given the prevalent attitude towards unmarried couples living together, we couldn't actually share a home and so she lived in a flat on the via Roma in Borgofranco. (In Italy, many but not all roads lead to Rome!) I spent a lot of time with her there, although I couldn't spend the night as I didn't want to compromise her reputation, returning home to my family very late. At first my friends were rather sceptical about Inge, although some of the young men did flirt with her in a spirit of competitive masculinity, trying it on in an effort to prove correct their own theories about foreign girls, but our love remained steadfast and eventually Inge was accepted into my circle of friends without a problem.

My trusty Vespa, however, was proving less steadfast and not up to the journeys I planned to make exploring the beautiful Val d'Aosta, its mountains and surrounding areas, showing my girlfriend my beautiful homeland as we spent every weekend together visiting different places. The time had come to buy a car, and with great pride I bought a Fiat. The Fiat 500 was designed by Dante Giacosa, another graduate of the

Politecnico di Torino, and had been launched as the Fiat Nuova 500 in 1957. It was marketed as a cheap and practical town car, measuring only three metres long with a tiny 479cc two-cylinder, air-cooled engine – but it was perfect for me and Inge and we made many memorable trips in this little car.

In 1959 we went all the way south to Vietri sul Mare, to visit the town of my birth on the beautiful Amalfi coast, and then travelled inland so I could introduce Inge to my grandmother Giuseppina, Aunt Dora and other relatives. It was an extremely happy time, and Inge loved Italy so much so that she was able to persuade her mother to come and live with her at the flat in via Roma without difficulty. Mutti was delighted. My mother and she got on very well, so Inge's family and my own became more closely integrated. At last I felt happy and content, and wanted little more than to continue living like this, but it was not to be. The following year life changed irrevocably for me.

Fritaten suppe

Zuppa con frittata

Very much in my cooking philosophy is Fritaten Suppe, *one of Vienna's simplest dishes. Is delightful and delicate, and so easy to make.*

Serves 4

2 large eggs, beaten
50 g (2 oz) plain flour
100 ml (3½ fl oz) milk
1 tbsp chives or parsley, finely chopped
2 tbsp olive oil or Vienna pumpkin
   seed oil.
1.2 litre (40 fl oz) chicken or beef stock
   (cubes are allowed)
Parmesan cheese (optional)
salt and pepper

Mix the beaten eggs, flour, milk and chives or parsley and salt and pepper.

Put 1 tablespoon of olive oil into a non-stick frying onto a medium heat. Pour half of the mixture into the pan and when brown, turn over, and set aside. Repeat with the remaining mixture. Roll up each frittata and cut into thin strips.

Pour the hot broth into bowls and add a quarter of the frittata and serve instantly with a few chives. If you want to make it more Italian, serve with some Parmesan cheese.

CHAPTER SIX

Vienna

n 26 August 1960, I drove to work at Olivetti as normal. It was late summer and the weather was hot, with only an occasional breeze off the mountains to freshen the morning.

Coming back to my workstation after lunch, I was surprised to hear that one of the directors of the company had been looking for me. Now I saw him coming towards me with a worried look on his face. 'Antonio,' he said when he saw me, 'I'm afraid there has been an accident and you need to go to your family at once.' He knew no more than that and so, bewildered and anxious and not knowing who had been hurt or what had happened, I left the factory and drove home immediately, turning over in my mind all the while what might greet me there. Was it Mamma or Papa who was ill, or worse? Or was it one of my brothers or sisters? It's hard to imagine now, in the days of mobile phones and text messaging, that I journeyed home without any real idea of what had happened. The only message that had got through was just an instruction to return as quickly as possible. Although it was only a twenty-minute journey it felt like an eternity to me. While I feared for the worst, I also hoped it was a false alarm.

But it was not. I walked in to find my mother unconscious from the shock of the news, my two sisters beside themselves with weeping and my two elder brothers equally ashen-faced and disbelieving. My cherished younger brother Enrico was dead. It was the worst possible news: of all my family I was closer to him than to any of the others, and this was something I had never anticipated. Enrico had been so young, vibrant and full of life, I just could not take it in. I could not believe that my dearest brother, to whom I was as attached as a parent to a child let alone a sibling, was dead. It made no sense to me. Apart from my sisters' sobs, no one was making a sound and it was hard at first to make out what had happened. Only Papa, equally distraught, managed to stay lucid enough to tell me that my brother had been swimming with friends in the lake and had drowned. Now Papa faced the daunting task of having to go to the mortuary, where Enrico's body had been taken, to make a formal identification and sign the release papers for his body. I immediately offered to go with him.

On that hot August day, my brother and his friends had gone where we'd all been regularly to swim in the summer months, to a nearby lake at Montalto Dora, which lies about halfway between Ivrea in the south and Borgofranco to the north, on the opposite side of the via Aosta from the River Dora. It is one of five alpine lakes in the area, all deep and tantalisingly cool on a hot summer's day. Enrico and his friends were competent swimmers, a skill learnt in early childhood and one I had taught my brother myself, so his drowning seemed inconceivable.

Bit by bit we were able to piece together the story from his companions. They had all been together, swimming and larking about in the lake, jumping in, diving underwater and resurfacing, splashing and calling out to each other, as happy and carefree as teenaged boys could be. Then someone noticed that Enrico had not reappeared from a dive. Initially they thought he was continuing his prank and would resurface at any minute, laughing at their consternation, but he didn't. As time passed they panicked, eventually running for help. Too late. His body was found floating face down in only two to three metres of water. He was just thirteen years old. When the fire brigade arrived, they tried mouth-to-mouth resuscitation but he was dead.

As the attendant gently removed the sheet that shrouded him, it was a terrible shock to see Enrico's young body so cold on the marble mortuary slab. His skinny legs were naked and motionless, his hair still wet and sticking up in an unruly fashion around his lifeless features. His mouth was slightly open. Papa silently nodded his head as he and I stood rigidly side by side, studying Enrico's expressionless face, before the attendant gently drew the sheet over him once more. The consensus was that he had swum too soon after eating and suffered a cramp that caused him to drown; it was deemed a terrible accident. My father's jaw was clamped shut, his mouth a grim line as he struggled to contain his emotions. I was too shocked then to cry, feeling not so much that I had to be strong for my family as completely numb. The weight I felt in my heart then was to remain with me for ever.

Enrico's body was brought home. We dressed him in his best suit, and gently combed and slicked back his hair from his pallid features. With his arms uncharacteristically still by his sides and his fingernails unusually clean from the water in which he'd met his death, we laid him in an adult-sized coffin which only seemed to accentuate his extreme youth and the tragedy of his early departure from this life.

As was the custom, the coffin was displayed in the sitting room next to the now silent piano, so that family, friends and neighbours could come and pay their respects before Enrico's funeral and interment. The local paper had published the news, and people came from far and wide. Because of Papa's job my family were well known in the area, and while many wanted to come to show support for us, each time someone visited I found their condolences and expressions of grief harder to bear. They seemed to make it more difficult for me to express my own. It was too public, and so I chose instead to sit alone with my brother through the night, occasionally wiping his face when some slight discharge leaked from his nose.

Keeping vigil in the still, small hours, I remembered all the happy times we'd shared but also tortured myself with memories of times I had lost patience with him, spoken sharply or dismissively, and the one occasion when I had showed irritation and anger by slapping him in the face. Now I wept bitter tears of self-recrimination as I considered Cicci's watery destiny and my own loss. In my bereft state I could find no self-forgiveness. I felt then, and it remains true even now, that as his elder brother I should have shown him only love and understanding.

It was a long night. In the morning they came to close the coffin, but not before my mother hugged his body one last, long time, trying to coax warm life back into him with her tearful embrace, and I slipped some of his favourite *baci perugina* – literally, small chocolate kisses – into his pocket. The sealed coffin was loaded on to the hearse and we began our slow procession from the railway station down the main road, along via Aosta to the church of St Maurizo Martyr on via Marini, the bell tolling all the while. Then, after the service, the cortège made its way back to the cemetery on via Montebuono, a huge number of people showing their silent solidarity, and the priest performed more rites for the interment as Cicci's coffin was slid into the *loculo,* a burial niche recessed into the wall.

This final act seemed to cauterise my heart with grief. It was the same for all those around me; my mother in particular seemed to collapse in on herself as if her life, too, were over. In a way, for all of us, life would never be the same again, but the grief we felt seemed to isolate us rather than bringing us together. Inge, with me throughout and desperately sad herself, found it difficult to reach me. I found it impossible to celebrate my brother's short life as his death seemed to blot out and bury any happy memories, while my own overwhelming remorse threatened to engulf me.

The following day dawned even more bleakly without the ceremony to focus on, leaving our family with just a big hole where Cicci's happy presence had once been. My mother had taken to her bed while my poor father had to return to work. I could not bear to be in the house with its claustrophobic atmosphere, and got up early. Before it grew too hot I took a walk into town, ending up at the market. Here I bought a huge bunch of fresh parsley, its densely green leaves still sprinkled with early-morning dew, its pungent scent evocative of so many meals. Along with this I bought a whole kilo of salted anchovies.

Returning home, I set to work. I carefully rinsed each anchovy under cold, running water, the salt stinging slightly when it touched any small cut or torn cuticle on my increasingly chilled hands. I dried the washed anchovies carefully on a clean, freshly laundered cloth. Then, taking a newly sharpened knife, I made a neat incision along the side of each small fish, peeling back the top portion to reveal the backbone. Using the tip of the knife gently to ease out and remove this from the fish's lower side, I slowly worked my way through the pile until the filleting was complete. Then I chopped the fresh parsley and layered the anchovies with it. It took several hours and I was glad of the distraction of the slow methodical work, painstakingly preparing the anchovies so that they could be made into the traditional Piedmontese dip *bagna caôda,* or another Piedmont speciality *salsa verde*; something simple that could be eaten with some bread and olive oil, its fresh taste stimulating the taste buds if and when a little appetite returned. This was perhaps the first time I remember actively turning to the preparation of food in an effort to create some sort of meaning and purpose in my life when otherwise there was none. I didn't know it then, but this process was to become a source of solace to me again many, many times in the future.

Among the numerous visitors to our home after the death of Enrico were the local Jehovah's Witnesses. In the past Mamma had given these people and their views short shrift; her Roman Catholicism was both cultural and spiritual and had served her well enough in the past, but now she was truly tested and I assume she found her original faith wanting. Vulnerable in her loss and aching with grief, somehow the teachings of this religious sect gave her something to hold on to, and she renounced her Catholicism and took up with the Witnesses. Why this, of all religions, should speak to her at this time – what with its ideas about fallen angels ruling the earth since 1 October 1914, and that we were heading for the end of the world; that there was no life after death and, when we eventually reached Judgement Day, only 144,000 souls would be resurrected to rule with Jehovah's main witness, Jesus Christ – is beyond me. From where I sat she seemed to be grasping at straws in the vain hope that one day she would see her youngest son again, jumping from one hypocritical institution – as I believed Catholicism to be – to another, and this one seemed even more bizarre in its views. But it took over her life until the end of her days, and created something of a rift in our relationship as she now viewed everything through the prism of her new religious beliefs.

I came to loathe the sight of the *Watchtower* magazine, which she read avidly, and chose to avoid any discussion of it that might arise, particularly disliking the Witnesses' evangelical need to try and convert others. She knew better than to attempt to persuade me of its teachings, but my sister Anna, seven years older than me, embraced them too. Anna had had a good, secure and rewarding job as a secretary which she'd enjoyed. Now she gave it up and became a Jehovah's Witness preacher, convinced that in the year 2000, when the end of the world was expected, she would be reunited with our brother. Throughout the years she has continued to try and convert me – even when the year 2000 came and went with no noticeable ending – and we argue endlessly about it, even while I have continued to support her financially. I was, and remain, completely agnostic, and actively sought excommunication from the Church of Rome many years ago. Now she is old and paralysed following a brain haemorrhage: even there her religion betrayed her as she refused the blood transfusion that would have made possible surgery to prevent paralysis.

My life changed again in December 1960 when Inge decided to return to Vienna for good. This was enough to persuade me to make a break from the sombre atmosphere that prevailed at home and, now that my German was good enough, join her there. I handed in my notice at Olivetti, and began to make my preparations. My parents were nervous about my giving up such stable work, and also of losing me so soon after my brother's death, but I was adamant that I needed a change. I felt that if I didn't leave now and try and make something more of my life, then I never would.

Even though I did so with a heavy heart, it felt like a whole new start for me when I packed up my Fiat 500 and drove to Vienna early in January 1961. I had the spare room at Inge's house in an area of the city known as Blumengasse, the literal translation being 'flower street'. Inge's mother was pleased to have her daughter home and equally pleased to welcome me, while I was happy to be reunited with my girlfriend and also to have a new life to explore after the sadness of the preceding months. I was committed to completing my exams, the equivalent of A-levels which I hadn't previously taken on account of joining the Navy, at the private Matura Schule Roland. But first I had to do a brief course at the university to obtain a certificate of competence in the German language, which was part of the school's admissions requirement. I was keen to read and write perfect German, and to lose the influence of the local Austrian dialect I had acquired, so worked really hard to do this in the allotted time before taking up my place. There were many students at the school, mostly a bunch of twenty-somethings who, like me, had dropped out of school and now wanted to complete their education.

In order to pay my way, I also needed to find a job that fitted in with my studies. Luckily there was an Olivetti Agency in the city and, trading on my previous experience and good track record with the company, I applied for work and immediately got a job repairing typewriters, calculators, washing machines and irons! So I worked at the agency in the morning and went to school in the afternoons, and this brought a renewed sense of order and stability to my life. I was also becoming fluent in a number of languages. Besides my mother tongue, my French was good because it was the second most-spoken language in Piedmont, and now my German was improving daily. Being fluent in a number of languages had long been a private ambition of mine as I believed it would make the world more accessible to me. I was delighted to be making good progress with this.

Vienna in the early 1960s was a vibrant and interesting place. Annexed and occupied by Nazi Germany in the Anschluss of 1938, when much of Austria had welcomed Hitler's policies, it didn't regain its independence from Germany until after the end of the war. Then Austria remained under the control of the Western Allies, and like the rest of the country the city of Vienna was divided and jointly occupied by the US, the UK, the Soviet Union and France, until Austria declared perpetual neutrality and finally regained full sovereignty in 1955. This internationalism had left its legacy.

By the time I lived there in 1961 the atmosphere in Vienna was extremely liberal. Austria had also benefited from the 1948 Marshall Plan in which American money was given after the terrible winter of 1947, to boost industrial production in an attempt to rebuild the European economies after the war and try to combat the spread of Soviet Communism. This was before the intensity of the Cold War was ratcheted up a notch with the Berlin blockade and the building of the Wall in August 1961. Being twenty-four years old and living in Vienna in the early 1960s, however, I'm afraid I was not so much concerned with global politics as with my own social life.

When I wasn't working or studying, a favourite place to meet friends of an evening was the Café Hawelka, a coffee house on Dorotheergasse in the Innere Stadt district. It was frequented by artists, musicians and writers, and famous for that and for its expertise in coffee-making. Here I spent long hours talking to my friends. We could enjoy a *kleiner schwarzer* or a *grosser schwarzer,* a small or large espresso made from a blend of Robusta and Arabica beans; a *kleiner brauner* or a *grosser brauner* where the addition of frothy milk gave it a lighter taste while retaining its caffeine kick; a large *melange* with its ratio of 1:1 coffee to hot milk was the closest equivalent to a cappuccino and a popular choice; while a *Maria Theresia* was a large espresso served with Cointreau, and a *flaker* or *einspaenner* with a shot of rum. The list of available coffees was as long as in today's American-style cafés, but before there was ever Starbucks there was Café Hawelka.

Leopold Hawelka had opened the café with his wife Josefine in 1939 although it had had to close during the war, re-opening in 1945. Josefine was responsible for baking the café's speciality, its *buchteln* dessert, still made today from the family's secret recipe. It is primarily a sweet, plum jam-filled dumpling, made from yeast dough and cooked in batches in a large pan. The plum jam used is a traditional *powidl* made without additional sweeteners or pectin, but using the ripest plums of the season to ensure a high sugar content, and cooked for several hours. It is in fact more like a thick plum stew than a jam. Topped with vanilla sauce or powdered sugar, and eaten warm, *buchteln* are delicious. In those days I was so fit and active I could eat them regularly with impunity, my waistline easily withstanding their calorific assault!

Coffee was always served with an accompanying glass of water, presented on a small metal tray. As well the *buchteln,* the other food that I relished eating there was the *zwei eier im glas* which was two softly boiled eggs, peeled and served in a glass, with salt and pepper and a slice of rye bread spread with pork lard. Nutritious, sustaining and delicious, this was another favourite of mine. Or there were traditional Polish sausages, *debreziner,* boiled and served with fresh grated horseradish, strong and fiery on the tongue, and *blaukraut* (braised red cabbage) or beetroot. The food menu was short, unlike the coffee menu, but the excellence of the ingredients and their preparation made the dishes something to savour.

Working with Leopold, who lived to be 100 years old before his death in December 2011, and his wife Josefine was Theo the waiter who had been there since before the war and had the patience of an elephant. Even when his clientele was a little the worse for wear and becoming raucous or sentimental with drink, he never lost his equanimity or his discretion. He was also an informal banker for impoverished students, lending them the money to pay for their *debreziner, buchteln* or *Maria Theresia:* to be reimbursed, without interest, a couple of days later.

The café was extremely atmospheric, its interior dark and smoky with worn velvet banquettes, wooden chairs and panelled walls hung with original art and concert posters. Patronised by writers, actors and artists, it was bohemian and convivial in equal measure and I loved going there to talk to its regular clientele of artistic and literary people, enhancing my cultural education with conversations about art, existentialism, literature and music. Vienna, home to the sort of bohemian counterculture epitomised by the Austrian painters Egon Schiele and Gustav Klimt, continued to inspire artists in the 1960s. I found the ambience quite intoxicating and many an evening ended late at Café Hawelka amid long, stimulating conversations with the likes of artist and architect Friedensreich Hundertwasser, famous for his extraordinary creations such as the Hundertwasserhaus apartment block in Plochingen in Vienna, and luminaries of Die Wiener Schule des Phantastischen Realismus (Vienna School of Fantastic Realism) like Ernst Fuchs, Wolfgang Hutter and Johann Muschik, all of whom were happy to expound their artistic theories to anyone interested enough to listen – and I lapped up this magical and invigorating intellectual atmosphere. I met also Oskar Kokoschka, the artist, poet and playwright who had spent the war years in Scotland. Café Hawelka remains in its original location, still serving excellent coffee and *buchteln*, but now run by Leopold's son Günter and grandsons Michael and Amir. Revisiting it today, I am instantly transported back to the vigorous, curious young man, eager for life, I was on my first visits there.

Initially I felt very positive about my life in Vienna. My studies were going well and I passed my exams; I had work, a stimulating social life and good friends. Along with Inge's mother, there was her older sister Jutta, with whom I got along very well, and other friends such as Peter and Leonie Manhardt to whom I was also close. Inge was passionate about classical music, and there were many performances to be enjoyed at the Vienna State Opera and the Vienna Philharmonic, both under the musical direction of legendary conductor Herbert von Karajan, who was famous for performing operas in their original language, rather than always in German, which I particularly appreciated. I also loved traditional *Wiener volksmusik*, and *schrammelmusik* played on an accordion and double-necked guitar. There was also *Wienerlieder* folk music, one example of which is the traditional Austrian *ländler*, a folk dance which featured in the Salzburg-based, 1965 film *The Sound of Music,* where Captain von Trapp dances it with Fraulein Maria the governess, played by Julie Andrews.

Inge and I also explored the lovely Austrian countryside in my trusty Fiat 500, visiting Lake Neusiedl south of Vienna on the Austria-Hungary border, and the Blau Valley of the River Danube with its apricot trees covered with delicate blossom in the spring, so well evoked by Van Gogh's painting of a similar orchard in Arles, and delicious fruit in the summer. All the beauties of nature that I had loved in my homeland were also here to be savoured in Austria, and as the seasons passed I became more and more at home.

One thing I did miss though was Mamma's cooking. I enjoyed the food eaten at home with Inge and her family; and *Wiener schnitzel,* a

Viennese cutlet of breaded veal, chicken or pork, fried and served with a squeeze of fresh lemon juice, is still something I enjoy and like to cook today. But I hankered for the *ragùs* of my mother's kitchen, the fresh tomato sauces and the pasta. This was hard to come by in Vienna; although they used noodles in soup, these were made from strips of pancake – *frittaten* – and weren't the same. Although you could buy almost anything at Vienna's famous food market the Naschmarkt, situated between Karlsplatz and Kettenbrückengasse, for all its extensive and diverse range of gastronomic delights, you couldn't find any pasta. Although it has always been dried and stored domestically, this was in the days before pasta was commercially produced and exported around the world in the vast quantities it is today. Then I discovered an Italian restaurant, Ristorante Roma on Kutschkergasse. The food there was delicious, and not only did they sell me a little pasta to take home, what was marvellous was that they also taught me how to make it.

But it wasn't until I moved out of Inge's family home that I really began to cook. Our love affair had palled, for which I take full responsibility. I had started to live a separate life from my girlfriend, not always available to accompany her when she went to a concert or festival, preferring instead the nightlife at the Café Hawelka. Instead of going out alone or with a female friend, Inge sometimes went to a concert in the company of a male friend. In stereotypical Italian male fashion – I was still young and foolish! – I took exception to this. I then decided that, as we were too young to be married, then maybe some time spent living separately might suit us both better. While wanting to opt for a single life, I also knew I didn't want to lose Inge completely, so with all the arrogance of my immaturity I asked her to wait for me. Amazingly, she agreed, and I found myself somewhere else to live. Initially I moved into the flat of a friend I'd met at the café, Michael von Wolkenstein, who came from an old and well-established Viennese family and went on to become a film producer and an important proponent of the Austrian film industry. His father was a doctor and for several months I slept in a room complete with glass cabinets full of medicines and surgical tools, which glinted in the light in a menacing way and were a little unsettling to sleep alongside.

It was here in Michael's home that I first started to cook regularly. There was a small kitchen with two burners on which to cook along with an oven, a fridge, some old saucepans, a mixed collection of cutlery, and a table on which to prepare food. It was here that I made pasta for the first time, mixing the durum wheat flour, eggs and water as I had been shown at the Ristorante Roma, working the dough very thoroughly to eliminate any air bubbles and make it smooth as silk, before rolling it out, the gluten in the flour stretching to an extremely thin but flexible sheet, and cutting it into strips for perhaps little tagliolini, tagliatelle, pappardelle or lasagne. I didn't have a roller to flatten the dough like they did at the restaurant, but I used a rolling pin instead. With practice I became good at rolling it out thinly and evenly on the well-scrubbed kitchen table, and cutting it with a sharp knife I had bought especially for the purpose, draping it in floured strips over the back of a kitchen chair to allow it to dry a little before cooking it quickly in salted, boiling water.

Here, too, I made my first Bolognese sauce. I took olive oil and gently fried a chopped onion before adding and browning the meat that I had asked the butcher to mince, followed by some wine, before stirring in chopped tomatoes and a little salt and freshly ground black pepper; all the while, tasting, tasting, tasting, to match the flavours of my memory with what I was cooking. I let it simmer for some time as I had seen Mamma do. When I was satisfied I asked Michael to try it, and when he too pronounced it good, I knew I was there.

Once I had the basics, I went from strength to strength. I wrote to my mother to ask her about certain ingredients, how to cook those dishes that I had watched her make so many times, occasionally calling her on the phone to check some detail or other. I became a regular visitor to the Naschmarkt looking for the ingredients I needed, from sage to courgettes, and often came home at the end of the day laden with quantities of seasonal, over-ripe tomatoes so that I could bottle *pomodoro* sauce from Mamma's recipe, to store and use later in my dishes. My repertoire was quite basic still – *pasta al forno, pasta alla carbonara, gnocchi al pesto, pasta e patate* – but I cooked with real appreciation for my ingredients and with a passion for the food I remembered, fast gaining a reputation for producing delicious, heart-warming, authentic Italian dishes, all the time discovering the alchemy that happens when particular ingredients are put together and combined with skill. I really enjoyed cooking for my friends, and their appreciation of my food was another reward.

I also cooked those Austrian dishes I enjoyed, too. And as I became more experienced, I would experiment or try to cook something I had tasted – in a restaurant, someone else's home, a dish of my mother's – by analysing and copying it. This is the basis of cooking, tasting and analysing and copying; combining those tastes that complement each other and understanding how to bring out the flavours of your ingredients, how to maximise these through the way in which you cook, whether you grill, boil or fry. All these skills can be learnt, but a cook's first teacher is taste and you develop this skill by using it! The rest is an art, learnt through love of food and the ingredients from which it is cooked, and love for those for whom the food is prepared.

It wasn't common for young men to cook in those days, although some students cooked rudimentary dishes for themselves. I was unique in my curiosity about food, and my willingness to cook in order to create something lovely to share, rather than just to satiate hunger. In spite of my minimal kitchen, but because Italian food is good for hearty, appreciative and large appetites, I often cooked for lots of people, preparing mountains of pasta and savoury sauces, and when meat was expensive I'd make it go further by adding bulk with vegetables, bought cheaply from the market at the end of the day. Not only did my fellow students grace my table, but also impoverished artists and writers. Sometimes I showed others how to cook my Bolognese or Neapolitan sauces, but I never had access to recipe books or wrote things down. At that stage it was all about eating for pleasure, and sharing that pleasure with others.

From Michael's flat, I moved on to another home, this time shared with two friends, one of whom was a kind Jewish philosopher, who often gave me ideas to think about. One story he told me, which has stayed with me to this day, is that if two people have one coin each, the use of each coin is limited. But if those two people put their two coins together, they can do more than on their own or if one person has both the coins. From this I learnt that sharing and circulating ideas – like coins – can be advantageous in that everyone benefits more than if you just hold on to your one idea, keeping it all to yourself.

By this time, however, I had virtually stopped seeing Inge. Expressing a desire that she should wait for me while I experienced freedom – in which I behaved rather badly, I might add – I found myself increasingly lonely. So much so that I got myself a dog, a dachshund that I named Baci, for company. I also started a new job working for a tourist bus company, Wien bei Nacht, which ran night tours of Vienna. I accompanied tourists on sightseeing excursions, including to the Moulin Rouge nightclub on Walfischgasse, in one of the oldest areas of the city, which had opened in 1884, five years before the Moulin Rouge in Paris. I got into the habit of working at night and sleeping all day, earning enough money to keep and entertain myself. I stopped cooking so often for my friends. I started drinking spirits rather than wine, thankful for the quick anaesthetic they provided for my bruised feelings, brooding over my loss of Inge, behaving like a dissolute poet.

One evening, out with friends in the Café Hawelka, I suddenly saw a beautiful young woman sitting on the other side of the bar. She had a lovely face, I thought, and as I gazed at her, she looked up and smiled at me. Some time later, we exchanged another glance then both stood up. I took her hand and we left the café together without having spoken a word while our mutual friends looked on in astonishment. It was a beautiful spring evening in May and we walked through the centre of Vienna, holding hands and talking. Eva was an art student from Munich, visiting Vienna for the Wiener Festwochen, an innovative cultural festival that was established in 1951 and occurs every May, with a diverse programme of plays, concerts, lectures and performances, both traditional and avant-garde. Not only did Eva have wonderfully expressive eyes, she had a perfect body too.

We were inseparable for three days. We went for a meal together at the Griechenbiesl, the oldest and most historic public house in Vienna, on Fleischmarkt next to the Greek Church. It was famous for its goulash and beer, and past diners were reputed to have included Beethoven, Schubert, Wagner, Strauss and Mark Twain! On the second day I took Eva to the Grinzing area of Vienna, famous for its *heuriger* wine taverns where we ate *backhendl,* a Viennese breaded fried chicken dish served with various pickles, washed down with copious quantities of the local *gumpoldskirchner* wine. On this occasion Eva drank so much that I had to carry her home. We were immediately lovers but while I wondered whether this was the proverbial 'love at first sight', a sense of having betrayed Inge niggled at me and suggested otherwise.

Eva returned to Munich at the end of her holiday and we agreed I would visit her there. The following weekend I drove the 300-plus kilometres to the capital of Bavaria, as promised, with Baci as my travelling companion. That night we didn't even go out to eat, but stayed in and ordered an Italian takeaway. We continued in this way for several months into the autumn and early winter months, heavily dependent on the physical side of our relationship. Then, one weekend, I had trouble reaching Munich because of a sudden heavy snowfall followed by a tremendous, bitterly cold hoar frost that crystallised the trees and made the roads lethal. Few other cars were visible as I drove gingerly through the silent white night, illuminated by a full moon that created a spooky atmosphere. Eventually I arrived, chilled to the bone, poor Baci snuggled close as we tried to keep each other warm. Happy and anxious to see Eva after my delayed arrival, I discovered that it was not just the weather that had frozen. Her greeting was quite subdued and, after I'd made love with her for what turned out to be the last time, she confessed to having slept with another man.

A knife through my youthful heart would have been less painful. Baci and I made the long, cold return trip to Vienna, with my emotions as numb as my feet. How could another love affair have gone so badly wrong? I wondered. I realised that I had been on the rebound after Inge, but that didn't make it any less painful. I was by now, I realise in retrospect, quite severely depressed, not eating properly unless cooking for friends, which I was doing less and less, drinking too much, spending too much, sleeping badly. Then I stopped going to work. Spiralling out of control, I was on the brink of breakdown. At this point, alarmed and concerned for my health, Inge did me another great favour: she called my brother Carlo, who took the first train to Vienna with my father to sort me out. After one look at the state I was in, they packed up all my belongings in my Fiat 500, sat me in the back with Baci, and drove non-stop back to Ivrea. Like many a young man before me, the Prodigal Son included, I returned home to my family in order to recover.

Acciughe in salsa verde

Anchovies in green sauce

Various salsa verde or green sauces have been developed over the years by non-Italian chefs, which may be delicious, but which do not always correspond to the Italian taste. We normally use parsley, basil or rocket as the green base, and this one is made with parsley. When you come home and feel a little peckish for something salty, these anchovies on toasted bread are miraculous. Naturally the dish can be served as part of an antipasto.

Makes a 300g batch
300g perfect anchovy fillets in oil
    (Italian or Spanish are the best)

Salsa verde
1 fresh white bread roll
about 2 tbsp white wine vinegar
1 big bunch flat-leaf parsley, very
    finely chopped, without the stalks
1 small medium-hot chilli, finely
    chopped
1 garlic clove, peeled and puréed
10 little cornichons (mini gherkins),
    very finely chopped
15 salted capers, soaked, drained and
    very finely chopped
extra-virgin olive oil, as required

Drain the anchovies, and put a layer of them in the bottom of a narrow ceramic container. You want to have several layers of anchovies, so don't use too large a dish.

To start the *salsa,* cut off the crust from the roll, and soak the inner crumbs in a little vinegar for a few minutes. Squeeze as dry as possible, then finely chop. Put into a bowl with the parsley, chilli, garlic, cornichons and capers, and mix well, adding enough olive oil to achieve a sauce consistency.

Cover the anchovies with a layer of green sauce, then top with another layer of anchovies. Repeat this until all the anchovies are covered with sauce. Add enough olive oil to cover everything, and keep refrigerated for a day, after which you can start to use them. Keep refrigerated for up to a week. Serve with cold meats or as a dip with many other canapé-type dishes.

CHAPTER SEVEN

Germany

I t was a long journey back from Vienna, with little conversation between my father, brother Carlo and myself. Watching the scenery flash past as we headed towards Italy, I dozed and brooded, cramped in the back of the Fiat as my brother steadily drove home, with all my possessions (such as they were) on board and dachshund Baci on my lap, wondering yet again what the future held for me. My parents had moved from the station house in Borgofranco to a flat in Ivrea after the death of Enrico, and I was glad not to be returning to my old home, which was so full of memories, or to be seeing old friends who might now look at me with disdain for what I felt was my return in defeat.

It is only from the distance of the years since that I realise my breakdown was probably a reaction to unexpressed grief at my brother's death. As a family, we had not shared our feelings. Instead each one of us tried to find our own way through the sorrow, but in isolation from one other. I had worsened this sense of isolation for myself by going off to live in Vienna, and then again when I'd split up from Inge. I didn't know how to deal with the terrible sense of loneliness in my heart, which stemmed not only from the loss of my brother but also my earlier separation from my family when I was five years old.

So I tried to obscure these sad, difficult feelings with the increasingly dissolute behaviour that had prompted Inge to call my brother. Drinking anaesthetised me for a while, but it was in itself a depressant and in the long term didn't help. Seeking love from women helped a little, but it was only a temporary respite and I know now that I probably over-romanticised the nature of these attachments. I wish I had known then that some reflection and insight would have been useful, but in those days there was not the ready access to talking therapies and bereavement support that exists now. Even a more ready acknowledgement from friends and family that a bereavement can have a profound effect on one's continuing life might have proved useful, not just at the moment of loss but for a long time afterwards. It is only in more recent years, when other emotional crises occurred and were examined more closely, that I have gained some perspective and, in the end, some peace. In fact, the very writing of this story now is in a way an investigation of who I am, and how and why I became that person.

Once back in Ivrea, however, with home-cooked meals and sleeping more regularly, I soon recovered, from my physical exhaustion at least. Finding work was the next step. Since I was now fluent in German, I approached a travel company in Turin, Transitalia. It was a privately owned company that organised travel and cruise itineraries, and I was immediately offered a job. Although this meant commuting forty kilometres every day from Ivrea to my office in Turin, I was pleased to be back at work and for such a reputable travel company.

My boss was Signora Giovanna Colombo Zamboni, and she was a member of AIDDA (Association of Women Entrepreneurs and Corporate Executives and Managers), founded in 1961 in Turin to support the development of women in business. AIDDA is still going strong with about 3000 companies currently belonging to the organisation and has recently celebrated its fiftieth anniversary.

During my time with Transitalia, we had to organise that year's World AIDDA Congress, with a conference, tourist and cultural events, and a gala dinner for about 300 people.

Twelve young women and myself put together a programme of events that included a theatre trip, several excellent restaurant meals and the gala dinner itself, along with visiting the Fiat factory at Lingotto in Turin. That was more exciting than it sounds because the factory, built on the via Nizza and designed by young architect Giaccomo Matte-Trucco, was the largest car factory in the world when it opened in 1923, and the building was described by Le Corbusier as 'one of the most impressive sights in industry'. It was built on five floors, and unusual in that the component parts came in at the bottom floor and, as the cars were built, they moved up to the top floor and eventually to a test track on the roof. Although Fiat moved its production from the Lingotto factory in the 1970s, the building was later converted into a public space, with a theatre, shopping arcade, the prestigious NH Lingotto Tech hotel, a convention centre and, in the eastern part of the building, the Automotive Engineering faculty of the Politecnico di Torino. The test track remains on the roof, and formed part of the getaway sequence in the 1969 Michael Caine movie *The Italian Job*.

We also arranged a visit to the Museo della Sindone in via San Domenico to see the extraordinary history, forensic investigations and photographic evidence of the famous Turin Shroud. Although the original relics are kept in the Duomo di Torino San Giovanni Battista and are not available for public viewing, the museum of the Shroud proved fascinating. It was a lot of work creating a stimulating cultural and social conference and entertainment for AIDDA, but ultimately a highly successful event with which Signora Zamboni was very pleased.

One of those attending the conference was a German businesswoman, Gertrude Silevich, who ran Ischia Reisedienst – a travel service from Berlin to Ischia, a volcanic island in the

Tyrrhenian Sea just off the coast of Naples. Ischia is a beautiful tourist destination that also benefits from hot thermal springs, around which a spa industry has been built up – making it particularly attractive to Germans who fully endorse and regularly engage in spa treatments. In her forthright and rather humourless way, Frau Silevich explained to me that she needed someone fluent in both German and Italian, which I appeared to be, to work for her. She had managed to arrange charter flights from Berlin Tempelhof airport to Naples where visitors could get a boat to Ischia. To have got even this far was a remarkable achievement, given that although the airport was in West Berlin, Berlin itself was in the middle of what was then known as East Germany or the GDR (German Democratic Republic) and travel there was highly restricted by the impact of the Cold War. Frau Silevich was based on Ischia, along with her son and a couple of employees, and determined to make a go of her business venture, but she needed a travelling tour operator to organise things between Berlin and Ischia. That, she suggested, was a job that would suit me.

It seemed like interesting work, which might also open up other opportunities for me in the travel industry, and maybe I could be more autonomous and less office-bound, so I accepted her offer. From Berlin I had to manage the itineraries of those travelling, accompany them on their flight to Naples then transfer them to the small seaside village of Marechiaro where we could board a ferry for the island. Here accommodation was arranged by Frau Silevich, but there was also further work for me as an *accompagnatore* or tour guide when trips for these German visitors could be arranged to other places, like Capri's famous *Grotta Azzurra* (Blue Grotto), the ancient Roman ruins at Pompeii, or a visit to the city of Naples itself.

I was a bit of an innocent concerning these trips, which often included visits to tourist shops selling jewellery and other attractions. It didn't occur to me to take my visitors to one shop or another, and receive a tip negotiated with the shop owner in advance for this courtesy, as many *accompagnatori* did. I also didn't take advantage of the many single women who travelled to Ischia on holiday, often looking for a little light-hearted holiday romance, as many other tour guides also did. For me the job was rather boring. It was nice enough sitting in the sun, chatting to visitors, but although the Blue Grotto is a breathtakingly beautiful natural spectacle, where the natural phenomenon of sunlight, filtered and refracted as it passes through a narrow opening into the cave, creates a deep silvery-blue effect, there's also a natural limit to how many times its wonders will amaze you.

Fortunately for me, another visitor, businessman Wolfgang Bruneman, saw me as a candidate for employment with his new company, and provided me with an exit from tour operating and the chance of a new occupation. On one of the various tourist trips I made with him on his visit to Ischia, we had been talking about my time at Olivetti and, because of my technical and electrical skills, combined with my fluent German, he offered me a job managing the regional service centres for the photocopying franchise he was setting up, importing Japanese photocopiers manufactured by Toshiba into West Germany. I would need to be based in West Berlin to do the job and we agreed that I should move there at the end of my summer contract with Ischia Reisedienst. This proposition was made even more attractive to me by the fact that, towards the end of my time working for Frau Silevich, I had met a very attractive woman who lived in Berlin.

Ursula had travelled alone to Ischia to spend a couple of weeks holidaying at one of the spa hotels there. We got to know each other a little during her visit and, learning of my impending arrival in Berlin to start a new job, she'd agreed to meet up with me once I'd arrived. It made me anticipate the move to Berlin all the more keenly to know that she would be there, with the possibility of a friendship between us at least or perhaps something more. At that point I wasn't sure. So

I arrived in Berlin with high hopes for my new future, soon finding myself a place to live and settling down into my new job.

The quality of the Japanese-produced Fertomat photocopier I was helping to promote was, for its time, quite something. Their new technology used a superfine black powder and photosensitive paper to produce an image, and although the machines were quite slow compared to the alternative Excel photocopiers, taking about a minute to copy and print each time, the quality of the reproduction was much better. Having been trained to service and repair the copiers myself, my job was to train employees and ensure quality control in the local service centres around Germany. So I would find myself travelling all week, catching a Pan-Am propliner plane from Berlin Tempelhof airport (also home to the USAF who still had a strong presence there) which I knew so well from my time with Ischia Reisedienst, but this time flying on domestic routes to Munich, Hamburg or Frankfurt. Air travel was the most efficient way to travel throughout Germany at this time, especially from West Berlin, using the Templehof airport in the Amercian sector, annexed as it was in the middle of the GDR, a fact exploited not only by the US's Pan-Am airline but also by British European Airways (BEA) as the former Western Allies competed for the lucrative market in German air travel.

Working for Wolfgang Bruneman's company Feracop was not the most scintillating of jobs, but weekends spent with Ursula were my consolation. Although she was married, she had no children and her husband was homosexual by preference, so her marriage no longer had any physical side. Ursula and he co-owned a knitwear factory and business, where she also worked, and she would not leave him for fear of losing her share of this. It was a situation that suited her very well but, after a while, I wanted to be more than just her weekend lover. I was in love with her and wanted to be able to make plans for the future and to live with her full-time. While I was happy with her and there had been hope for a future life together, I had tolerated life in Berlin, the endless travelling and tedious work. Now it began to pall on me.

Berlin in the late 1960s was a divided city caught in the middle of a repressive Cold War. I had been used to being able to travel freely wherever I liked in Italy and Austria, without the sort of controls imposed by the totalitarian regime of the communist GDR. As an Italian national I was, allegedly, free to travel through Checkpoint Charlie, but the Volkswagen I was now driving was almost taken apart as police on the border checked to see if I was smuggling through anything illegal. The most depressing experience though was driving to West Germany down a 'corridor' through the GDR, which was heavily policed. At the time the law stated that if you saw a car with a blue light, you had to stop. Any car that didn't was fined ten *Deutschemarks*, and the police were using this technicality to cash in on the more valuable Western DM, which gave the lie to any commitment they professed to feel to their own regime. It was exasperating and expensive in equal measure.

Not only that, but Herr Bruneman's business was not going well. The Feracop company was fast losing out to Xerox and after a time production on the Fertomat copier ceased. However, my boss was not without other entrepreneurial ideas and had moved his company into the whole new market of microfilming. Again, with my technical expertise, I was recruited to work on this. In the 1960s Zeiss Ikon had merged with Voigtländer, the oldest camera manufacturer in Germany, to become the biggest phototechnical company in West Germany and world leaders in microfilm.

Using a special Zeiss Ikon camera, I discovered it was possible to film the entire works of writer, poet, playwright and essayist Johann Wolfgang von Goethe – not just his famous *Faust* – to be reproduced as microfiche at some later date as required.

Initially I found what was essentially rather boring, repetitive work fascinating, especially when dealing with a subject like Goethe. The most interesting job I worked on, however, was microfilming hundreds of antique drawings and designs for old naval steam engines, the originals produced on parchment and stored flat in very large map drawers. They were becoming brittle with age and needed to be stored on microfilm for posterity. The originals measured 2 x 1 metres. One by one they were photographed, and the image reduced to just 8mm wide. It took quite some time to carry out the job, but it felt good to be involved in something that was so important – the preservation of these marvellous originals. Unfortunately, much of my work was focused on more mundane material.

I still had to travel for work, and on one occasion found myself based with a colleague – another technician at Feracop called Schneider – in Hanover. One evening, watching television in the sitting room at the hotel, I met an interesting woman. We got talking because we had both taken some leftover bread from dinner with which to feed the carp in a nearby city pond. These fish were obviously well enough fed, some of them looked to be at least ten kilos in weight, but were very entertaining as they snapped away with gusto at the bread thrown to them. We got talking and I discovered that Gerda had quite a prestigious and high-profile job: she was the sales director for an Italian wine company. It was wonderful to talk about wine from my home country! She was based in Hamburg, and travelled all over for work. I liked her; she was very elegant with her well-cut black hair, but quite reserved. Talking to her as we fed the carp together, I saw an intelligent, cultured side to this woman and very much appreciated her willingness to converse with me about things that seemed to matter to both of us, like art and music – and wine!

When I left for Berlin I took a note of her phone number in Hamburg and asked if I could take her for dinner when I was next at the Feracop

Agency there. This I did, and during our conversation then Gerda suggested I might consider working for the Bisotti wine company as a sales manager, which sounded a very attractive idea. I not only had an interest in wine, but also some knowledge of the subject, growing up as I had done amongst the vineyards of northern Italy. My papa, too, had worked with the local winemakers, distributing their wine by rail, and I told Gerda how he'd been suspected of spying during the war in his efforts to support the local wine trade.

I was, however, still trying to have a relationship with Ursula. She didn't like the idea of my leaving Berlin, in spite of the excitement I felt about finally doing some work that was of far greater interest to me than microfilming. Come with me, I said, but she still refused to leave her husband, risk losing her share of their company and make a new life with me. We reached an impasse and had yet another of our increasingly stormy conversations about it all. This time I saw red and, without telling her my plans, I gave up my job at Feracop, my flat in Berlin, and moved to Hamburg to secure the job at Bisotti Wines.

It was immediately a relief to be in Hamburg, away from the intensity of Berlin. Hamburg is an extraordinary city, the second largest in Germany, built on the mouth and tributaries of the River Elbe, its many streams, rivers and canals crossed by over 2000 bridges – more even than in Venice or Amsterdam. It's also an enormous port with over forty kilometres of docks, positioned on the southern point of the Jutland Peninsula, with Scandinavia to the north, the Baltic Sea to its east and the North Sea to its west. I found it a vibrant city, with an atmosphere of liberty and freedom and quite a high immigrant population, so I felt less isolated and more at home here than I had in Berlin.

There had been a policy in Germany of recruiting migrant workers into industrial jobs because of the acute, post-war labour shortage, a programme known in Western Germany as the *Gastarbeiterprogramm,* where 'guest workers' were known as *gastarbeiter*. In East Germany there was a similar programme that referred to the workers as *vertragsarbeiter*. The original description had been *fremdarbeiter*, literally 'foreign worker', coined in Nazi Germany when most workers were brought against their will, as forced labour, from German-occupied Europe, so this term was dropped because of its negative connotations. A lot of *gastarbeiter* came from Italy, whole families of them, and worked mainly in industry. Then came the Spaniards, and after them the Greeks then the Turks.

We were, however, all subject to *meldezettel*, the residence registration form that had to be assigned a unique twelve-digit residence number and signed not only by the person registered, but also by whoever provided the accommodation where they lived, usually the landlord of a rented apartment. This *meldezettel* had to be registered at the local police station and, as a foreign national, whenever you moved accommodation, you had to re-register with the police. It was a rather tedious form of state control, and had the effect of making us feel that we were there on sufferance when, in fact, post-war Germany desperately needed an enhanced workforce to help rebuild it.

Some Germans could also be quite conservative and intolerant of foreign workers, but this didn't affect me particularly because not only was my spoken German very fluent, it was also very correct and I spoke with what was referred to as a 'high German' dialect from southern Germany, rather than a 'low German' dialect from the north. So even if I was initially judged as an Italian *gastarbeiter*, the minute I opened my mouth to speak my accent meant that I was accepted. This was another reason why the work I did in Germany, from being a tourist operator to a technical manager to a wine salesman, was so successful – not only did I have the expertise, I also had the language. But it was more than that. I liked to watch how people worked together, how they operated, people's relationships in the workplace, and the subtleties of selling; all skills that would prove invaluable to me in later life. No experience is ever wasted, whether good or bad, if you learn from it in the end.

I was much happier in Hamburg than I had been for a while. The waterfront was beautiful, as were the historic buildings and considerable parks and gardens – the Alter Botanischer Garten being a particularly lovely place in which to walk – all of which made it an attractive place to live. It also had a diverse and stimulating cultural and social life, with a variety of annual festivals. And let's not forget that the Hamburg music clubs were infamous in the 1960s. It was here that the Beatles honed their early performance skills – playing a forty-eight-night booking at the Indra Club on Grosse Freiheitstrasse, opening on 17 August 1960. Although this was some years before my arrival in the city, it still had a reputation for its lively music scene although my taste was more towards classical and jazz than pop.

The majority of the food I ate was still German, of course. Hamburg is ostensibly home to the original hamburger, which seems to have developed from the local *frikadelle*. The Hamburg dish is made from a mixture of minced beef, chopped onion, seasoning, stale bread and beaten egg to bind it altogether, and then pan-fried and served with potatoes and other vegetables. Enclosing it in a bread bun seems to have been an American addition, and hamburgers today are thinner than was traditionally the case. Food in Hamburg also bore the influence of neighbouring Scadinavia and I quite liked *labskaus*, a mixture of corned beef, mashed potato and beetroot, the latter giving the dish a rather unfortunate colour. It seemed to be a staple of the seamen who frequented the port. By contrast I found the traditional *birnen, bohnen und speck* – green beans cooked with pears and bacon – quite strange at first.

I did however like *franzbroechten,* a sweet pastry a bit like a cross between a Danish pastry and a croissant or *pain au raisin*. Made of croissant-type dough, then rolled thinly and spread with butter, sugar and cinnamon before being folded and cut and baked in the oven, these delicacies are said to have appeared in Hamburg after Napoleon's occupation between 1806–14, their allegedly French origination reflected in the name – French bread translates to German as *Französisch brot*. Variants of the *franzbroechten* include the addition of chocolate, raisins, poppy and pumpkin seeds, and these are delicious for breakfast or a mid-morning snack with a large cup of excellent espresso. It was here in Hamburg also that I first drank *alsterwasser*, a mixture of lager-like beer and fizzy lemonade, like an English shandy.

One thing that was found a lot in Germany, and which I learnt to cook, was a soft noodle, made with eggs, flour, a little water and salt, called *spätzle*. You take the dough mixture and squeeze it through a sort of mini-colander or *spätzlepresse,* like a potato ricer, or a coarse grater called a *spätzlehobel*, before cooking the noodles in boiling, salted water where they rise to the surface as they are cooked and can be scooped off and served as an accompaniment to other foods, combined with other ingredients or added to soups. *Käsespätzle* is served with cheese, typically Emmental, and fried onion; *linsen, spätzle und saitenwürstle* is noodles served with lentils and frankfurter sausages; or *krautspätzle* is noodles with *sauerkraut* (pickled cabbage). Similar noodles appear in Swiss cooking where they are called *spätzli* or *knöpfle*, although *knöpfle* means 'small buttons' which explains the shape of the Swiss version; and in Hungarian cooking, where they are called *nokedli* or *galuska*. You can buy dried *spätzle* but they're not the same. Freshly prepared varieties are now making an appearance in some European supermarkets.

A dish I particularly enjoyed was *eisbein* – literally a cut of pork from the hock or knuckle joint – a dish made of pickled ham hock braised on the bone, rather similar to boiled gammon but usually cured or smoked beforehand. It has a delicious, intense flavour. Sometimes the skin of the joint is given a honey or caramelised glaze in the oven after braising, and it can be served with *spätzle* or mashed potatoes, anything substantial enough to soak up the juices, along with sauerkraut and mustard. I was not, however, quite so keen on the traditional *aalsuppe*, it's name indicating that it could literally be made with 'all' or anything, because *aal* also means eel, and it was often made with those! I found a lot of food in Hamburg to be pan-fried, like *braatkartoffeln* (pan-fried potato slices) or *finkenwerder scholle* (pan-fried plaice). This food was very different from the emphasis placed on fresh vegetables, fruit and fish in my southern Italian birthplace, and olive oil wasn't imported much either so frying was done in lard or vegetable oil. It was still a while before post-war globalisation really revolutionised the food available in our shops. In the meantime I was quite happy learning to cook German recipes, while continuing to entertain my friends with my repertoire of Italian dishes, too.

I started work as a sales manager for Bisotti Wines and began to become reacquainted with the Italian wines that had once been such an everyday feature of my life. Growing up in Piedmont, I was surrounded by vineyards growing the famous *Nebbiolo* grape from which the great Italian red wines Barolo and Barbaresco are made. Also from the same area is another grape, the Muscat or *moscato,* from which the sparkling white Asti wines are made. The story of my childhood experience of drinking too much of that in its early stages greatly amused Gerda. To the east of Milan the Valpolicella reds and Soave white wines are produced, and with all these I was quite familiar. But I soon discovered that the Germans had a quite different taste in wine, and many had discovered and developed a liking for Marsala from Sicily. Someone told me that it was the sweetness of it that was so appealing because they had been deprived of sugar for so long during the war, but I don't know if that is accurate. It's true that the traditional German wines, like those made from the Reisling grape, tend towards being sweet but light, unoaked and low in alcohol, but Germany produces wines in a variety of styles – dry, semi-sweet and sweet white wines, rosé wines, red wines and sparkling wines called *sekt*. The only wine style not commonly produced is fortified wine. Maybe this is why they took to Marsala – and in great quantities – creating an excellent market for Bisotti Wines.

Named after the city in Sicily from which it originates, Marsala is a fortified wine (typically between 15–20 per cent proof) similar to port or sherry, and aged in wooden casks. It is produced in the province of Trapani from the Catarratto, Pignatello, Nerello, Calabrese and Grillo grapes and comes in three different levels of sweetness – *secco* or dry, *semisecco*, and *dolce* or sweet – with a number of different varieties depending on colour and ageing classification. *Oro* is golden, *Ambra* is amber in colour from the *mosto cotto* (grape juice syrup) sweetener added to the wine, while *Rubino* is reddish. Then there are four levels of ageing in the barrels before it is bottled: *Fine* Marsala only has a year's ageing, while *Superiore* is aged for at least two years, *Superiore Riserva* for at least four years, and *Vergine Soleras* for at least five years.

Marsala is something I have used extensively in my cooking ever since these days. *Scaloppine al Marsala* is a real favourite of mine. Tender, thin, small slices of veal – the *scaloppine* or *fettine* – are dusted with flour and fried in hot butter, with the addition of a little stock, white wine, Marsala, garlic and parsley. You can also cook *fegato*, liver, in this way – calf's liver is best for this dish – again cut in thin slices and dusted with flour. And, of course, Marsala is used in the preparation of *zabaglione* – the light, foamy custard confection made by whisking eggs, sugar and Marsala together over a gentle heat – which is also the basis for one of the nicest ice creams I've ever made. Marsala is gaining in popularity again today though it tends to be drunk chilled as an aperitif, or occasionally as a dessert wine, but in the 1960s the Germans seemed to drink it with everything and sales boomed!

As sales manager for Bisotti Wines I travelled around West Germany, visiting wine departments in various stores to run promotions, training and supporting the internal sales staff to run tastings – offering samples to shoppers to try, alongside snacks to nibble, and persuading them to buy. It was interesting work, and I had responsibility too for the advertising, information material and general promotion, but I particularly enjoyed developing my salesmanship, based on knowing the product *and* the market, and working with sales teams to bring the two together with elegance and grace.

While I was working with Gerda, a certain tenderness developed between us. She was a divorcee, without children, and in time we decided to live together. We worked hard and at the weekends enjoyed each other's company, often having Gerda's niece Audrey to stay with us, creating a sense of family – something I missed and longed for. Although there wasn't a great passion between us, there was a gentle happiness and living together was very easy. We also travelled to Ivrea together, and so Gerda got to meet and know my family a little. Mamma professed confusion with my numerous changes of girlfriend – Inge, Ursula and now Gerda – but was pleased to see me content, for the time being at least.

One day in 1968, while I was working from home, Gerda called me on the telephone. What about getting married? she asked. I was a little surprised at first but after living together for three years, the suggestion was not totally unexpected. I could think of no immediate reason not to so I said yes, but without any great conviction, I'm afraid. Then she said that she felt, in fairness, there was something she should confess to. I couldn't think what it could be but she told me she was actually older than she had let on. In fact, she was ten years older, and at that point aged forty-one. Given that we had been together for three years by now and it hadn't mattered before, I couldn't see why it might matter now or even in the future, so we got married and both my parents, brother

Carlo and sister Anna came to Hamburg for the wedding. Then Gerda and I went to Salerno for our honeymoon, visiting my birthplace at Vietri sul Mare and meeting up with various relatives – Aunt Dora, her husband Gianni and my two cousins Sonia and Umberto amongst them – whom I had not seen for many years.

Back in Hamburg, my professional life took another turn. I was enjoying considerable success with Bisotti Wines, but had also extended my work into a more general sales consultancy, working on other projects. News of my professional reputation as a good salesman, and my personal reputation as someone of intelligence and good and easygoing character, had somehow reached a company called Investors Overseas Services. I was contacted by one of their consultants who visited me and explained to me how IOS operated in Germany. The company was described to me as a mutual fund, an investment savings programme for a future pension, and at that time was showing quite considerable and, in Germany, unprecedented financial success.

IOS had been set up by Bernie Cornfeld in the 1950s. The company was legally incorporated in Panama, although its principal offices were in Switzerland with the main operational offices in Ferney-Voltaire, France, a short drive across the French border from its Geneva-registered office. Then in 1962 IOS had launched its 'Fund of Funds', with investment in shares of other mutual funds, including some of IOS's own. Cornfeld's one-line pitch, 'Do you sincerely want to be rich?' became a by-word for success and during the next eight years IOS raised in excess of $2.5 billion, bringing Cornfeld a personal fortune that was estimated at the time to be over $100 million.

At its peak, IOS employed around 25,000 salesmen who sold a series of mutual funds door-to-door all over Europe, especially in Germany, originally targeting US expatriates and servicemen who couldn't access US investing, but the main growth area of the business was actually small-time investors, who until then hadn't had easy access to investment opportunities of this kind. Cornfeld called it 'the people's capitalism'.

After some initial intensive training, I became one of 3000 IOS consultants in Germany, working for a company I believed to be sound, not just because it showed such good financial results but also because Erich Mende, a highly respected ex-politician and for a time Vice-Chancellor of the German Bundestag, was involved. Since 1967 he had tirelessly promoted IOS's opportunities to the German public, with an ensuing increase to around 5000 consultants and around 200,000 actual investors in the company's products. I had no reason to doubt the legitimacy of IOS, or to suspect that anything could go wrong. In fact, it seemed initially to be an excellent move for me to become an IOS consultant, exploiting my various skills and interests, and within six months I had achieved the position of Manager, with a turnover of about $1 million a month.

This was extraordinary for me, as money had never been either a personal or professional motivator before. As a romantic, I believed that my personal happiness in life would come primarily from relationships, from the love of a good woman, a happy marriage and family life. I felt I had already achieved that but I found this new financial success to be very exciting and realised that happiness could also come from feeling inspired by the work you do, and the rewards, material and otherwise, it brings. This was a revelation to me and, with all the energy and commitment of a young man of thirty-two, I embraced it. I was now earning very well, and it made a big difference to my life.

I rented a much larger flat in a lovely old building on the Sierichstrasse near the Alster lake, a very nice residential area of Hamburg, where Gerda, Audrey and I lived together as a family, and where I also had my office, a beautiful space in which to socialise and entertain not only friends but customers as well. This was an area of

Hamburg where there were numerous consulates and embassies, a very upmarket district with a good reputation. Our flat had a bit of garden, and wasn't far from a particularly attractive park by the lake and some smart shops. I bought a pony for Audrey, learnt to ride myself at the stables where it was kept, and we regularly rode together in the countryside near Hamburg. I was, it would seem, living the dream – far outstripping anything I'd imagined on first leaving Italy for Austria ten years before.

There were other successes too. I became involved with a town-twinning project between Lüneburg, not far from Hamburg, and my home town of Ivrea in Italy. Town twinning began after World War II in an attempt to forge links and friendships between communities in different countries. Its central idea was to create international co-operation and understanding within a diverse cultural framework, and special emphasis was placed on the involvement of young people, the idea being that this would serve as a good foundation for a peaceful future.

Another important goal of the scheme was the exchange of ideas and innovation between the partner cities, for the benefit of all sections of the twinned communities. Along with assisting with the communication between the mayors of the two towns, with my fluent German and Italian, I also organised for the *Coro Alpino Eporediese* – Ivrea's Alpine Chorus (a singing group which was set up in 1953 and is still going today, and in which my brother Carlo sang) to give a concert in Lüneburg as part of the twinning celebrations. It felt very good to be organising this, all the travel arrangements and flights for the twenty men in the choir – including Carlo – to come from my original hometown to my adoptive one.

The concert was lovely and the visit was a great success. I even took the choir to the Reeperbahn, to see a bit of Hamburg's famous nightlife in the red-light district which had legal prostitution on certain streets.

We went, in fact, to the courtyard of one of the brothels, where the choir sang a song. As it resonated around the walls, the girls came out from behind the windows in response to this lovely serenade, clapping and applauding the men afterwards for sheer pleasure in their singing.

While the choir was staying in Germany, I invited them all to my home for a meal I cooked myself – the traditional *eisbein* – made from a huge boiled ham hock, garnished and roasted and served with *bratkartoffeln, spätzle* and *sauerkraut* – with a *rote grütze,* made from raspberries, red and blackcurrants, and cherries with lots of fruit juice, liqueurs and whipped cream, to follow. I wanted to create a delicious meal of German food – Italian food they could get any day at home, but for this meal I wanted them to appreciate the food of the host country. I felt very proud to be offering them this and for them all to see how well my life was turning out, particularly my brother Carlo given that he had also witnessed me in less successful days. At this point, I couldn't have been happier, but my life was soon to change once again.

Scaloppine al Marsala secco

Veal escalopes with Marsala

The glorification of the Marsala wine from Sicily is reflected not only in the classic dessert zabaglione but also in this delicious recipe. It was made popular by Garibaldi, who landed in Marsala to liberate Italy, but also by the initial trade from a British company who were using the wine to make sherry in the eighteenth century.

Serves 4
500g (1lb 2oz) veal escalopes, cut
    5 mm (¼ in) thick
plain flour, for dusting
6 tablespoons extra virgin
olive oil or 50g (2oz) butter
1 glass of vintage dry Marsala
salt and pepper

Dust the escalopes in flour on both sides, shaking off the excess.

Heat the oil or butter in a large heavy frying pan. Fry the veal for a couple of minutes on each side, cooking in batches so as not to overcrowd the pan.

When all the escalopes are done, put them all back in the pan and add the wine and some seasoning. Stir for a few seconds; the meat should become lightly glazed because of the combination of flour and wine. Serve immediately.

CHAPTER EIGHT

Jan

fter the exuberance and optimism of the late 1960s, the decade that spawned a thousand clichés, the swinging sixties among them, 1970 dawned rather differently. It was the year Colonel Gaddafi formally came to power in Libya, and the Beatles split; the year the UK Government introduced a bill for women to be given equal pay, and General de Gaulle died; the year the first jumbo jet landed at Heathrow airport, and actor Laurence Olivier was made a life peer. By March 1970, when Simon and Garfunkel's 'Bridge Over Troubled Water' was top of the singles charts in the UK and US, my marriage and the IOS share price were both in serious trouble.

Accepting the age difference between Gerda and myself, and the sad truth that we would never be able to create our own family, was one thing – we were fortunate enough to have her niece Audrey living with us full-time – but there was something else. As she grew older, Gerda became less and less interested in the sexual side of our relationship. She was only in her early-forties but her libido was seriously in decline while mine, in my early-thirties, wasn't. We discussed what could be done about it and the only solution she thought viable was for me to take drugs to suppress my sex drive. This, I'm afraid, was not something I was prepared to do, absolutely not, although I didn't know what other solution could be found. It was a cause of considerable friction between us, however, and eventually our whole relationship began to deteriorate as we spent less and less time together. In retrospect, the writing was on the wall, but I felt desperately that I wanted to keep things happy and stable, not least because the IOS situation was going from bad to worse.

In fund management, investments can go down as well as up (as the advertisements say) and the American market was performing badly at the beginning of 1970. In the previous decade, IOS had raised $2.5 billion, due in part to its 'Fund of Funds'. This investment opportunity had been very popular and while the market was bullish – when there was a lot of investor confidence and consequently investment – it was fine, but when confidence diminished, as it did at the end of the 1960s, the resulting bear market was disastrous. The IOS share value decreased from $40 to $18 to $12 in the spring as everyone started to sell. Then it dropped to $2. American financier Robert Vesco, who at the time was also in financial trouble, offered help to Cornfeld. Vesco proceeded to take over the management of IOS, ousting Cornfeld, and used $500 million worth of IOS money to cover his own investments in a number of Latin American companies. When this was discovered, he fled to the Bahamas. IOS shares dropped to 40 cents and the company collapsed.

I was fortunate insofar as I personally hadn't invested a great deal, although I knew many who had and felt very badly for them. I got together with a number of other IOS managers and we sought to find a way to form another business, this time creating investment opportunities in properties in Spain and the Balearics, which were relatively cheap at the time despite the fact that they were increasingly popular destinations for Germans. My role in this new venture was to take on the sales and marketing, and to locate areas where property was available for the investors. Ibiza (or *Eivissa* to give it its official,

Catalan, name) and also Gran Canaria were identified as being good options, still very beautiful and unspoilt, with a lovely climate year-round. Here, the company built groups of twenty to fifty small villas around the coastal resorts, mainly in the south, to accommodate tourists and owners alike.

Besides its indigenous population, Ibiza had long been a popular location with artists, writers, poets and other bohemians, who had bought old *fincas* and created their own eccentric communes decades before this. In the 1970s it became an easily accessible and cheap destination for groups of idealistic young people, many from Germany and also from the US, where avoiding being drafted to fight in Vietnam was a consideration. These young people migrated to the island from the old hippie trails through India, Pakistan and Nepal, or perhaps Turkey, Syria, Jordan, Iraq and Iran, where they had been busily rejecting the old capitalist lifestyle and embracing a new alternative one. Now it seemed they needn't travel so far in order to do that. In the late 1960s, renting a *finca* on Ibiza could cost as little as $30 a month, while a bottle of wine was 50 cents. Many of these young people were relatively rich by comparison to the local inhabitants, so could easily afford to live in the simple, whitewashed houses set against a backdrop of boats, sunny skies and deep blue sea. These hippies were looking for a way out of the nine-to-five work ethic and there was, inevitably, quite a lot of sex, drugs and rock 'n' roll as they refused to conform to established society. This was not my scene, but it was part of the backdrop to life on Ibiza at the time. I preferred drinking a glass of wine or a *café con leche* while sitting at a harbourside café, watching the boats come and go and the fishermen mending their nets.

As part of my role in the property investment company, I would advertise the newly built properties for sale in Ibiza and Gran Canaria through the travel, property and investment pages of the German newspapers, finding prospective customers whom I would then accompany to the individual destinations in order to close the deal. It was pleasant enough work and I was relatively successful at it. Again, I was utilising all the skills I had gained to date – sales, marketing, investment, and now property dealing – but I wasn't convinced that my heart ultimately lay in property speculation. In addition, some of my colleagues were rather unscrupulous about adding commission on top of that already incorporated into the price, which I believed was unethical even while it was commonplace. I told myself I could always go back to being a wine merchant, which I had loved, if this enterprise didn't work out.

During this time Gerda and I visited Ibiza together on one occasion, and it was then that I acquired a new dog. My Baci, the dear little dachshund that had accompanied me home to Italy from Austria, before I moved to Germany, had long gone. My new dog came from Ibiza and was originally one of the many strays that congregated back then on the island. Sometimes they were fed and petted by the tourists, but these street dogs, as they were known, could become quite a nuisance when they formed feral packs. So, at the end of the season, they were routinely rounded up and destroyed by the local authorities.

One day, I noticed a small dog, a puppy in fact, curiously ugly but quite endearing, who regularly came to the bungalow where we were staying, looking for scraps. With no collar or any other indication of ownership, the dog was abandoned, the cleaner asserted. So every day for the two weeks we were there, I fed this abandoned pup, named Jan (pronounced Yan) by the locals, and grew fond of him. I didn't like the thought of what might happen to him at the end of the season, so I decided to keep him and take him back with us to Hamburg. This required a trip to the local vet to make sure Jan was healthy, that he'd had the right immunisations and that we had the correct paperwork in order to take him with us. He adapted to life in his new home in

Hamburg very well, immediately becoming good friends with a black cat named Bammel, which we also owned at the time.

But Jan was absolutely my dog and became a dear companion to me through some very difficult years ahead, even moving to England with me later. He turned out to be a Picardy shepherd dog, loyal and sweet-tempered with a perpetually tousled look. He lived for thirteen years. Though generally I'm not sentimental about animals, I loved that dog and even dedicated one of my first publications, *The Complete Mushroom Book,* to him.

By this time my marriage was over. I knew it, and I suspect Gerda did too, but we continued to live together although leading increasingly miserable, separate existences. It was a dismal time for me, and couldn't have been any more pleasant for Gerda either, but she didn't want a divorce and I didn't know what to do.

During this time I was travelling quite regularly to Ibiza, then a very simple, peaceful place in comparison to today. The airport building was just a hut and you had to pass through a wooden gate to walk across the tarmac and board your plane. Today nearly six million tourists a year use the island's airport. On one of the last occasions that I went to Ibiza for work, I was taking a friend, accompanied by his girlfriend, to visit a property. They were enchanted by it and we closed the deal, deciding to celebrate with a meal at Sant Antoni's harbourside promenade, the Passeig de Ses Fonts, a short drive from Ibiza Town. Allegedly the birthplace of Christopher Columbus, Sant Antoni de Portmany had originally been a small fishing village, but because of its lovely natural bay and port had become a popular tourist spot even then, with numerous very good restaurants.

On our way there, I slowed down at a crossroads to give way to another vehicle: there was a woman driving it. For a moment we were both stationary and I caught her eye and smiled. This beautiful woman smiled back at me and, in a moment of apparent madness, I leant out of the window and invited her to join us for dinner. She looked perplexed as did the two friends I was with, surprised by my sheer nerve in inviting this total stranger to dinner. But I took a chance and repeated the offer in German, judging it to be her first language, and laughingly explained we were celebrating at a particular restaurant and, if she would like to join us as my guest, she was more than welcome. At this point she visibly relaxed and replied – in German, as I had correctly surmised – that she would think about it, before smiling back, giving me a wave and driving off. My friends laughed again at my nerve and joked that I would be lucky if she did come, teasing me that she was too beautiful for the likes of me! But I couldn't help hoping that she would show up.

So as we sat drinking our aperitifs and eating our appetisers of *los caracoles*, small snails simply cooked but exquisitely seasoned with garlic, butter and parsley, I was hoping against hope that the mystery German woman would show up. Suddenly I saw her walking on to the balcony of the restaurant. She was wearing a sleeveless white dress, which showed off her slim, suntanned arms and shapely brown legs. I saw her removing her dark glasses as she looked around. I stood up to greet her, introducing myself, and she told me her name: Christa. Although she was German she lived in London, but was currently on the island locating a holiday villa for her husband, a property dealer. I'm afraid to say that even though she told me she was married, with two daughters, my interest in her didn't diminish, so I was greatly relieved when she revealed, after further conversation long into the night once my friends had left us, that she and her husband were on the verge of separation. Romantic that I am, by the end of the evening I was already envisaging our future together. Meeting Christa was the catalyst I needed finally to end my marriage with Gerda, hard though that was and even while I did not yet know whether Christa felt the same.

I returned to Hamburg feeling invigorated after this chance

meeting and sensing new possibilities ahead of me for the first time in ages, although I couldn't yet see my way through to a life away from Gerda, the property business and Hamburg. Christa was becoming something of an obsession with me by then. After the way the passion had gone from my marriage, I was very excited about this attractive woman and the possibility of seeing her again. Initially I continued with my job, relentlessly pursuing this new relationship by phone but keeping it secret from Gerda while I started to think how to change things. IOS was completely finished, and property dealing was not the way I wanted to go.

Crunch time came one day when, after weeks of poor performance in the property business, a deal came good and I received a cheque in payment. Determined to celebrate what I thought might be an upturn in my fortunes, I decided I would cook myself a delicious steak. I went out to buy the ingredients for the meal. It had been a while since I had had enough money to buy decent food, so I bought the most wonderful piece of meat, the best vegetables and fruit, freshly baked bread and a good bottle of wine to complement the meal. It would be a feast and my mouth watered at the prospect. I came home, cooked the food to perfection and had sat down to eat when I realised I had forgotten the bread. Returning to the kitchen to fetch it, I didn't see Bammel the cat jump on to the table and take the steak from my plate! As I turned and saw what was happening, and shouted at the cat which was attempting to carry off the large, hot piece of meat, it dropped it on the floor. Quick as a flash, Jan shot out from under the table, grabbed it and wolfed it down in a couple of huge bites. My steak! Gone. I didn't know whether to laugh or cry as I sat down to eat the bread, salad and fruit, the centrepiece of my lovely banquet devoured with little appreciation by my thieving dog.

It was a turning point nevertheless. Over that lunch I made a decision to resign completely from the property company and return to the wine business, and so I began to put out feelers and re-establish some of my wine contacts. One of these, Herr August Keller, ran his wine business from the small town of Bad Bramstedt about forty-two kilometres from Hamburg – famous for its statue of Roland, the legendary first-century warrior and nephew of Charlemagne, for its rheumatism clinic, and nowadays for being the place where fashion designer Karl Lagerfeld went to school. Hearing of my interest in returning to the wine business, Herr Keller offered me a job as his sales director. This was just what I needed and I started work with great enthusiasm.

Keller was more an old farmer than a businessman, but he had a good working knowledge of wine and a reasonable acumen for business. What's more, he was prepared to take on someone who could add something to his company, through their skills and knowledge, without feeling threatened by them. The German passion for Marsala had diminished. Germans had begun to appreciate the finer, dry wines of Italy, creating a new market on top of the previously established one. I was pleased to be doing something based again on real knowledge, and enjoyed discussing with Keller not only the ways of the world but also which wines we should import. Sharing as he did my passion for food and wine, he was as happy to hear my recommendations as my customers were. As sales director I was involved in virtually every aspect of the business, and was also travelling widely again. I was finding many new customers, especially as Italian trattorias, pizzerias and restaurants were by now proliferating in Germany. The *gastarbeiters* of the past had become better integrated into German society where the excellence of Italian food and wine was increasingly being recognised. These customers were pleased to deal with a fellow Italian, as Keller had foreseen when employing me.

I was much happier once I had work I enjoyed. I was earning a decent wage and was also travelling throughout Germany again, which often took me away from home and Gerda, to Munich or Berlin, always accompanied by my dog, the faithful Jan. And at weekends I began to travel regularly to London, to see Christa. My next step was to learn another language, English, because I was already planning my move. I began to read books about London, in which I was becoming interested, its history, customs, and people too.

I increasingly enjoyed my visits to the city, and remember taking a charter flight for the first time from Hamburg to Luton, where Christa picked me up in her Mini. Joining the M1 motorway at Junction 10, we sped the thirty-two miles into the city, probably more quickly then than we would do now as there was far less traffic. Then we drove down Edgware Road and around Marble Arch, zooming down Park Lane where the speed limit increases to 40 mph – the only inner-city road where it exceeds 30 mph – and around Hyde Park Corner, where today's Lanesborough Hotel was then St George's Hospital, and then down busy Knightsbridge, admiring the fashionable shops along the way.

I stayed initially at the Park Tower Hotel in Knightsbridge, now the Sheraton Park Tower, not far from the Cheyne Walk home on the banks of the Thames that Christa shared with her two daughters. I was introduced to them as a 'friend from Ibiza'. Actually on Knightsbridge itself, my hotel was also only yards away from Harvey Nichols and a few minutes' walk from Harrods. I could hardly believe the opulence of the food hall there the first time I saw it!

But the situation wasn't easy for me. I didn't yet speak English, and although I relished the time Christa and I spent together, and kept in touch with her by phone and letter when we were apart, I was still stuck in my old life and becoming increasingly depressed about it. And when Gerda found out about Christa, unsurprisingly the arguments accelerated. The more depressed I became, the harder I worked; the less I slept, the more exhausted I became. I was also drinking heavily. Looking back, I should have recognised the symptoms from my previous breakdown, but I didn't. I always put on the relaxed and jovial persona of a lover when I saw Christa, but emotionally I was just hanging on by my fingertips. One night, alone at home at the flat in Hamburg and feeling increasingly isolated, I drank my way through a bottle of whisky and with its last dregs swallowed the contents of a bottle of sleeping pills. It was the only way out I could see at that moment. But I didn't want to die in the flat where Audrey might see my body, so I went out into the streets of Hamburg, weaving my way towards the lake near where we lived, thinking I could as a last resort throw myself in.

Luckily I didn't, collapsing unconscious on the bank before I had a chance to do so. I was found and taken to the emergency department of the local hospital. I regained consciousness to find myself strapped to my bed and feeling terrible. My stomach had been pumped and traces of charcoal from this clinical procedure still smeared my tear-stained cheeks. Christa was called, probably by Gerda, and she flew over from London. I was released from hospital into her care and, still feeling very sick, went with her to a nearby hotel where we spent the night. Long discussions ensued about what I should do next. Should I move to London? How would I find work? Where would I live? Nothing, it seemed, could be resolved until I took the first step and moved out of the flat I shared with my wife. Reassured of our future together by Christa, I took the final step away from my marriage.

August Keller came to my rescue once again, finding me a flat on the eighth floor of a block in Bad Bramstedt, which although sparsely furnished would serve me well enough for the time being. On the last day I ever saw Gerda, we sat down at the table of our home in Hamburg, discussing our separation and working out what to do with our joint belongings. She was crying and upset, but at the same time telling me determinedly what was hers and not mine, wishing to keep everything really, and an argument broke out. This felt like the last straw to me. I stood up, tipped the table towards her and said, 'Take it all, I want nothing of this life,' before walking out with only a small case of clothes, the dog and my car. Once again another chance at the good life I had hoped for was ending badly. I felt as I had done on leaving Austria, all those years before, depressed and defeated. My family knew only half the story but guessed I was unwell. They offered support that I was disinclined to take, preferring instead to soldier on alone.

My new life consisted of working all week and flying to London to see Christa at weekends. August Keller continued to be a supportive friend, and although my new home in Bad Bramstedt was rather spartan at least the rent was cheap. I was still travelling a great deal and regularly went to Berlin, driving along the frustratingly anachronistic 'corridor' through the GDR and into West Berlin, where I had numerous good customers and a second small flat in which to stay when I was there. By now I was mostly living outside the city, however, and in the countryside I was able to take long walks with Jan when I had time off, and forage for mushrooms and other delicacies in the woods and surrounding areas. I relished being back in regular contact with the natural world, and slowly its restorative magic did its work. I began to recover both my equilibrium and my enthusiasm for life.

I also rediscovered the passion for cooking which I had looked to for solace in the past, and did so again now. I was cooking regularly for myself, and sometimes for friends, the simple Italian dishes of old that I loved so well – *ragù* of various kinds and *salsa di pomodoro alla Napoletana* (Neopolitan tomato sauce), vegetable dishes like *zucchini alla scapece* (marinated courgettes) and *melanzane fritte* (fried aubergines), and *crostini ai funghi* with the wild mushrooms I found, and *tofeja del Canavese*, a pork and borlotti beans dish from Piedmont cooked in a terracotta pot, and *osso buco alla Milanese*. Christa came to visit me, too, and although the ambience of my home was not very luxurious, we had a good time together, sharing some lovely walks with Jan, and I would show off my culinary skills and knowledge of wine to her.

On one occasion my boss planned a party, to which I was invited, and asked me to make all the food. I toiled away all day on a variety of finger foods to complement the wine and other drinks. I made lovely antipasti of delicious salamis, focaccia with olives, bruschetta brushed with olive oil and crushed garlic or rosemary, and my masterpiece – *fritto misto alla Piemontese*, a variety of bite-sized meats and vegetables dipped in beaten egg and flour and shallow-fried in hot olive oil until golden brown and crisp. Finally I was delighted to lay out all this lovingly prepared food on a number of trays ready to serve. I could only carry two at a time down in the lift from my eighth-floor flat to where the party was being held.

An hour before the guests were to arrive, I proudly took the first two trays down. Entering the flat on my return, I discovered that my naughty dog Jan had surpassed himself by jumping up and knocking the remaining trays to the floor where he'd gobbled up what he could. What remained was such a mess it was impossible to retrieve. I was upset and angry, exhausted after my endeavours, and shouted at him loudly, cursing his stupidity – and my own, for leaving temptation in a dog's way. Such was my anger that Jan knew better than to stay within view and hid under the bed for a full twenty-four hours. Needless to say the food, although in short supply, was much appreciated and my apologies were gracefully accepted once the guests heard the circumstances. I learnt a valuable lesson too: never trust a greedy dog. Or, at least, shut them in another room when there is food about!

My divorce from Gerda was finalised, and Christa's divorce from her husband also came through. We were now both free to share a future together and I began to look at ways in which I could come to London full-time. I had been taking English lessons and this, together with my frequent weekend visits, was beginning to give me an initial grasp of the language. I was convinced that my future lay in the wine business and surmised that if there was a market for Italian wine in Germany, there must be one in the UK and, more specifically, in London. On my visits I had been following up contacts, checking out the newly emerging Italian restaurants, especially those around Soho and the theatre district of the city. I just needed to find a way to secure a working life there, and believed the best way would be through wine.

Eventually my tenacity paid off. It came about through one of the clients I was representing in Keller's business in Germany, Marchesi de' Frescobaldi. A Florentine family with a 700-year history of producing Tuscan wines, they continue to run five wine estates in the Chianti region to this day, producing a fantastic range of red and white wines. They put me in touch with their British-based importer, Ciborio, a company that had been bringing the best of Italy to Britain since 1951. It was a happy day for me when I was offered a job in the sales department there and could at last make my move to London. It was 1975 when I packed up my car, by this time a BMW, with my dog, a rug and a few personal possessions, and took the ferry from Hamburg to Dover. Here, Christa had arranged quarantine for Jan. He was whisked off the boat before disembarkation and taken off to Farringdon Kennels in Hampshire for six months.

On the journey over, I considered my life. It was August 1975 and I was thirty-eight, divorced, and embarking on a new life in a new country, speaking excellent Italian, French, Spanish and German but only the rudiments of English. True to my father's dreams, I had travelled and worked further from home than any other member of my family, but I was also keen to emulate what my parents had had, and to create what I craved most: a happy family life, based on a secure, intimate relationship with Christa. By now I had known her for several years, but we had not yet lived together full-time. I was optimistic, but also knew from experience that life's dreams don't always pan out exactly as we would like. I did, however, fervently hope that my new life in England would be the culmination of my dreams. As the ferry sailed overnight from Hamburg to Dover, I sat on deck with a cigarette and a glass of wine, gazing at the harvest moon and considering all these things.

Salsa di pomodoro alla Napoletana

Neapolitan tomato sauce

This is one of the most simple sauces and makes the perfect base for other more elaborate dishes. I really like it on some spaghetti.

Serves 6
90 ml (3 fl oz) extra-virgin olive oil
2 garlic cloves, crushed
1 kg (2 ¼ lb) ripe tomatoes, peeled, deseeded and chopped
6 basil leaves
salt and pepper

Heat the oil in a pan and gently fry the garlic for a few minutes without allowing it to colour. Add the tomatoes and fry, stirring constantly, for 5 minutes, allowing just the excess liquid to evaporate.

Add the basil and salt and pepper to taste and the sauce is ready to use.

CHAPTER NINE

London

I felt a little adrift when I first arrived in London. Living there was quite different from coming for a visit. I drove off the ferry with feelings of trepidation about my new life. Christa had not been able to meet me at Dover, so I had to drive alone to London in my left-hand drive car, on the left-hand side of the road, while also trying to understand the road signs . . . all of which was quite stressful. But the other drivers seemed friendly enough, I thought, as one by one they smiled at me. It turned out that they weren't so much smiling at me as at my car licence plate. Registered in an area of Germany called Segeberg, my licence plate read SEX 613. I smiled back, impervious to the reason for their amusement. I just thought it was a good omen for my arrival!

The mid-seventies was a time of global change. The Vietnam War finally finished, and the Spanish dictator Franco died. The British Conservative Party had a new leader, Margaret Thatcher, the first woman ever to lead a British political party – at a time when only 27 of the 635 elected MPs in the country were women – and with a huge majority. The Suez Canal reopened for the first time since the Six Day War, and the IRA continued to bomb London, murdering the co-founder of *The Guinness Book of Records*, Ross McWhirter, and, along with issuing endless bomb threats, succeeded in bombing the London Hilton Hotel. This was the year inflation ran at 25 per cent and a gallon of petrol cost 72 pence, but at least I was no longer living in a country divided by a wall and could freely travel around. England felt amazingly open and friendly after the confines of Germany, and for that I was thankful.

In spite of my slight trepidation about my new life, I was very pleased that my job with Ciborio was secured before I arrived. It meant that I had work immediately and the possibility of building upon and extending my business contacts and earning a decent wage to support my new family and myself. But moving in with Christa at the lovely Cheyne Walk house which had been her marital home made me feel a little uncomfortable. It felt as if I was in another man's house, but the Chelsea area was such a good place to live it seemed sensible to stay put for the time being.

Cheyne Walk is an historic street between the Thames Embankment and the fashionable King's Road. It was then and still is a very fashionable area, with beautiful early-eighteenth-century houses overlooking the houseboats berthed on the river. I loved these houseboats, which made such attractive, cosy-looking homes, especially at night when the lights from their interiors were reflected across the water. Cheyne Walk was renowned for being home to many artists and musicians. Dante Gabriel Rossetti had lived at number 16, while the painter JMW Turner had died at number 119; the Rolling Stones' Mick Jagger had lived with Marianne Faithfull at number 48 in 1968, and Keith Richards had lived at number 3, now a National Trust property. Ralph Vaughan Williams had written the beautiful music for The Lark Ascending at number 13, and the author of *Cranford*, Elizabeth Gaskell, had been born at number 93 in 1810. The publisher Lord Weidenfeld has lived in Cheyne Walk since the 1960s, and both engineering Brunels – father Marc Isambard and son Isambard

Kingdom – had lived at number 98 in the nineteenth century. It was an amazing, historic street.

Not yet being fluent in the English language, however, did make me feel quite insecure. Although I could speak German to Christa and Italian with much of my client base, I knew I needed to get to grips with the English language as soon as possible. I immediately enrolled at St Anthony's Language School in Earl's Court, which specialised in teaching foreign and business students, and spent several nights a week there, for two months, working hard. It was tough. Even though I knew Italian, Latin, French and German, I found English to be such a hybrid language with so many different grammatical rules that even today, after living in England for nearly forty years, my German is more correct in many ways and, of course, Italian is still my mother tongue. But these were just temporary feelings of insecurity, I reasoned. Once I got to grips with the language and my new work, they would soon pass as I settled down to enjoy life in London.

In order to help my English, I occasionally watched television. The nine o'clock BBC News was excellent, I thought, with its carefully enunciated consonants and vowels. *Upstairs, Downstairs*, an ITV costume drama series about an upper-class family and their servants in London, gave me an impression of old England, while *Fawlty Towers*, created by and starring John Cleese of *Monty Python's Flying Circus* fame, gave me some insight into the contemporary one in which I now found myself. More entertaining than particularly accurate, no doubt, both were amusing in their own way, although I sometimes found it quite hard to follow what the butler Hudson, played by Scots actor Gordon Jackson, was saying, in the drama about life above and below stairs in Edwardian England.

There wasn't much time though for watching television, as my working and social lives intermingled. London in the mid-seventies was an exciting place to be and I was kept busy trying to build my business contacts, which were inevitably in the restaurant and hospitality business and therefore convivial and enjoyable in themselves There was a big Italian restaurant scene emerging in London that had developed from both the Italian coffee houses at the turn of the twentieth century and the waiters in the big London hotels of the 1950s, who had left to start up their own restaurants in the 1960s. One of the first Italian restaurants to become famous, not least for its celebrity clientele, was La Trattoria Terrazza in Romilly Street in London's Soho district, opened by Franco Lagattolla, originally an Italian waiter, and Neapolitan wine waiter Mario Cassandro, whose first job on arriving from Naples in 1947 was at the provisions store Parmigiani Figlio in Old Compton Street.

If you want to get an idea of an Italian store typical of this era, look no further than Lina Stores on Soho's Brewer Street, with its beautifully preserved 1950s exterior in green Vitrolite and ceramic tiles. It is still open today and sells a range of imported Italian produce that includes olive oil, porcini, lentils, beans, Seggiano chestnut honey, *Sapori panforte* and *Paccheri* pasta, besides having a deli counter with great olives, cheeses, hams, salamis, truffles, marinated artichokes and anchovies, as well as its own handmade pasta and sausages, while spaghetti then came wrapped in instantly recognisable dark blue waxed paper.

There had been Italian cafés in Soho for years and their popularity had soared with the arrival of the first Gaggia espresso coffee machines in the early 1950s as well as the jukeboxes imported from the USA, which naturally drew in a younger clientele. This Italian café culture was the precursor to the Italian trattoria and restaurant scene of the 1970s. By then Soho was associated with the vibrant music, film, advertising, publishing, photography and fashion industries, which provided a clientele keen to spend long boozy lunchtimes entertaining their contacts on business accounts. Together with the business lunchers, many artists and writers from Soho's fifties past remained regular visitors to the area, from Lucian Freud to Eduardo Paolozzi, George Orwell to ex-advertising man and author Len Deighton. I liked nothing more than walking down Berwick Street on an early summer's morning, en route to meeting my restaurant clients just as the market traders got going. I'd pass the vegetable stalls and Ron's flower stall (still there to this day), and Fratelli Camisa (now gone), the Italian deli on the corner of Peter Street, originally opened in 1929, from where I could pick up some freshly ground coffee or authentic, home-made ravioli.

Pizza was another Italian speciality that had arrived in Soho with a flourish when Peter Boizot, a vegetarian entrepreneur originally from Peterborough, brought a pizza oven over from Naples and a pizza chef from Sicily and opened the first Pizza Express restaurant in Wardour Street in 1965. He also combined live music with serving food, opening a jazz club in Soho's Dean Street Pizza Express which over the years has hosted the likes of Ella Fitzgerald, Amy Winehouse, Jamie Cullum and Ravi Shankar's jazz singer daughter Norah Jones. With Boizot responsible also for Kettner's in Romilly Street, Pizza on the Park, and the now closed Condotti restaurant in Mayfair, it was not until 1973 when the American Pizza Hut chain arrived in the UK that there was any serious competition to his pizza restaurants.

Although the credit for post-war culinary development in Britain is often handed on a plate to Elizabeth David, who first published *A Book of Mediterranean Cooking* in 1950, the BBC television cook Zena Skinner, on air from 1963 and author of five recipe books and packs of recipe cards, can also take some credit. It was Skinner who told her TV audience that spaghetti was ready to be eaten when a piece of it was, '. . . thrown at the wall and it sticks . . .'. And it was Robert Carrier who provided the recipes that graced many a dinner party in the 1970s, courtesy of the publication of his wipe-clean, easy-to-follow cookery cards, with recipes for dishes previously considered 'gourmet', like *coq au vin*, pork chops baked in a mushroom and cream sauce, quiche Lorraine and even ratatouille. The British finally took to using foreign ingredients like garlic and avocado, as well as lots of cream and butter with which they were more familiar.

The 1970s was also the era of Smash, a freeze-dried mashed potato product, and let's not forget Vesta curries, which were also made from dried ingredients, and Angel Delight, an instant pudding mix made by adding cold milk. Cinzano Bianco, Mateus Rosé and Blue Nun wine were all considered to be sophisticated drinks. Personally, I believe the biggest revolution in popular culinary taste arose from the Italian influence in late-1970s Soho, where food was increasingly appreciated for the simplicity and authenticity of its ingredients, flavour and presentation. The emerging media industry frequented the area's restaurants, liked what it found, and relayed it to the country as a whole, weaning them away from their packets and tins.

My entrée into London life was not the easiest of times for me personally, and I think I underestimated at the time how stressful I was finding it. I loved London, with all its friendliness and opportunity, but I was a long way from home and everything I knew in Italy and Germany. Speaking English was still a bit of a struggle for me, and every weekend when I visited Jan, quarantined in kennels outside London, it was always an emotional wrench to leave him – with resonances of all the other losses I had known over the years. The only benefit to me from these autumnal forays outside the city was that I discovered the English countryside. I loved to walk there, even without my dog, and in doing so I discovered an abundance of wild mushrooms. Beech hangers, for instance, provided exactly the right conditions of leafy humus-rich soil for *Boletus edulis* or cep mushrooms. I was thrilled to discover a source of them, not far from London, and from then on continued to indulge my passion for mushrooms.

I began to collect them on these weekly trips, at first just for myself, but increasingly for others. Unlike the English, who at this time regarded most wild mushrooms as potentially fatal toadstools so wouldn't risk foraging for them, I was experienced and knowledgeable enough to collect them safely. This meant that, in season, there were rich pickings to be had, and my Italian friends and restaurant clients were delighted to receive them. And I, in turn, learnt to make the pastry necessary to create a delicious *torta di funghi* – a wild mushroom tart – in order to extend my culinary range yet again.

I had been living here for about three months when, one evening, Christa and I went out to dinner at the Italian restaurant Santa Croce on the Chelsea Embankment, not far from where we lived. I had been feeling a little under the weather, as the English like to say, but over dinner I started to feel extremely nauseous, chilly and sweaty, with a very heavy feeling like bad indigestion, as if an elephant were sitting on my chest. I couldn't think what it could be, except perhaps that I was getting the flu, but had never felt so physically dreadful before – or indeed since. So we came home and I was very sick.

It got so bad that nothing I could do would relieve the increasing discomfort – lying down or standing up, it was just as bad – and Christa decided I must go to hospital. She dialled 999 for an ambulance. I was taken to the Accident and Emergency department of the Brompton Hospital (now the Royal Brompton since the granting of its charter by Queen Elizabeth II in 1991) on the Fulham Road, where they diagnosed a heart attack – a heart attack! I was only thirty-eight and pretty fit, not then overweight, and this was a young age for anyone to have a heart attack, but fortunately I received the best of treatment, courtesy of the English National Health Service, and made a good recovery.

I was quite shocked, though, as the doctors carried out their tests and treated me: the stress of the last couple of months had obviously been greater than I'd realised, and I felt quite depressed about this, even while the doctors reassured me that I would in time make an absolutely full recovery – which I did, in spite of my fears for my future health. Christa was also quite shocked, wondering no doubt what she'd taken on – first my suicide attempt in Hamburg, and now this. I thought it prudent, though, not to tell my parents about my being hospitalised with a heart attack, as there was no point in worrying them. I did tell them later, but only when I was quite recovered.

I'll never forget a fellow patient in the opposite bed at the Brompton Hospital, Martin Cummings, who'd had a heart valve replaced. Because his mother was Italian he spoke a little of the language, which was greatly consoling to me as I made my recovery. Not only that, his mother used to bring in food for her son, and once she knew I was Italian too, she kindly brought in some for me as well. I don't think I have ever savoured a finer Neapolitan version of the *pasta e fagioli* soup she brought in one day. It quite restored both me and my will to live, this wonderful taste of my homeland.

I was discharged after about a week, but had to wear a portable ECG for a while to monitor my heart rate. I wore it when I went back to work too. I was instructed not to overdo it and to take 'gentle exercise', which meant walking along the Embankment rather than making love, about which I was initially a little nervous! Once the period of monitoring was over, I received a final discharge from the cardiologist, with the confirmation that all was well and I could resume my usual lifestyle again – both Christa and I were very relieved to hear this.

I was still feeling my way in my new home city but beginning to make friends and business contacts as I visited London's restaurants to sell wine. The majority of my customers initially were Italian, and over the years many grew to be close friends. As I became more accepted by them I was invited to a monthly lunch meeting of all the restaurateurs, held at San Frediano, jointly owned by Mino Parlanti and his brother-in-law Franco Buonaguidi, on the Fulham Road. In time, my Tuscan friend Alvaro Maccioni of La Famiglia on Langton Street, Walter Mariti at the Pontevecchio, who also co-owned the Meridiana with Enzo Apicella, all became my friends. And I was beginning to include English customers among my friends, too – in particular Allan Martin, owner of My Old Dutch, the chain of popular pancake houses that continues to prosper on the King's Road and elsewhere in central London.

It was, however, the Italian artist, interior designer and political cartoonist Enzo Apicella who first introduced me to good whisky. A single malt whisky called Laphroaig, to be precise, from the distillery of the same name on the Scottish Isle of Islay. I immediately liked it and discovered it was one of life's great joys after a day spent hunting mushrooms in chilly autumn weather. Enzo was not only the co-founder of the Meridiana, co-owner of the Condotti in Mayfair, and the designer of 150 restaurants, including the famous Arethusa Club, he was also responsible for the corporate identity for the Pizza Express chain. The London *Evening Standard*'s restaurant critic Fay Maschler credited him with being the first to throw out the raffia-clad Chianti bottles and plastic grapes hanging on fabric vines from the London trattoria, in a successful effort to create a new market for a more authentic and less faux-rustic Italian style. Today, he is still a prolific political cartoonist.

As the months passed, I was building something of a reputation for myself among the gastronomic community of London, not least because of my knowledge of wine and interest in food. I was particularly interested to see what was being offered, in terms of Italian dishes, in British restaurants. A lot of the menus were quite simple, which was fine, but seemed to be designed to give customers what they thought they wanted, rather than authentic Italian cooking. It was what I came to call Britalian food: dishes like spag bol rather than *tagliatelle al ragù Bolognese*, made with minced beef, rather than from minced veal and pork with herbs added. *Petto di pollo sorpresa* made an appearance, courtesy of La Terrazza – breast of chicken stuffed with garlic butter and deep fried in breadcrumbs. Although popular with customers, it wasn't Italian at all, but an adaptation of Chicken Kiev. It later featured in Franco Lagattolla's recipe book, *The Recipes That Made a Million.* There were other dishes unheard of in Italy, like *pera avocado con gamberetti,* half an avocado filled with prawns in a *salsa aurora,* which was mayonnaise mixed with tomato ketchup. And for dessert you might find *arancio caramellato* slices of fresh, peeled orange served in orange syrup sweetened with caramelised sugar and given an Italianate name, or profiteroles stuffed with whipped cream and covered with a chocolate sauce – a typically French dessert, not to mention Black Forest gâteau which has never been Italian but rather an English version of the German *Schwarzwälder Kirschtorte.*

It was in this gastronomic climate that I sold wine. Many restaurateurs were, like me, keen to introduce diners to new varieties other than the well-known Chianti, Frascati, Valpolicella and Barolo. In addition, there were also restaurateurs who wanted to create a little more authenticity in their menus – the same restaurateurs who welcomed my supply of foraged mushrooms – and I watched as those who truly cared about food began to ensure greater integrity in the ingredients and recipes that they used. As my friend Alvaro Maccioni said: if you can cook like your mother then you are a good cook, but if you can cook like your grandmother then you are a great cook. It was a sentiment I applauded, and reflects the same love of authenticity that I brought to bear when developing the first menus for the future Carluccio's Caffè.

At home I continued to cook, for myself and for family and friends. One of my favourite dishes to this day is one of the simplest, *spaghetti aglio, olio e peperoncino* – spaghetti with olive oil, garlic and chilli. It's the quickest, easiest and cheapest recipe, and so delicious. And it's the base recipe for many variations – a few capers added maybe or some sundried tomatoes – making it easy to ring the changes. Now that it was possible to get good-quality ingredients from the Italian delis in Soho like Lina Stores, Fratelli Camisa or *Parmigiani* – unlike in Hamburg where they had still been difficult to source – I was happy. And I had many new friends with whom I could converse about the varieties of Italian cuisine and the regional specialities that were becoming increasingly popular.

Perhaps one of the greatest contributors to this understanding of regional cooking was Pellegrino Artusi, who published his book *La Scienza in Cucina e l'Arte di Mangiare Bene* (*Science in the Kitchen and the Art of Eating Well*) in the nineteenth century. It was the first book to highlight all of Italy's wonderful regional specialities – and that's why I like it, because, in a sense, 'Italian food' doesn't exist – it has always been a cuisine with marked regional differences.

The milieu in which I lived and worked in London suited me. It reminded me a little of my time spent in Vienna, when I had enjoyed the company of the artists, musicians and writers who frequented the Café Hawelka. This time, however, I was older, better established, better paid, with increasing gastronomic knowledge and a measure of authority in the wine-importing business. These happy circumstances were contributing not only to my immediate sense of wellbeing, but also – though I didn't yet know it – to the future I would go on to create for myself.

Living in London with its great cultural heritage also gave me many opportunities to explore and develop my artistic interests. With free access to wonderful places like the British Museum, the National Gallery, and the Tate (now the gallery known as Tate Britain), which was only a little further up the Embankment from where we lived, I started to enjoy and actively engage in these interests. I had always drawn and sketched as a child and young man; now I returned to it and started to paint, too. I found the contemplation and relaxation it afforded very pleasurable, along with the sheer sensual pleasure of working with paint on canvas. I not only enjoyed the actual painting, but also the pleasure of hanging my finished work on the walls. It was greatly appreciated by Christa and added to the ambience of what, at last, felt to be my home.

Christa and I also enjoyed holidays together away from London, during the winter in Austria and in the summer by the sea. She went back home to Italy with me, where she met and was welcomed by my family, who were happy to see me settled at last.

While I worked, Christa furthered her studies, taking a BA in literature at the North London Polytechnic. After this, wanting to use her degree professionally, she decided to take a course to teach languages one-to-one, enrolling in a class to do so. She then got a job and would leave early in the morning, returning home after her day's work to be welcomed with a glass of wine and some divine Verdi aria from *La Traviata* on the record player as I perfected a dish of *osso buco alla Milanese*. Jan, by now long out of quarantine and also happily ensconced with us, would always be pleased to see her. We were very happy with life, I thought, and when Christa decided to sell Cheyne Walk and buy a new house in nearby Harley Gardens, also in Chelsea, it seemed that the foundations on which we were building our life together were secure. I was to discover that this was not the case with a terrible jolt, shortly after the beginning of 1978.

On that cold January evening Christa didn't arrive home from work as scheduled. Supper grew cold on the table. I began to worry about not hearing from her as this was very out of character. Her daughter, at home at the time, was also worried about her mother, so we eventually decided to go and look for her, driving to the building where she worked in the West End. The place was shut and the lights were off, but there in the doorway, illuminated by the streetlights, stood Christa kissing a man I didn't recognise. I stopped the car and looked on in astonishment before calling out to her. She broke away, startled by my voice, and immediately got into the passenger seat of the car. The three of us drove home without saying a word.

I was furiously angry and mortally hurt by her betrayal, although she made no excuse except to tell me that it was not what it seemed. The man – who turned out to be the principal of the school where she had enrolled for her course – had merely been keeping her warm on a cold night, she said. I didn't believe her, trusting instead in what I had seen with my own eyes: the intensity of his kiss and her response to it. No one ate anything when we got home. Frustrated by Christa's stonewalling, I started to drink my way through a bottle of whisky, becoming increasingly upset as I did so. I could think of no other way to numb my chaotic feelings. Then, when the bottle was finished, I took myself out of the house and got into the car, determined to smash myself up on the motorway, such was my desperation to end my whisky-fuelled pain. It sounds like complete madness now, and of course it was. I was mad with hurt and rage. I accelerated my powerful BMW hard up Gunter Grove and Finborough Road towards Earl's Court, which were thankfully free from traffic at that time of night, heading for West Cromwell Road and the A4, jumping red lights all the way. Suddenly, and luckily for me, the car's engine made a terrible grinding noise and shuddered to a halt. The crankshaft had gone.

I couldn't believe that my suicidal intentions had been thwarted like this. Drunk though I was, I got out of the car and, fuelled with rage now, pushed it to the side of the road before walking home. Although I had been gone less than an hour, by the time I got back I saw that the man I had previously seen kissing the woman I considered to be my wife had arrived at the house and was sitting on the sofa with his arm around her, as if it were his rightful place, not mine! Furious and humiliated yet further, but trying not to make a scene in front of Christa's poor daughter, who was herself by this time quite distraught as she was fond of me and saddened by what was happening, I left again

– this time intent on throwing myself off Battersea Bridge – and she followed me, begging me not to do it. Obviously still drunk and out of control, my behaviour as I tried to climb the railings frightened her to such an extent that she alerted passers-by who stepped in, somehow persuaded me otherwise and accompanied me home. And the man was still sitting on the sofa – taking my place already! I couldn't believe it. I wanted to punch him in the face. Instead, I took out this destructive urge on myself.

Going upstairs, I took down all my paintings and brought them into the sitting room. In front of Christa and the interloper, I systematically destroyed each one, ranting and raging as I did so. It was not a pretty sight. Then I took another bottle of whisky and washed down a bottle of Valium with it – another suicide attempt, resulting in another hospital admission to the Brompton, another session with the stomach pump, and another terrible sense of loss as another relationship imploded, leaving me struggling with feelings of abandonment once again. It may sound over-dramatic now, but at the time I was devastated. I left hospital the following morning still feeling sick and chilled to the bone. Unable to go home, I took myself off to my friend Luigi on the Fulham Road. He took me in and gave me sanctuary in the equally cold upstairs back room of his home, where I immediately crashed out for several hours. Christa's new lover Martin had – as I feared – absolutely taken my place. He'd moved in with her straight away, as I discovered when I went to collect Jan. It was an emotional reunion with my dog who immediately ran to me, delightedly licking my face in welcome, the closeness of his warm furry body giving me some much-needed comfort in a time of great sadness.

With the help of friends I pulled myself together. I found a furnished flat in nearby Ifield Road, owned by one of my restaurant clients, where I was able to move in immediately. An Italian garage owner from the Portobello Road, who was a mechanical wizard and managed miracles with the BMW's engine, recovered my car from the side of the road and returned it fully functioning to me along with a large bill. I never saw Christa again: she sent my few possessions round in a taxi. I heard later that she and Martin moved to Wales, where she had another baby – having told me that she wanted no more children – and they bought and ran a mini-cab firm, which subsequently failed before they eventually split up.

Looking back, I still have no idea what her betrayal and desertion was all about, some sort of madness perhaps but without any discussion possible between us I will never know – and even her own family didn't really understand it either. We had seemed so happy before it happened, it made no sense to me. Martin was German too, so maybe there was something they shared that I didn't understand. At the time, I was so emotionally bruised by what had happened I just wanted to put it behind me – not least because these events had led to another major depression for me.

I don't think I recognised it then because mental-health issues were seldom discussed and there was not the awareness of them that there is today, but I recognise now that I have always been prone to quite serious bouts of depression. There had been several depressive episodes by this time that I had more or less ignored, and two suicide attempts which I couldn't, not to mention the risky behaviour associated with doing things like drinking and driving. I dealt with these dark feelings by dismissing them and just getting on with life. If you had asked anyone who knew me then they would in all probability have described me as a jovial man, highly knowledgeable about wine, who had a dog called Jan, drove a BMW and brought mushrooms as a gift whenever they were in season. That was me, I believed; or rather the version of me I liked to project, using jokes and jollity as a screen while underneath ran a current of deep unhappiness and depression that I sought to conceal.

So I got on with work, and in fact prospered at it. My strategy of ignoring my own feelings worked – more or less – until the next time. I changed jobs, leaving Ciborio to take over sales at Eurowines, a company established by Alfonso Addis in 1965 and run by him until 1995. Alfonso was a Sardinian wine merchant who, like me, wanted to import better-quality wines from Italy. The company is still run by his son Leo today.

I worked hard, and saw my friends. I took Jan for long walks around the Serpentine in Hyde Park. I studiously avoided thinking about what had happened, believing it to be counter-productive, concentrating instead on being good company to my friends and customers while inside my emotions still raged. How could Christa have done this to me? Denied me children, then gone off to have a baby with another man. Left me homeless. Abandoned me. When all I had ever wanted was a happy home and family life . . . In the midst of this turmoil, and with no professional help to balance my emotions, there was also no hope of my reflecting on and re-evaluating my own learnt patterns of behaviour that could have contributed to the demise of yet another relationship. I felt desolate, believing I would never find another love or create the family life I dreamt of.

Better instead to put my faith and trust in my dog, whose unconditional love was a great consolation to me. Jan, at least, would never let me down.

Spaghetti aglio, olio e peperoncino

~~~~~~~~~~~~~~~~~~~~~~~~~~~~

Spaghetti with garlic, oil and chilli

This is probably one of the most popular recipes for native Italians. They like to eat it at any time, but it's probably the prime dish to be eaten for a midnight feast, when they arrive home late and hungry. It takes only about 6–7 minutes to cook the pasta, while the 'sauce' is ready in less than half that time. You don't even have to grate any Parmesan, as the pasta is better without.

Serves 2
salt
180 g (6 oz) spaghetti or linguine
6 tbsp olive oil
2 garlic cloves, peeled and finely
     chopped
1 small chilli (the strength is up to
     you), finely chopped, with seeds

Put plenty of water in a saucepan, add salt, bring to boil and throw in the pasta. Stir, then cook for about 5–6 minutes, until nearly done.

Now start the sauce by heating the olive oil gently in a deep frying pan. Fry the garlic and chilli and fry for a few seconds, or until the garlic starts to change colour, taking care not to burn it.

The pasta will be ready and al dente in those few minutes. Drain it well and put in the pan with the 'sauce', adding a little salt and perhaps 1–2 tbsp of the pasta cooking water. Stir a couple of times and serve (without Parmesan).

To make it more special...

For people who think this is too simple, you could add a further burst of flavour by including a couple of anchovy fillets. Fry them along with the garlic and chilli, and they will melt into the oil. You could add a teaspoon of tiny capers too if you like, or some very finely cubed green olives. Or, at the end, you could grate some *bottarga* (dried and salted tuna or grey mullet roe) over the top of each portion.

CHAPTER TEN

A Wedding

f 1978 had started badly I was, on the face of it at least, reasonably optimistic about my future. In spite of my sadness about the abrupt termination of my life with Christa, I enjoyed living in Ifield Road with my dog, socialising with my friends and customers, walking in the woods outside London foraging for mushrooms, and whittling my hazelwood sticks. I continued to cook and really appreciated the access I now had to the fresh ingredients that a cosmopolitan city like London imported. Getting my hands on really good olive oil, for example, was no longer restricted to my visits home, and staples like garlic were beginning to find their way regularly on to supermarket shelves as well as market stalls. Herbs I could grow myself, and there were increasingly good butchers locally, too, while the Italian delis provided fresh pasta when I couldn't be bothered to make it myself.

I also enjoyed good English food, when I could find it, and was a regular at one of my favourite restaurants, the extremely popular Hungry Horse on the Fulham Road. Here the traditional English roast beef was spectacularly good and they would prepare a special side order of freshly steamed spinach with a little olive oil and lemon, the Italian way, to accompany it at my request. They also served jugged hare and that great English classic Spotted Dick, the lightest of suet puddings stuffed with juicy currants and served with piping hot custard. Some evenings the Hungry Horse would become the rendezvous for a number of off-duty Italian restaurant owners and managers, who would gather together for a game of poker. I often joined them and we gambled together, but only for small stakes – no one had the money then to risk large sums. It was a social thing only, but I enjoyed that frisson of excitement, the tension and anticipation that comes from gambling when you know you have a good hand. And it was a fun way to share time with my friends.

London's Fulham Road in the late 1970s was in fact a very social place. It had a number of popular pubs including the Queen's Elm and Finch's, but a new social phenomenon began to take off – the wine bar – and one in particular which I visited often, Bray's, run by my friends Judy and Julian Bray. Wine bars were proving very popular, and provided a good new market for salesmen like myself, especially those of us who were interested in sourcing good but less commonly known wines.

They were also at the forefront of the Beaujolais Nouveau race, to get the first bottles of that year's vintage back to London. It was a marketing ploy really, dreamt up by Georges Duboeuf who had learnt his trade on the family vineyard in the Saône-et-Loire, and went on to create Les Vins Georges Duboeuf. He had almost single-handedly created the annual phenomenon of the race, and was not nicknamed *le roi du Beaujolais* for nothing.

Beaujolais Nouveau is produced from the *Gamay noir à jus blanc* grape, and is ready to drink within eight weeks of its harvest – making it great for cash flow if a demand can be created for this very young wine, which is best drunk chilled. Bray's was one of the wine bars that participated in this event; it was a bit of fun and created some light-hearted competition between the different businesses. I can remember Judy coming in triumphantly, after an overnight drive back from France, and putting up a poster in the bar window that announced: '*Le Beaujolais nouveau est arrivé!*' The wine itself was not particularly to my taste, however, I preferred to drink whisky instead – but wine bars were not licensed to sell spirits so we got round this small problem by pouring my whisky into a wine glass, in order to disguise it. As a consequence I had to put up with Julian's endless jokes about the flatulent nature of my dog, but it was a small price to pay to be able to drink good whisky in the company of congenial friends.

It was here in the wine bar that I met a woman one day – she was a friend of a friend of mine, who used to let and manage properties abroad. I was always interested to hear news of the foreign property market, although glad no longer to be involved at first hand, and he and I got talking. Through him, I came to know Francesca. A few years younger than me, she was divorced from her Spanish husband and had a young daughter who was growing up with her grandparents in the north of England. Francesca was good company and seemed to enjoy being with me. It also seemed we had a lot in common, sharing an appreciation of food and wine, but also of art and music too, and conversation between us was always lively. I asked her out, and we started to see each other every day. Friends warned me not to get too serious too soon, but within a short time we were lovers and, after only a month of knowing each other, we decided to marry.

At the time I was quite pragmatic about it. For me, this was in some way an act of defiance against all that had so recently gone wrong, and a means of keeping my depression at bay. I *could* still be happy, and I would show this to the world. Francesca was very keen to marry me, I was flattered, and it put an end to my living alone, for which I was grateful. We travelled north to see her parents, and for me to meet her daughter, a very sweet, pretty young girl. And we made plans. Again, I think my yearning for a family and the chance of a child with Francesca clouded my judgement, and in spite of protestations from various friends who thought I was being very rash, we went ahead. Even though at the time I privately thought we had only a 50/50 chance of the marriage working out, I still thought it worth the gamble.

We married at Chelsea Register Office on the King's Road, where countless marriages are celebrated with photographs taken in front of the porch on the famous steps outside this attractive Neo-classical building. It was here that actor David Niven had married his second wife, Swedish model Hjördis Paulina Tersmeden in 1948, Judy Garland had married Micky Deans in 1969, and more recently Michael Winner had married his long-standing girlfriend Geraldine. Afterwards, we enjoyed a lengthy wedding breakfast on the terrace of the Meridiana restaurant on the Fulham Road, owned by my friends Enzo Apicella and Walter Mariti. Walter was originally from Tuscany, and the cuisine of his restaurant reflected the regional specialities of this lovely area of Italy, as La Terrazza reflected Neapolitan cooking and San Lorenzo in Beauchamp Place focused more on the cuisine of northern Italy. I forget what we ate that day, but it probably included Tuscan specialities like *cacciucco,* a fish soup from Livorno, *quaglie allo spiedo*, quails cooked on a skewer, *tortellini al brodo di carne* which is a particular favourite of mine, tortellini cooked in a meat broth, and no doubt a slice of panforte – traditional Tuscan cake from Siena – to go with a postprandial cup of espresso and glass of *grappa*.

After we left the restaurant, with congratulations ringing in one ear and dire warnings in the other, Francesca and I set off on our honeymoon. Our destination was the Périgord region of France – famous for its truffles, *foie gras* and walnuts – driving in my repaired BMW and taking the overnight ferry to Cherbourg, hoping to arrive at our destination of Sarlat, a wonderful old town just north of the beautiful Dordogne river, for a late lunch. I had planned what I thought would be a wonderful trip to share with my new wife, with lots of excellent opportunities to eat good food and drink delicious wine, which I thought we would both enjoy. Boarding the ferry, we slept separately in the bunk beds of our cabin, without consummating our marriage on our wedding night. This, it turned out, was something of an omen for the trip to come.

Waking the next morning, I found the ferry had obviously docked so I got up and left the cabin to find that my car was the only one yet to disembark. I hurried back to our cabin to wake Francesca and tell her we needed to make haste and leave. She looked at me as if I were stupid and asked why the staff hadn't woken us? What staff? I couldn't understand her response, and her manner towards me was so disdainful that I hardly recognised her. She was, she pointed out, accustomed to travelling first class, not in this unexpectedly makeshift manner. My heart sank and, not for the first time, I thought that my 50/50 gamble might not pay off.

I was right. The journey to Sarlat, planned with such happy anticipation, was a nightmare. Francesca was consistently cold and patronising towards me, treating me as if I were some country bumpkin who knew nothing about life. Whether or not she was right about that was not the issue. She had not shown her contempt for me previously, or I would never in a million years have married her, but with a ring safely on her finger she showed it now. I was deeply upset by this turn of events and hoped against hope it was some passing aberration, but in my heart – and gut – I think I knew then that I had made a terrible, terrible mistake.

When we finally arrived at our hotel, Francesca took herself off and phoned her mother, returning in a slightly calmer and less argumentative mood. I breathed a sigh of relief and we set off for dinner. Here, Francesca ate crab and it upset her stomach. Another disaster that was patently my fault and another night spent in separate beds in silent apathy after another furious row. The following morning she was still feeling unwell so we agreed to cut our losses and return home, cancelling our honeymoon. Driving back, we decided to break our journey overnight at La Rochelle, a really stunning and unspoilt old seaside port on the Atlantic west coast of France, staying at the five-star Le Yachtman hotel on the quai Valin, at the foot of the lighthouse, with its views of the old harbour towers of this historic town. Francesca was still feeling ill and immediately took to her bed, leaving me free to spend my evening as I chose.

I took a walk around the quayside of this charming old port, and ate dinner by myself at the hotel. I ordered the largest *plateau de fruits de mer*, an exquisite plateful of fruits of the sea – fish, crab, lobster, oysters, the full works – it was wonderful, especially washed down with some delicious Sancerre. Here I was treated with courteous charm and sympathy for my new wife's delicate stomach, leaving me free to enjoy the company of the waiters and even the chef, who not only entertained me by showing me how to hypnotise a lobster, but also demonstrated how to make *sorbet à l'estragon* – tarragon sorbet – a surprising but spectacular palate cleanser to follow the *fruits de mer*.

A day later we were back in London, moving into a house in Chiswick that I had rented before our departure in preparation for our return. It was not a happy homecoming and, although we continued living together, we more or less began living separate lives immediately. The daily rows continued, however, and our sex life was negligible, so there was little pleasure to be had from this arrangement. And there were fresh complications. Because we had married at such short notice, no one from my family had been able to get over from Italy to attend the wedding so I had promised to visit them all with my new bride shortly after our return from France. I was loath to let them know that I had made such a colossal mistake – from the moment we returned from our honeymoon I'd planned to divorce Francesca – but I felt a complete fool and I didn't want my family to know just yet the magnitude of my mistake. I insisted to Francesca that we should go ahead with this trip, and the travel plans were made. It was a mad idea but we went, out of some misguided idea of mine that I could pull it off. Within hours of arrival, my brother Carlo took me to one side and said, 'Where the hell did you get that woman from?' I could conceal how disastrous my new liaison was from the rest of the world, perhaps, but not from those who really loved me and knew me well.

On our return from this grim visit to Italy we moved again, this time to a mews flat in Earl's Court, but it was absolutely over. I knew it and I am sure Francesca did too. I filed for divorce, after just seven months, and fortunately it was granted immediately. At that point Francesca tried to claim maintenance from me for her daughter, who had never even lived with us. I was very relieved when the judge ruled that a marriage, and certainly one which was obviously a mistake from the start such as ours, was not a meal ticket for life. I never heard from Francesca again.

I moved back to Chelsea, to the Ifield Road flat to which I had retreated after my split from Christa. There was a good reason why this road was called the 'road of the singles', I discovered – it was full of small flats and divorcees. It felt quite surreal, as if the previous twelve months hadn't happened at all, and it seemed almost as if I could blot out the episode with Francesca completely. A second chance, but this time I would learn from my mistakes, I thought determinedly. So I decided to focus on creating the sort of life I really wanted to lead: working hard, walking my dog, painting again – and choosing, for the time being at least, to avoid a close relationship with a woman. This plan served me well enough for a time, and then, at the end of 1980, I met a woman who was to change my life for ever, but this time in a very positive and long-lasting way.

From time to time, once I was sure I wouldn't run into Francesca, I ventured back to Bray's wine bar and on one occasion I got talking to a very nice woman there called Lobby Green. She was beautiful and vivacious with an exotic face, and was very good company. It was, and remained, only ever a good friendship as neither of us was interested in taking it further – once bitten, twice shy was relevant to us both at the time – but we did share many interests and talked about everything under the sun. I liked very much having a female friend, and occasionally we would accompany each other to events where having a partner was useful, and that was fun too.

One day, driving down Walton Street towards Draycott Avenue, on my way to the Fulham Road, I saw Lobby crossing the street and entering the Conran Shop. I parked and hurried over to say hello to her. She was, she told me, popping in to see someone she'd met on a flight from Paris and become friends with. Come with me, she said and we went through to the shop's office, and there I met Priscilla Patrick, one of the directors and a buyer for the shop. She was very gracious and charming, offered us coffee and we all chatted, remarking on the fact that with the Christmas season upon us it was a bore to be single and divorced when the festivities placed such emphasis on family life. I had, I said, half planned to go to Italy to visit my family, but with the pressure of work at this time of year, had decided to stay put and visit them in the spring. At this point Lobby suggested that we all get together for a festive drink at the bar opposite, after Priscilla had finished work on Christmas Eve. It was agreed, and I felt good knowing that I had this small festive event to look forward to.

Christmas Eve arrived and we all met again as planned. I liked this English woman Priscilla and her sweet smile very much. She had a gentle nature although I could see that, as with many English women, there was an underlying strength. Her slight bossiness hid a kindness and vulnerability, and that strength had helped her not only to train as a photographer but also to run a business in France importing English furniture and, after her divorce from her architect husband, to successfully raise their three children alone. She obviously had a very good eye for design and an appreciation of beautiful things, and relished her job at the Conran Shop. I was impressed and, somewhere along the line, must have impressed her a little too as when she heard that I was in London over New Year, she invited me to her home for a New Year's Eve drink and to have supper with her and her children. Much later she told me that I had made a positive impression on that first evening when she had mentioned a cocktail she liked and I had not only picked up on what she'd said, but known how to make it and gone to the bar to organise it for her. She had been quite touched by the trouble I'd taken to please her, and I was very touched by her generosity in inviting me over for New Year's Eve, and happy to accept.

Christmas Day that year I spent alone, apart from Jan. At lunchtime I cooked us both a steak, and fresh green beans with a little garlic and mint to accompany mine. Then I poached a dish of pears in red wine before opening a new bottle of Laphroaig and settling down to spend the afternoon painting. With Maria Callas on the gramophone turntable singing '*O patria mia*' and other arias from *Aïda*, I spent a happy few hours painting a portrait of my dog looking longingly at a Christmas tree decorated with cutlets, sausages, ham and bones, by which time the whisky bottle was half-empty and I went to bed and slept well. I still have the painting to this day and it's a lovely memento of my faithful dog.

The following day, Boxing Day, I was invited to visit friends but chose instead to stay home and continue painting, nursing a little bit of a hangover too, I have to admit. I cooked a large *pasta al forno,* a pasta dish baked in the oven which is one of the best of comfort foods, nourishing and tasty and perfect for the day after a surfeit of whisky the night before. It is a dish from my home in northern Italy, and traditionally cooked in a wood-burning oven when it would be called *pasta al forno di legna*. The pasta is cooked first in boiling water before being mixed with a meat sauce (a *ragù Bolognese* is good) and covered with a *besciamella* sauce and topped with cheese, taleggio is my choice, with perhaps a little parmesan too. Because the pasta is, effectively, cooked twice it's very soft, not al dente, and the dish is all the more comforting for that. So with pasta to eat, lots of water to drink, and a long walk with Jan on Wimbledon Common afterwards, it was another very pleasant day.

As New Year's Eve dawned, I was feeling a little apprehensive about meeting Priscilla again – or, rather, I was particularly concerned because I knew her children would also be there. As I was not so familiar with teenagers, I wondered how the conversation would go. I needn't have worried; they were friendly and curious, and very much appreciated the panettone I brought, while their mother appreciated the wine. Priscilla lived in a flat in Covent Garden, accessed by an alley that cut between Long Acre and Floral Street, overlooking the box office of the Royal Opera House. Immediately I found myself happily occupied in the kitchen helping her prepare a huge pile of prawns, customary in her family for New Year's Eve celebrations, and whipping up egg yolks and olive oil into the necessary mayonnaise to accompany them. Back in my comfort zone, I relaxed. Next we prepared *escargots*, snails with garlic and butter, a simple recipe that Priscilla had learnt while living in Paris for a couple of years.

It was a delicious meal and fun to be sharing it with Priscilla and her children, Granby, Lucy and Ben, who were interested in my stories about my dog, and polite enough to laugh at my jokes. I needn't have worried after all. What they didn't like, however, was my smoking and I was persuaded to make giving it up my New Year's resolution for 1980. I told them how, in some regions of Italy, it is the custom to throw out of the window anything old and not useful so as to start the New Year with only the new. Midnight came and we raised a glass of champagne to toast the beginning of not just a new year, but also a new decade,

1.

1. *Foraging for mushrooms in New Forest, 1995.*

2. *It was fantastic to visit my Aunt Dora while filming* Italian Feasts *in 1996. She was still as spritely as ever.*

2.

1.

2.

3.

1. *Sharing a joke with Anna-Louise, my manager, on her Wedding Day in December 2008.*

2. *Me with my dear friend and brilliant chef Raymond Blanc, showing off our OBEs in 2007.*

3. *At a mushroom market in Italy in 2008.*

1.

2.

3.

1. *Me and Truffle posing for our 2010 Christmas card. My whittled sticks can be seen to the left of the picture.*

2. *With Dame Tessa Jowell at my O.B.E Ceremony.*

3. *Enjoying hospital food after my knee operation in 2011.*

1. *I still have a wonderful friendship with my ex-girlfriend Inge.*

2. *Tanya Marzola, my ex-assistant, and me in 2004.*

3. *Outside the Neal Street store in 2004.*

1.

2.

1. *Writing my memoirs in Oualidia, Morocco, 2012.*

2. *Me and legendary photographer Elsbeth Juda, 2011.*

3. *The marble stone that was outside the first Carluccio deli now lives on my front doorstep.*

3.

Image courtesy Jake Eastham.

1.

1. *Carluccio's Managing Director, Simon Kossoff, and me at the opening party of the Nottingham restaurant.*

2. *I've always loved wearing bright colours. Here I am at the Music and Food festival in Pulgia, 2010.*

3. *Sunday lunch has always been a big affair in the Carluccio household. I love cooking for friends and still do it frequently.*

2.

3.

1.

1. *Gennaro, Sandrino and me whilst filming* Two Greedy Italians *in 2011.*

2. *My Alpine rock garden.*

2.

1. *My dear friend Fabrice Moireau created a Carluccio coat of Arms for my seventy-fifth birthday present.*

2. *With Sophia Loren, my adopted pig, in Malton, North Yorkshire, October 2011.*

and I threw my packet of cigarettes out of the top-floor window. Then I turned to kiss my hostess. To the surprise of myself and Priscilla – and the children, I think – it turned into a proper kiss, and the good wishes we exchanged for the New Year were completely genuine and heartfelt. The year to come was the year of the Moscow Olympics and the music of Abba, the death of John Lennon and Jean-Paul Sartre, and the year we caught our first sight of an eighteen-year-old kindergarten teacher, Lady Diana Spencer, photographed in a see-through skirt with a child on her hip and instantly christened Shy Di. In the early hours of this new decade, Priscilla and I drove to Putney to wish a Happy New Year to the mutual friend who'd introduced us, Lobby, before going our separate ways.

I returned home with a lot to think about. The evening had gone from the cautious meeting of two potential friends to the possibility of something far more. I had found my encounter with Priscilla fascinating and had been surprised by her kiss because I'd had no inkling from her previous behaviour that she might respond to me so favourably. That she was a highly intelligent, sophisticated woman, I could see. A little reserved in her ways, perhaps, which I liked, but she obviously had a good business head and was also very direct in her opinions, which I admired. She spoke fluent French, was well travelled and had a real appreciation of good design, all of which also appealed to me. In spite of my previous intention to steer clear of any romantic involvement, I could see that this slightly vulnerable but poised woman was someone out of the ordinary. I decided to take things slowly with her and remain open to whatever that might bring.

We started to see each other, cautiously at first but more kisses followed. I invited Priscilla to my home and cooked her a meal, taking great care to show the pleasure it gave me. She was very interested in my paintings even while she condemned my landlord's choice of furniture, her professional designer's eye seeing my furnishings for the tacky items that they were. We enjoyed walking my dog together on Wimbledon Common or in Richmond Park and, when her children had returned to boarding school, meeting up at her flat where the proximity to the Royal Opera House meant that we could enjoy hearing operatic rehearsals as spring turned to summer, the weather becoming warmer and the windows open. She loved the ballet too, so much so that she had taken extensive lessons as a girl, which still showed in her elegant posture and deportment.

Tentatively, I began to see a future for me with Priscilla. We were both in our early-forties, with much to share and to enjoy. She confided in me that she had hoped to meet a wise old man as a future companion. I didn't feel I was either old or particularly wise, but I did feel I had a down-to-earth philosophy of life, something that we in fact shared, and that we had a similar appreciation of art, travel, food, wine and nature. Eventually I let my passion for her develop and we became a couple. It felt good, harmonious and peaceful, with the promise of so much more we might accomplish together.

Pere al Vin Santo

Pears in Vin Santo

I adore cooked fruit. Indeed, I adore fruit point blank. The cooking of some fruit happens to make a dish more sophisticated. You can substitute the pears for peaches, plums or apples.

Serves 4
4 Comice pears
1 x 750 ml (25 fl oz) bottle Vin Santo
100 g (4 oz) caster sugar
rind of 1 lemon
3 cloves
1 stick of cinnamon

First, peel the pears so that they can absorb the taste and golden colour of the wine, but leave them whole. Put them in a stainless steel saucepan, just large enough to hold them, and cover with the wine. Add the sugar, lemon rind and spices and poach for 40 minutes with the lid on.

Remove the lid and cook for a further 10 minutes. Remove the pears from the liquid and set on one side.

Boil the remaining liquid fast to reduce it to a thicker consistency pour this sauce over the pears. Allow to chill and serve.

CHAPTER ELEVEN

Mof Mof

y the spring of 1980, my relationship with Priscilla was going well. For the first time in years I felt at peace. My wine selling business was flourishing and although there was by now much more competition, there was also much more wine being drunk and the restaurant scene that I was helping to supply was booming.

The social climate had changed greatly over the last ten years; people ate out much more regularly, not only for pleasure but also for business, especially in London. Expense-account lunches fuelled a lot of business, particularly in the media centres and, increasingly, in the City – the business area of London. People were also generally travelling more; there was greater interest in and appreciation of wine, and all this had extended the potential market for me – from restaurants to wine bars and even pubs, which were now beginning to serve wine, and decent wine at that. Restaurants now took more trouble over their wine lists, looking for greater expertise from their suppliers, and all this was good for a wine merchant like myself.

So I was busy, and Priscilla was busy. As creative director of the Conran Design Group she travelled a lot, not just in Europe but also to India, to source merchandise and see suppliers. I sometimes went with her and enjoyed those trips very much. Priscilla sourced a lot of textiles and other products through a company called Fabindia, set up by a visionary American entrepreneur called John Bissell and his wife, the Delhi-born and delightful Bim. Their business was completely ethical in its approach, years before Fairtrade became as fashionable as it is today, and they were very committed to promoting all that was good and beautiful in India's heritage through its fabrics and artefacts. The Bissells ensured that any products, fabrics or carpets that were sourced for their customers were of high quality and complied with strict principles about the use of child labour and fair prices for work done. They had also set up a school in Delhi. The Fabindia business continues to this day through the work of their son William, while their daughter Monsoon is an acclaimed film-maker.

Through the Bissells we had a wonderful entrée into Delhi's artistic and intellectual elite, as well as to the equally fascinating, less luxurious side of Indian life as our visits afforded us the chance to meet some of those responsible for the lovely work that was being sold back in the UK. We also enjoyed the most amazing food: some of the tastiest pakoras, samosas and chapatis I've ever eaten, along with subtly spiced curries and beautifully prepared vegetables, washed down with chilled, locally brewed Kingfisher beer.

We also visited Ahmedabad, where we met and got to know Asha Sarabhai who had set up her own fabric and clothing design business, creating lovely quilted silks and cottons, and from whom Priscilla bought stock for the Conran Shop. A graduate of modern languages and sociology from Cambridge University, Asha had returned to India and realised that its rich textile and craft traditions were quickly disappearing. She felt indignant about the way skilled craftsmen were being turned into mass producers and her concern led her to start workshops in the compound of her husband Suhrid's family in Ahmedabad, employing around a hundred craftsmen and their families. Their use of vegetable dyeing, handblock printing, hand and machine sewing, produce unique household textiles and clothing of charm and simplicity.

With her children away at boarding school, Priscilla could fit her business trips into term times, and then be around for them during the holidays. With all this coming and going, we worked hard to create time to spend and enjoy together, but it wasn't always easy. In time, I was living more and more at her Covent Garden flat, so that eventually she suggested I give up my home in Ifield Road and move in. It made more sense so I did, and it was at this point that our commitment to each other became obvious to all. I had been concerned about how Priscilla's children would react, but they were glad to see their mother happy and so I relaxed and was content. In fact, being part of the family gave me great pleasure, watching the three children grow up and create their own lives. Their school had special open days every term, and in the first summer after Priscilla and I started living together, she invited me to visit the school as her partner. It was a great honour to be accepted into the family like this, but I can't pretend I wasn't nervous. What should I say to the headmaster, I queried to Priscilla, if he should address me? I was worried about my still rather awkward English, and how easily I could be marked out as a foreigner. I didn't want to cause any embarrassment to anyone, least of all her children. She laughed and advised me, 'Just say "Oh, good Lord!" in response to anything he says, and that should see you through.' She was right, of course, and the day went without a hitch.

It was the custom on these school visits for each family to have a picnic together on a blanket on the grass in the school's grounds so I had prepared all sorts of lovely Italian picnic treats with Priscilla's children in mind – *cannolicchi con frittella*, a typical Sicilian pasta dish with artichokes, broad beans and peas, which makes a delicious cold salad, along with some good olives, cheeses, salamis and *focaccia* bread, and *pane casereccio*, which is a wonderful rustic Pugliese bread stuffed with cheese and salami, and of course some freshly made *pizzette Margherita* with tomato and mozzarella topping. There was not a Scotch egg or fish paste sandwich to be seen in our picnic basket, and we had a very different spread from the other families, of which the children were very proud and appreciative. This became a regular event, and I always went all out to surpass myself with the *scampagnata* on their behalf – including a nicely chilled bottle of Verdicchio for Priscilla and myself to enjoy with our food.

Jan, too, would accompany us on these picnic forays, delighting the children but driving the rest of us mad as he had an unerring eye for a stray sausage roll or sandwich crust. On one occasion he was threatened with being locked in the car, for getting too close to a neighbouring family's unwatched picnic basket!

The children's school, Bryanston, was just outside Blandford Forum in Dorset, a beautiful area of the country, and the long drive from London took us through the magnificent New Forest. It was good to be able to share my love of foraging for *funghi* with Priscilla, who also had an interest. Growing up as she did in Liphook in Hampshire, she and her brother had found an excellent spot for mushroom-gathering near the golf course there. So, travelling to and from the school, we would break our journey and explore the New Forest, moving on to the area around Liphook, taking the opportunity for a little foraging along the way. In season, we easily picked a rich harvest of wonderful mushrooms – porcini, cep, chanterelles and puffballs among them – and these we cooked or shared with friends, or my restaurant clients, where I knew they were particularly appreciated.

Priscilla's own appreciation of food and my cooking was something I greatly valued in her. Sharing my life with someone with such similar interests was a great pleasure. It was at her suggestion too that I entered the *Sunday Times* Cook of the Year competition in 1981, where I got through the regional competitions and, very much to our joint satisfaction, ended up in the final. The judges for this event were Michael Bateman, food campaigner and editor of the *Sunday Times'* Lifespan section, food writer and author Arabella Boxer, and food writer, restaurateur and chair of the judges Robert Carrier. They were an impressive bunch and all, in their own way, very much at the forefront of promoting food at the time, in particular through the pages of the *Sunday Times* newspaper. There wasn't quite the fashion for food writing and restaurant criticism then that there is now, but it was heading that way. For the final of this competition, all five of us contestants were given three hours to prepare a dish that had to be based on fish and vegetables.

Participating in the competition was an interesting thing to do, and devising a dish based solely on these two foodstuff helped clarify my own ideas about what made food good and delicious to eat. I was a cook, not a chef, and a self-taught cook at that. I was innately convinced of the value of good ingredients and of working with them, rather than disguising them with fancy techniques or sauces. I was wholly convinced of my own ethos: minimum of fuss and maximum of flavour (*mof mof*), choosing the best ingredients possible as well as those that worked well together, keeping things simple and allowing the food to 'speak' for itself. This was rather at odds with the fashion in cooking in the early 1980s, which had become massively over-complicated to my mind. This was the time of *nouvelle cuisine* and *cuisine minceur* and the era of elaborately produced dishes: the opposite of my *mof mof* philosophy! In any event, I thought three hours rather a long time in which to prepare just one dish, although I realised this reflected the expectations around what constituted competition-winning food at the time.

So I decided to stick to my guns and prepare a simple but sophisticated dish, not exactly Italian, but with an Italian sensitivity to ingredients and with definite Italian panache. My recipe was called sole and salmon *barcarola*. The combination of these two fish together, the delicate white fillet of sole and the slightly chunkier salmon, is an excellent one. I prepared the fish and then placed it in several large courgettes, cut in half with their seeds scooped out, and covered by a savoury zabaglione – egg yolks whisked with dry Marsala and a little lemon juice rather than sugar, rather like a piquant mayonnaise – to flatter and bring out the subtle flavours of the fish which was to be baked in the oven. The shape of the courgettes was like a little boat or *barca,* hence the recipe's name. To accompany this dish, I prepared a purée of chickpeas with little cubes of pancetta, and a salad of roasted peppers with garlic and parsley. With everything done in an hour, and nothing else to do, I gave a hand to one of my co-competitors. She was struggling with a very complicated dish of fish, algae and sunflowers when she dropped the lot on the floor while transferring it from one pot to another. While she was verging on the distraught at the mishap, I was able to help her rectify the situation and carry on.

I didn't win the competition, which was fine. But while acknowledging my success as a runner-up, Robert Carrier said something that struck me as quite strange. He said I hadn't achieved first place because, apparently, I was too keen to win, which seemed like a very odd reason for not choosing me. Instead of some inadequacy in my choice of dish or its execution, the reason that he gave was that I was too keen to win? It didn't make any sort of sense to me. Given that the nature of competition is that it requires a desire to win, and we were all participating in a competition, I would have thought this was true of all five of us. As it was, winning hadn't actually been my primary motivation. The competition was a way in which I could show, and for the first time publicly, my own philosophy of cooking and how good and simple an authentic Italian approach to food could be. Also, I wanted to reward Priscilla's faith in me by getting to the final at least, which I had achieved. Winning would just have been the icing on the cake. But no matter, because although surprised by Carrier's opinion, I was very pleased to have got so far and to have my efforts receive the acknowledgement and acclaim that they did. Years later Michael Bateman, who I came to know, confided in me that I would have won that year but for the fact that in the previous three years it had been won by a foreign man, and for reasons of diplomacy they needed it to be won by an English woman. Because of this and Carrier's opposition to me, for reasons I didn't really understand, the first prize had to go elsewhere . . . I wonder where that woman is now?

Indirectly, the competition also brought me to the attention of some influential people who would, it turned out, be instrumental in helping me in the years to come. There were follow-up articles in the press about me, and my cooking, and increasingly about my interest and expertise in mushrooms, and how I was supplying some of London's top restaurants with interesting and delicious *funghi* I was gaining something of a reputation not just as a wine merchant but also as the 'mushroom man'. So failing actually to win the *Sunday Times'* Cook of the Year competition did no damage to my career, quite the reverse in fact.

Shortly after the competition was over, Priscilla and I were invited to her brother's home in Berkshire. I hadn't met him before, but in fact his wife was food editor on the *Sunday Times* and had had to pull out of being one of the judges on the Cook of the Year competition when I'd made it to the final, in case it was seen to be a conflict of interest. It was in fact for her brother's business, the Conran Design Group, that Priscilla worked as creative director. And, she explained to me, it was her brother who was also responsible for Habitat, the popular home furnishings store that was renowned for, amongst other things, its chicken bricks, huge circular paper Japanese light shades, Sabatier knives and storage jars for dried pasta. This was the man who had made duvets accessible to the British public. The man who had democratised good taste and made it affordable to 'those on a teacher's salary', as the story goes, opening his first Habitat store on the Fulham Road in 1964. He had previously opened a restaurant, the Soup Kitchen, in Chandos Place just off the Strand in 1953, with a second-hand Gaggia coffee machine, quarry-tiled floors, stripped pine tables and chairs. This was someone whom I immediately expected to like, not only because he was Priscilla's brother but also because he had an obvious interest in food and design – which I shared – but at the time of first meeting him, I literally had no idea how significant Terence Conran had been, or would continue to be, to the world of British design.

Terence had bought his home, Barton Court in Berkshire, in 1971 when it was derelict, and he and his second wife Caroline had transformed the thirty-two-room, redbrick, seventeenth-century manor house into a beautiful home. Not only was there a wonderful sunny kitchen, with an Aga and long dining table, but a large and well-stocked, walled kitchen garden. In many ways the house, situated in extensive grounds beside the River Kenet, was the epitome of Englishness, but it was also a modern and well-loved family home full of beautiful objects, paintings and furniture, antique and modern, from a Thonet, bentwood chaise longue to a Castiglioni Arco light.

As her elder brother, Terence was naturally protective of Priscilla and no doubt keen to see what I was like, having heard about this Italian wine merchant and cook who had moved in with her. It was a full family gathering when I first met them, and I was glad that day of the company of my dog Jan, who was a natural icebreaker especially with the children. Terence was wearing one of his favourite dark blue – *bleu de travail* – shirts, the colour of traditional French workmen's dungarees. Besides Terence, Caroline and their three children, Tom, Ned and Sophie, there were Terence's two sons, Sebastian and Jasper, from his previous marriage to Shirley Conran of *Superwoman* fame – a sort of contemporary Mrs Beeton, whose household guide for women was first published in 1975. Her philosophy of cooking was: *Life's too short to stuff a mushroom*. Not in my book, I thought.

The Conrans were generous and convivial hosts, even if their family felt quite reserved in comparison to the Italian equivalent I was used to. On subsequent visits I was invited to cook or join in with the preparation of meals, and enjoyed being in Caroline's kitchen and spacious larder, where you might find a brace of pheasant, some freshly caught trout, jars of recently made pickles, quinces from the garden, and plaits of home-grown onions and garlic. It was very much designed as a kitchen to work in. Here, a gift for food or for cooking a particular dish was greatly appreciated by Caroline, and I immediately felt more at home. I also discovered there was a table tennis table at the house, and was challenged to a game by Terence – not an entirely easy game for him, as he only has vision in one eye following a childhood accident – but he played very competitively all the same and lost no time at all in beating me!

My own family was much on my mind at the time. Spending time over meals with another big family made me think about those spent with my own relatives, all those years ago, and while I felt happier generally with my life, I also felt quite nostalgic for the rumbustiousness of my extended Italian family, into which I fitted more easily. Sometimes, in spite of the welcome I was given, I felt like an outsider still, and in this household my lack of complete fluency in the English language also meant that I missed some of the subtleties of the conversation and the irony of the jokes as the lively conversation ricocheted around me.

Around that time, on one of my regular calls to my mother in Italy, she told me that my older brother Peppino wasn't well and had been taken to hospital for an operation on his stomach. The problem turned out to be much more serious than was first thought, as there had been some error in diagnosis. By the time they did an exploratory operation, about half of his stomach had become gangrenous and needed to be removed. I was horrified by the seriousness of this news and immediately said I would fly over, but she suggested I wait and see how things progressed over the following few days as he seem to making good progress. I thought I would wait to see him when he was home from hospital, and we could spend some time together as he convalesced. Then came a phone call with the totally unexpected news that he had suddenly taken a turn for the worse. Before I could make the trip, he died. I was desperately sorry to have missed seeing him, but the fact that his wife and three children had been at his bedside when he died brought some comfort.

I was worried as to how my mother would take the loss of another son, and so soon after my father's death two years previously. Papa had been ill for several years, nursed at home by my mother, and it had taken its toll on her. My last memory of him, so small and thin on what turned out to be his deathbed, was brought back to me by this latest news and I felt very sad and far away. Thankfully my other brother Carlo was still able to hold the fort and keep me abreast of how my mother was really coping, but I felt a great sense of homesickness in spite of my current happiness, and promised to visit them as soon as I could.

That year, Britain was gripped by royal wedding fever. On 29 July 1981 Prince Charles, the Prince of Wales and heir to the British throne, married Lady Diana Spencer after a short, five-month engagement. Escaping the event, however, Priscilla and I were on holiday with her children and Terence and his family in Sardinia. Terence had successfully floated his seventeen-year-old Habitat business and had decided to celebrate by renting a large villa in Porto Rotondo, right on the seafront, inviting us all to join him.

Porto Rotondo is a wonderful seaside village on a natural inlet of the Costa Smeralda near Monte Ladu, and has beautiful beaches, pink granite rocks eroded by wind and water, and a really perfect, glittering blue-green stretch of the Mediterranean Sea. I was thrilled to be back in Sardinia, not far from La Maddalena where I had spent time as a young man in the Navy. I was also delighted to share my memories of this with Priscilla. The village of Porto Rotondo itself had the very attractive Piazzetta San Marco with lots of shops and lively bars, and several pretty streets to explore, making it perfect for the evening *passeggiata*. But during the entire fourteen-day holiday we ate out only twice, taking this splendid opportunity to cook at the villa. We had a wealth of expertise between us to do so, as well as an abundance of wonderful local produce to enjoy.

We excelled ourselves. Not only was Caroline a fine cook, specialising in French and English food, but Terence also had friends staying in a neighbouring villa, Lisa and Rodney Kinsman, and Lisa was a connoisseur of Chinese food so we had her contribution as well. I, meanwhile, specialised in simple, authentic Italian food – completely at home in this milieu – while we took it in turns to go to Olbia to shop for ingredients and investigate the good local wines. One night we surpassed ourselves by barbecuing a piglet with myrtle berries, *porceddu al mirto,* but I also remember how wonderful it was to enjoy the exceptional quality of the local vegetables and the sun-ripened fruit again. Many of our meals remained very simple because of the excellence of the ingredients – I shared my *mof mof* approach again, and by now it was clear to everyone where the roots of my food philosophy lay.

Returning to England, Terence then asked me if I would consider cooking for his fiftieth birthday party in October. I was of course delighted by the suggestion, and readily agreed. It was quite an event. A large marquee, with twenty tables seating ten people each, and a stage and dance floor, was erected on the lawn at Barton Court. A separate tent housed the cooking area and barbecue. Terence and

I agreed the menu: lobster to start, followed by barbecued lamb and vegetables, then fruit salad and a splendid birthday cake. Magnums of Krug champagne were drunk. For later, I also prepared a huge pot of kedgeree and an equally large pot of fiery Serbian soup, to keep the guests going in the small hours of the party. They were both much appreciated around four am.

It was a terrific event and the organisation for it all went very smoothly, helped by staff from Terence's Neal Street Restaurant. The legendary jazz singer and raconteur George Melly entertained us. There were numerous famous friends present, including the designer Mary Quant (Terence had been at school with her husband and business partner, Alexander Plunket Greene) for whom Terence had designed her first shop in 1956, and the sculptor Eduardo Paolozzi (with whom he'd set up a furniture-making workshop in the East End in 1949), an Italian like myself, and with whom I became good friends until his death in 2005. Eduardo too loved *cucina povera* – simple Italian food – so we bonded over that as well as our mutual interest in art. Years later I sculpted his head in clay, greatly encouraged by him in my artistic endeavours. The dancing went on until the small hours, when the kedgeree and soup was served to the remaining, hungry guests. I finally joined Priscilla, already asleep in bed in a guest room in the house, at about five am.

We also had something to celebrate and look forward to. While we were on holiday in Sardinia, one evening Priscilla and I had gone for a quiet meal by ourselves, as there was something I wanted to ask her. I loved her and had for some time felt that she and I made a good partnership, sharing as many interests as we did, and so I asked her if she would consider marrying me. I remember her surprise at my question but, blushing a little, she'd said yes, and I felt very happy at the prospect of a future with her, immediately ordering champagne to toast our happiness. I had thought long and hard about asking her to be my wife, in view of my past mistakes, but finally felt sure we could make this work. I loved her calm, straightforward approach to life, in contrast to my more emotional ebullience. I admired her hardworking attitude and gentle humour, tinged with a steely determination. I was delighted she had said yes, because I hadn't for one moment been sure that she would take me seriously as husband material. At the same time, I wondered how well I could support the family on my income as a wine merchant. Priscilla's children's school fees were paid by her ex-husband, so I didn't have to worry about those, and of course her own work was financially well rewarded, but that didn't stop me feeling it was my role, as husband, to provide for my new wife and her family. But Priscilla had also benefited financially when her brother floated the Habitat business, and the proceeds were enough to buy a house in Fulham that would become our new home.

Shortly after we had told our family and friends that we planned to marry, which to my immense pleasure everyone thought grounds for celebration and not the reverse, Terence asked Priscilla to ask me if I would consider taking over the management of the Neal Street Restaurant for him. The restaurant was jointly owned by Terence and two friends, fellow designer Oliver Gregory and art dealer John Kasmin (whose clients' art often adorned the walls), with its front of house team having been run by the extremely jovial Charles Campbell. Terence loved to recall how Charles was not only responsible for Francis Bacon eating there but also how, on one occasion, in greeting a guest with open arms, he had let drop the unbelted trousers he had been surreptitiously holding up. They had been a good team, and very influential in the success of the place.

It was a very generous offer, but it was important for me to consider fully as it would mean giving up my independence as a wine seller to do so. Also, while I loved to cook, and in particular for friends and family, I really didn't want to cook in a restaurant and I made this clear, saying that I would only be prepared to take on the general management, the culinary direction of the food, the ambience and the PR. So this is what we agreed and, shortly after Terence's birthday on 4 October, I proudly started work as Managing Director of the Neal Street Restaurant.

Based in London's busy Covent Garden, not far from where Priscilla and I were living in Hanover Place, by 1981 the restaurant had been running for ten years. Located under the offices of Terence's design consulting business, housed in a nineteenth-century converted banana-ripening warehouse, with the pulleys for hoisting heavy loads to the upper floors still in place, the restaurant's frontage was painted the same *bleu de travail* as Terence's favourite shirts, with a white-painted brick interior, starched white linen tablecloths, and the sort of cane chairs that were comfortable enough to invite long, leisurely meals. It had an excellent reputation for its food and ambience and an extremely loyal and lively clientele amongst the arts, media and business types who enjoyed either lunching or dining there.

The historic street itself had been built by the seventeenth-century MP, entrepreneur and gambler Thomas Neale, who made and lost two fortunes before dying insolvent in 1699. Neal Street runs virtually north to south through Covent Garden, from Shaftesbury Avenue to Long Acre, and at the time was also home to Frank's Café, a market-barrow repair shop, a wonderful kite shop, and the Food for Thought health-food restaurant, which was part of the Neal's Yard co-operative, their takeaway salads being a staple of office girls' lunches in the area. Covent Garden is bordered by Drury Lane on one side, and St Martin's Lane running down to Trafalgar Square on the other, not far from Shaftesbury Avenue and Soho, and close enough to the West End and theatre district of London, as well as the Royal Opera House, to benefit from many evening visitors. Not only that, the development and opening of the old Covent Garden Market to create the new piazza and shopping centre in 1980, with its shops, bars, craft market and street performers, had revitalised the area. It was without a shadow of a doubt an excellent location for a restaurant.

The restaurant had originally been conceived as a canteen for those working in the offices above, and only after this initial use had it been opened to others. With its innovative design and style, and reputation for good food, it had quickly become successful. David Hockney had done the illustration for the menu, and we kept to the design for this as it reflected the style of the place so well. The original illustration, inscribed with Hockney's favourite Neal Street Restaurant meal – *Beluga Caviar, Watercress Soup, Truite au bleu, Chateaubriand Sauce Béarnaise, Mangetout, Haricots vert, Cheese, Crème Brûlée; Wines: Gewurtztraminer, Château Lafite, Château d'Yquem* – was sold by Sotheby's in 2007 for a staggering £48,000.

When I came on-board at the end of 1981, the chef was Santiago Gonzales, the most patient and capable chef I ever met, and the menu was a hybrid of English and French cookery, specialising in dishes like steak and kidney pie, which was reputed to be the best in London. My job was to liaise with the chef and generally supervise the food, write the menus, manage the already beautiful and stylish ambience, the staff and service, and run the PR side. I would start my week with a four am trip to the Nine Elms Market in Vauxhall to get the flowers, having a bacon roll and cup of strong – or as the English say *builder's* – tea with the other early risers at the market cafe: a workers' cafe not a café, for sure. Then I would return home and catch another hour's sleep before starting at the restaurant, arranging the flowers and attending to the demands of the restaurant's working day, which would always go on until well past midnight.

Things in the kitchen were always good, thanks to the excellent Santiago, but I had a problem with one of the waiters within my first week. There had been a general truculence in the service one evening that I wasn't happy about, and then at midnight when I had asked him to set up for the following day, this particular waiter had refused and started arguing with me. I realised that if I was to have any continuing authority with the staff I had to address this situation immediately, so I asked him again, and then warned him about his behaviour, but he continued to argue and insult me. At which point I sacked him with a month's wages, on the spot, for insubordination. He was still shouting at me as I escorted him from the premises, threatening to cut both my throat and my dog's. It was a good decision to stand up to him, as the restaurant didn't need staff with that sort of attitude extended towards fellow workers or diners. The other staff recognised this and respected me for it.

I seldom had trouble with them after this, although I did later have to dismiss one member of staff, having discovered his petty theft, which over the years came to a considerable amount of money. But this was part of my new role, I soon realised, managing the staff, and I was always very clear with them what I expected: a very professional, friendly approach to the clientele, without being servile or arrogant or over-effusive. No flourishes or *bella signora* here, as was practised in some of the restaurants of the time, while laughing at the customers behind their backs. The waiting staff's presence was not to impinge on their customers' experience of dining, but to enhance it by being attentive and respectful, and nothing more. This was important as increasing numbers of celebrities and well-known people came to eat and, knowing they would not be exposed to inappropriate attention, were able to relax and enjoy their meal with us. Of course there were some customers who would expect, or demand, more personal attention, and we were also able, often very discreetly, to provide this, too. But the initial welcome and service extended to all customers had to be the same, whoever they were – it didn't matter whether they were a prince or a bricklayer. This was my ethos, based on how I would like to be treated in a restaurant myself, and it paid off as I saw customers return time and time again.

One of the first things I had to do, because it really let us down, was to address the problem of the coffee offered at the end of a meal. David Hockney had once said of it, 'The coffee – it's a killer.' And he was right. I soon discovered why. Cirano the barman, who was responsible for it, made the coffee at the beginning of service and then *kept it warm* rather than making it fresh each time. That explained a lot! The coffee used was a Neapolitan one, reasonable enough, but I wanted something better for our guests. I found an Italian coffee-roasting company locally and, taking in a tin of Illy, asked them to copy its taste. This they did and became our suppliers. Freshly made from then on, the problem of the killer coffee was solved.

Over time, and in discussion with Santiago, Terence and Oliver Gregory, I began to bring my own ideas on food to bear in the restaurant. I started to introduce the occasional, authentic Italian dish, to see how it fitted into a menu that many regular diners had come to know and love. There was no point introducing something unless it enhanced the menu, and this gave me the chance to work out what worked and what didn't without jeopardising the good reputation we already had.

The first dish I introduced was a parcel of Cornish crab. I found an excellent source of fresh crab from Cornwall, and had this poached with a little brandy, served with a touch of homemade mayonnaise and parsley, and then parcelled up in the lightest of pancakes secured with a strand of al dente spaghetti. It was an immediate success. One regular and appreciative customer was comedian, BBC Radio One DJ, television entertainer and *Top of the Pops* presenter Kenny Everett. When he first ordered this dish and it arrived in front of him, he took a stamp from his wallet and stuck it on the crabmeat parcel for a joke, which made us all laugh. He was a man as spontaneously funny in life as he was on screen. I found that I really relished the social life of the restaurant as the same gregariousness that had enhanced my ability as a wine salesman came into play here, too. While it was a job, and a job I took seriously, running the restaurant also afforded me great pleasure and it was a privilege to meet the people I did without losing the professionalism it was so important to maintain.

At the same time, my personal life too was very happy. Priscilla and I got married on 22 December, exactly and deliberately on the anniversary of our very first meeting the previous year. The night before we married, as a sort of stag night, Terence had taken me out to dinner at Harry's Bar. It was an interesting choice of venue. Harry's Bar was established in 1979 as a fine dining, private club serving northern Italian cuisine, and was the creation of Mark Birley with financial and other assistance from Hotel Cipriani in Venice, home of the very first and world-famous Harry's Bar. Birley also owned and was famous for Annabel's nightclub, named after his first wife, Lady Annabel Vane-Tempest-Stewart, who went on later to marry financier James Goldsmith. I felt that perhaps Terence was not only wanting to welcome me into the family in his own rather reserved way, but also to show me that I was marrying into a family of some considerable social clout and connection and consequence. It didn't actually matter to me whether I was dining with the upper echelons of London society or, as I had done for lunch, polishing off a sack of oysters with my brother Carlo and Priscilla's son Granby in the new, but as yet unrenovated, house we had bought in Fulham to be our family home. To me it is what people are that matters, not where they come from, who their parents are or how much money they have; it's their decency, respect and affection, and the way they treat other people, that counts in life.

There was snow on the ground as I waited with my best man Phil Cutler, my brother Carlo and his wife, for Priscilla to arrive at the register office, accompanied by her friend and ex-boss Elsbeth Juda, known to her friends as Jay.

Elsbeth is an extraordinary woman. She had fled from the Nazi Germany to London with her husband Hans in 1934, with two suitcases – one full of clothes, the other of books – and Hans' precious violin. Here they had to create a new life for themselves, and from 1934 to 1963 they founded and worked on *The Ambassador* magazine. Elsbeth had learnt photography from Lucia Moholy, the ex-wife of László Moholy-Nagy of the Bauhaus design movement, and developed all her photographs in the bath of their small apartment. It was she who had taken the photographs of Winston Churchill for the ill-fated portrait (allegedly burnt by Churchill's wife after his death, as he apparently hated it so much) painted by Graham Sutherland in 1954, as a gift from the nation to the great man on his eightieth birthday. Born in 1911, Elsbeth is still one of my greatest friends and calls me her 'toy boy'.

After the simple marriage ceremony at the register office, we went to the Connaught for lunch. Here we were joined by Terence and Caroline, and some other friends along with restaurateur and author of *La Cucina Veneziana*, Gino Santin (to represent my restaurant clients and friends), for a lunch prepared by renowned *maître chef* and fellow truffle aficionado Michel Bourdin. The food was excellent, but the ambience was rather formal and, as we found out, the taking of celebratory photographs was forbidden. After our long, leisurely wedding meal, Priscilla and I left for our Christmas honeymoon in the snowy mountains of the Aosta valley, taking her youngest son Ben with us.

Focaccia

*This delicious bread can be eaten plain or, as they do in Genoa, made
into a sandwich with some mortadella while still warm!*

Serves 6–8

30 g (1 oz) fresh yeast

about 175 ml (5 fl oz) lukewarm water

500 g (16 oz) type 00 flour

2 tbsp olive oil, plus extra for the
    baking tray and for drizzling

pinch of salt

25 g (1 oz) coarse salt

Dissolve the yeast in the water. Put the flour in a bowl, then add the oil, yeast liquid and pinch of salt. Mix together, adding more water if necessary to obtain a very soft and smooth dough. Knead for about 10 minutes, until elastic, then place in a bowl, cover and leave to rise in a warm place for 1 hour or until doubled in size.

Preheat the oven to 200°C/400°F/gas 6. Lightly oil a large baking tray. Knock back the dough, then dip your fingertips in olive oil and gently press out the very elastic dough until it covers the whole tray. It should be about 2 cm (¾ in) high. Brush with olive oil and then make small indentations here and there in the dough with your fingertips. Sprinkle the coarse salt over the top and bake for 25–30 minutes, until a golden-brown crust has formed. As soon as the bread comes out of the oven, drizzle more olive oil on top; this will be absorbed, giving a wonderful flavour.

Allow to cool, then cut into squares and enjoy.

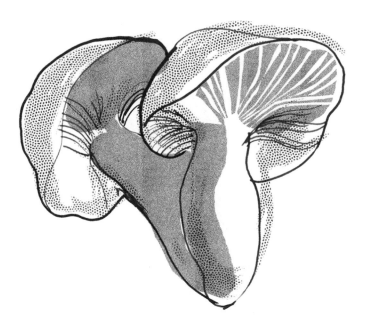

CHAPTER TWELVE

Mushroom Man

After our marriage, Priscilla and I (and Ben) travelled to Champoluc, a mountain village about ninety minutes' drive from Turin at the end of the Valle d'Ayas, for our honeymoon. The hotel in which we were guests, owned by my old friend Nina Burgai, was high in the mountains at about 2000 metres, very well positioned for skiing with lots of excellent snow, beautifully warm with its wooden interiors and with lovely views over the snowy mountains.

This was all very appropriate for Christmas but, alas, the altitude began to affect me and I started to feel quite unwell. After a few days my headaches and feelings of nausea got so bad that we had to move to another hotel further down the valley. At which point I began to wonder if I was actually cut out for honeymoons, or whether it was just bad luck given our choice of location, but it was a shame to be ill and I have avoided high altitudes ever since.

Priscilla and I returned in January 1982 and moved into our new home in Landridge Road, a very nicely positioned, three-storey Victorian, end-of-terrace house in a residential street, between Fulham Road and New King's Road, not far from Putney Bridge. It was quiet there, very different from the hustle and bustle of the flat in Covent Garden. Although we missed the singing from the Royal Opera House rehearsal rooms, we didn't miss the food smells from the restaurant Café des Amis du Vin that had recently opened beneath our flat, and it was nice to have a garden at last. There was quite a lot of work to be done on the house to get it as Priscilla wanted it – redecorating, enlarging the kitchen and creating the garden – and she was soon planning the renovations and making the house into a spacious and lovely home. I liked the area and the fact that these were family homes where people lived for a long time, and I happily contemplated doing the same with mine. Our next-door neighbours had actually been born in the house where they still lived. As an important part of the family, my dog Jan was happy enough, particularly as there were a couple of nearby parks for walks, Bishop's Park and Hurlingham Park, although he did miss spending his day with me, travelling around in my car and visiting my wine customers – but the Neal Street Restaurant was no place to bring a dog!

Initially I spent long hours at the restaurant, but I also started to get involved in other projects. Arabella Boxer, one of the judges of the *Sunday Times*' Cook of the Year competition in which I'd participated, asked me to contribute some recipes for a new book she was working on. My task was to devise and prepare party food recipes for twenty-five people, which I successfully did, and she was very pleased with the result. My first published recipes. I was very proud of them, too, and of my first steps into publishing on which I was later to build. Then I was asked to provide fifty-two recipes for the 1983 Habitat promotional calendar – a much bigger job – prepared by me and photographed for publication by Priscilla in the kitchen of Terence's home as the one at Landridge Road hadn't yet been completed to photographic standards. This was quite something and everyone was extremely pleased with the results. It was also in 1983 that I made my first TV appearance on BBC2, reporting on the health benefits of the Mediterranean diet. TV was a medium I found I was quite comfortable with, but it was to be another five years before my regular appearances on the BBC's *Food and Drink* programme began, which would eventually lead to the commissioning of the first of several TV series and documentaries of my own.

My passion for mushrooms flourished as I made many new discoveries in the English countryside I had grown to love. Mushrooms also became a feature of the restaurant as I started to incorporate more of my own Italian recipes – including those I could make with freshly gathered *funghi. Lepre con funghi e polenta* (hare with mushrooms and polenta) made its first appearance, followed by *rombo con chiodini* (turbot with honey fungus), *nocciole d'agnello con vescia* (noisette of lamb with puffball cubes), and *supreme di fagiano al tartufo* (supreme of pheasant with truffle). I was keen to honour the abundance of good game and wild mushrooms found in my adoptive country, and recipes like these helped me make my mark at the restaurant and also to effect the transition towards the authentic Italian food I wanted to share with my customers at the restaurant and a wider audience. It also meant using seasonal foods, not then the fashionable idea that it is now, which also tied into the very transitory nature of mushrooms. This made regular promotions focused on our menu possible too: we could advertise and promote the restaurant through our seasonal 'specials' as it were, which both the press and our customers were always keen to pick up on.

In season, I always had a large basket of freshly picked mushrooms on display at the door of the Neal Street Restaurant, and was now routinely called the 'mushroom man' because of my increasing expertise, knowledge and culinary application. To further my own knowledge and research I joined the British Mycological Society, which afforded me access to further expertise and information and also enabled me to get involved in the promotion and protection of British mushrooms. This was important because with the publication of Richard Mabey's classic book *Food for Free* in 1972, and then of Roger Phillips' popular mushroom books in the early 1980s, plus my own enthusiasm for and published articles about the joys of mushroom-foraging, there was a danger that damage could be done not only to native British fungi, but also their surrounding habitat if pickers became too zealous. In time, the British Mycological Society published a Code of Conduct for mushroom pickers, designed to protect the best interests of native fungi and those of us who enjoy and promote them, which I fully endorsed.

My work at the restaurant was so demanding that I could no longer source all the mushrooms myself, so I had the idea of contacting London's Polish community, because I knew that eastern European cultures also valued the mushroom, to see if there was any surplus to be had for my use. I put a small advertisement in a London-based Polish community newspaper asking for help and, after that, I had about ten suppliers coming in quite regularly with, say, a kilo of mushrooms. The system worked well, and then one day an Italian man came to see me. His name was Gennaro Contaldo and he had heard of my interest and arrived with a big basket of really splendid mushrooms – here was a man after my own heart! – for which he wouldn't accept payment, insisting instead that they were a gift from one mushroom lover to another.

Gennaro and I had a drink together and he told me he was from Tuscany, which made me laugh because I recognised from his accent that he was not. Being born in the south of Italy myself, although raised in the north, I was familiar with it. I told him he couldn't fool a fellow Italian on that one. But I understood why he did it: the old Italian preoccupation with the north of Italy somehow being superior to the south. I suppose he wanted me to think he was from the north because of that. So I understood why he did it, and it didn't matter to me and I told him that. So there was another bond, together with his help in supplying mushrooms, which was fantastic, especially later when I needed to find some to photograph for my books or TV programmes.

For the first year of this arrangement, however, Gennaro continued to refuse payment for the mushrooms he supplied, so I was always trying to find ways to give him a gift – sometimes a large salami, or some wine, or something for his family as I knew he had three children to support – while at the same time making a note of what money I would have paid him. At the end of the year I told him he had supplied me with £6,000 worth of mushrooms and I would like to reimburse him – but, no, he still wouldn't accept it! So this time, I was about to change my car, and I said, would you like it? This he finally accepted – then drove it to Italy and sold it there, a left-hand drive BMW, so that made sense, I suppose. Eventually I said I would like him to work with me but that he needed to learn some cooking skills and I would send him to Westminster College to learn to make bread, for example. So he agreed and we did that, and he became for a time an invaluable member of my staff, very important to the Neal Street Restaurant and later to the Carluccio delicatessen and shop.

In 1983, after the Habitat calendar was published with my recipes and I was doing more publicity for the restaurant, journalists began writing about my food philosophy and recipes. It was then that I had an approach from a book publisher. Colin Webb had been art director at publishers Weidenfeld & Nicholson when he teamed up with lyricist Tim Rice and broadcaster Michael Parkinson, to set up a new publishing company, Pavilion Books. I knew all three of them as they ate quite regularly at the restaurant, but one day Colin and I had a conversation, as he was waiting for his car to pick him up, when he said, 'Would you like to write a book?' So we talked about it and decided on the contents and how it should be done. A contract was drawn up and I wrote my first book, *An Invitation to Italian Cooking,* which was published in 1986 with a lot of very good publicity. The next book, which was an obvious one for me to do really, was *A Passion for Mushrooms,* which was published in 1988, and like the first has been constantly in print ever since. Both books were published in several languages and really struck a chord with readers, selling very well and further enhancing my professional profile as both restaurateur and food writer. Because of this, I started doing quite regular slots on TV, too – on the BBC's *Food and Drink* programme, a five-minute slot on the cuisine of various countries including Italy, and other similar TV and radio food programmes. I had also become the media's go-to man for the culinary use of mushrooms, and found this extraordinary: that my absolute passion and love for wild fungi, spawned as a child in the Piedmont woods of Italy, should years later become something of such commercial and media interest.

Those coming to the Neal Street Restaurant often came because of their own passion for and interest in mushrooms, and we had for a time a supplementary menu entitled *Festa dei Funghi* in consequence. One morning I got a call from the *Sun* newspaper. Did I know, they asked me, that Sarah Brightman, dining at the restaurant the night before with her (then) husband Andrew Lloyd Webber, had been taken ill later and admitted to hospital. Was it the mushrooms she'd eaten? they asked. Had I inadvertently poisoned her? I was aghast. This was the first I'd heard of it and I was horrified to think that something she might have eaten in my restaurant had caused her a problem. I said to the reporter I didn't know anything about it, but I was very sorry to hear that she was ill. As it was, later that day, Andrew Lloyd Webber's chauffeur came by the restaurant with a hand-written note for me. It said, much to my relief, that Sarah's illness had absolutely nothing to do with what she'd eaten the night before, and he apologised in case the news had caused me concern. I can't pretend that it hadn't, but I was very relieved that I had not poisoned her with a mushroom – and I can safely say, so far, that my record on this holds good!

The only other minor scare I ever had on the mushroom front was when several large jars of preserved mushrooms in the restaurant, from which we served our guests, inexplicably started to go mouldy. I couldn't understand it as the recipe I used for preserving them did not seem to be a problem elsewhere. In throwing out several batches, as they were no longer fit for use, I discovered that the alcoholic brine in which they were preserved had been drained off and replaced with water! No wonder they had gone mouldy. But I was perturbed. Was this a deliberate act of sabotage by a disgruntled member of staff or, worse, was someone out deliberately to discredit me? The truth turned out to be more mundane. A barman with an inclination towards dipsomania had been draining off the alcoholic preserving juice to drink, replacing it with water so that I wouldn't notice. Just as well that I did.

In spite of occasional and minor hiccups like these, the following years were spent in a very contented fashion. I ran the restaurant, which I really enjoyed, and was developing the menu until it reflected much more of the Italian food style I personally endorsed, *mof mof,* alongside the more traditional dishes everyone expected. It takes time to make a change like that; you don't frighten the horses, as my English friends would say, with too much, too soon. And it was my aim to work with the excellence of what I already had, not to throw the baby out with the bathwater. However, the more I put into the restaurant, the more convinced I became that we should move towards excellence in one style of food, rather than continuing with this hybrid menu. It seemed like the right time, especially on the back of my recently published and successful books, to focus on excellence in Italian food. My food philosophy and ethos, so clearly expressed in my first book *An Invitation to Italian Cooking,* should be extended to the restaurant, in order to refresh it and maximise its reputation. The restaurant was nearly eighteen years old by now, and I felt the time was absolutely right to create a contemporary but authentic Italian restaurant, building on what was there and what I had already done over the preceding eight years.

I discussed my ideas with Terence and he was in agreement. He saw it was the way to go, continuing to build on the restaurant's current and future strengths. Then he surprised me by also suggesting that I buy him out of the restaurant, so that I would not only be the Managing Director but the actual owner. It was an unexpected and generous offer, and in a way it was also an honour to be entrusted with something that had been so important to him, one of his very first successful restaurants. It was a splendid plan. Priscilla, too, was pleased with the prospect of my commitment being so justly rewarded, especially as it was one I had made in good faith but without any thought for benefiting personally from the success I had made of it.

I talked it through with her and checked with Christina Smith, the freeholder, about the rent. I went to the bank. Then I went back to Terence to confirm the deal between us so that we could draw up and sign the contract.

Once the deal was done, I continued with my efforts to make the restaurant's ambience, reputation and success my own, with the support of the excellent staff around me. Gennaro was still working for me, and we took on a young pastry cook, Jamie Oliver, although he didn't stay long, moving on to Rose Gray and Ruth Rogers' River Café within the year. The River Café was an interesting venture, given that neither woman had been a professional chef or even a professional cook before. They were friends before they were business partners. Ruth Rogers is the wife of the architect Richard Rogers, who had converted the former Duckhams oil storage facility on the north bank of the Thames, just off Fulham Palace Road, for his architectural partnership practice, and Rose Gray had originally trained as a fine artist and had even designed a self-assembly paper lamp shade that sold in Habitat, Liberty and Heal's. She had also trained as a home economist and I first met her when Arabella Boxer recommended her to do some work for me, checking the 250 recipes for my 1986 book *An Invitation to Italian Cooking*. When Rose went to New York some time later to work for six months in the kitchen of a newly-opened, Italian-style restaurant called Nell's Club, she asked if she could use some of my recipes.

When they first opened the River Café in 1987, it was as a canteen for Richard Rogers' architectural practice employees, in much the same way that Terence Conran had originally opened the Neal Street Restaurant. What was fascinating to me was that along with the innovative open-plan design of the restaurant, where the kitchen was clearly visible, and its lovely gardens complete with fresh herbs overlooking the river with Hammersmith Bridge to the right and Putney Bridge to the left, the two women focused their menu on the flavours of Italian home cooking, with an emphasis on sourcing excellent ingredients and keeping the menu simple.

Although I was sorry when Jamie, still mentored by Gennaro, left to go and work at the River Café as a *sous chef*, it was to be the making of him. He made an unscripted appearance in a BBC documentary, *Christmas at the River Café,* and caught the eye of Pat Llewellyn, a TV producer whose production company Optomen specialised in cookery programmes. This led to his own TV series, *The Naked Chef,* that won a Bafta for best television series in the features category in 2000, and the publication of his book of the same name. Pat went on to make celebrity chefs out of Gordon Ramsay and Heston Blumenthal, too.

By the end of the 1980s, the Neal Street Restaurant, my two books, the publicity we were getting from these and my television work, were all paying off and the restaurant was thriving. Our particular style of service, discreet and without unctuousness, relaxed but highly professional, combined with excellent Italian food and a wonderful wine list, attracted a diverse clientele which, partly because of its location in the popular and revamped Covent Garden, began to include more and more celebrities – from Mick Jagger to Joan Collins, Elton John to Robert de Niro, Casper Weinberger to Nicole Kidman, the Queen of Denmark to Kenny Everett. They all came to eat in Neal Street, which did us no harm at all. In fact, Prince Charles came with Princess Diana, and his second cousin King Constantine of Greece and his wife Queen Anne-Marie, for dinner one Valentine's Day; and on several occasions Luciano Pavarotti, with his gargantuan but appreciative appetite, came for a late dinner after singing at the Royal Opera House. Because of this I was later asked to do the catering for 1200 people for a Three Tenors – Luciano Pavarotti, Plácido Domingo and José Carreras – concert at Wembley Stadium on 5 July 1996.

In 1990 Priscilla decided, for one reason or another, that it was finally time to leave Habitat. At around the same time, the Conran Design Consultancy had moved out of Neal Street, relocating as Conran Holdings in Shad Thames, Butler's Wharf, and leaving a downstairs space, which had previously been their reception area, free. This gave me an idea. I went to the landlady, Christina Smith, and asked if I could rent the space to use as a shop, selling wonderful Italian food. I had for a long time wanted to import directly from Italy various products and ingredients for use in the restaurant and, eventually, for sale to the wider public. I knew there was a market for them because I was always being asked where it was possible to buy dried porcini, really good olive oil, sundried tomatoes – culinary delights not then available from the supermarket shelves. Christina agreed and, because I also wanted to sell freshly prepared foods in the delicatessen part of the shop, we needed to completely revamp the space to link it to the restaurant kitchen and make this possible.

Next I began to look for specific products. The first was a very special olive oil. Priscilla and I had been in Turin when I'd bought a bottle of olive oil from the Pastificio Defilippis shop and, in conversation with the owner, taken the details of the artisan company in Liguria that was producing it. I had been struck by the very good, velvety texture and light, peppery taste of the olive oil. It was really excellent, so I made an appointment with the company and visited them to discuss possibilities. I wanted to sell their stock exclusively. At first they were a little reluctant because at the time the shop was just an idea in my head, not yet realised. But this exceptionally good olive oil did indeed become the first of many products sourced and sold by Carluccio's, when it came into existence.

Priscilla meanwhile was looking for something to do now she was free from the Storehouse group and, with Italian designer Paola Navone, set up a new company Due Mani (Two Hands) to create luxury, Italian-designed goods produced in India for the European market. It seemed an excellent idea for her to have her own company, completely under her personal direction, and one that had nothing to do with either her brother or myself. She'd often complained of being seen as an appendage to us, so this would set her free at last.

We then moved my office from the basement of the restaurant up to the first floor next door, over where the new shop, Carluccio's, was to be. Priscilla's company shared this office space too, so we were effectively working together although initially on separate projects. However, when her design company failed to thrive, she moved her attention and energy to Carluccio's, and together we created the brand, shop and delicatessen.

It wasn't easy at first, because as with any shop you need a lot of products on the shelves and this requires investment. This was a new, niche idea. People also needed to know that the products were there to buy, and that they were good and worth buying, which required publicity. This, I thought, would not be so difficult to achieve, based on what I already knew about food and wine and the media contacts we already had. So Priscilla, with all her business acumen, negotiated with the banks at the same time as designing the distinctive look of the brand, the typeface for the name, the use of colour – the same dark blue associated with the Neal Street Restaurant and the *bleu de travail* of traditional working men's shirts.

I meanwhile was ensuring the quality of the products that were to be branded, because our reputation as Carluccio's would very much rest on their excellence. At the same time, using the extended restaurant kitchen, the by now well trained Gennaro was making food to sell in the shop's delicatessen – *focaccia* was, for the first time, made and sold, along with freshly produced pastas and raviolis – plus antipasti, Italian cheeses and salamis. Products that were dried, like our diverse range of penne, pappardelle and tagliatelle as well as spaghetti, or sold in jars like *crema di porcini e tartufi* (porcini and truffle), *ragù di cinghiale* (wild boar ragù), were easier to stock. But we also had our own-brand virgin olive oil from Liguria that I had discovered, along with freshly roasted coffee beans, delicious sweet biscuits like *cantucci* to dip into a glass of *vin santo*, or chocolate treats like *baci di dama* (ladies' kisses), panettone at Christmas time, and Italian wines. In time, we also stocked kitchen essentials like espresso coffee-makers, ravioli-cutters, beautiful olive-wood salad bowls and even a Carluccio's mushroom knife! Then I had to set to work to make sure that everyone knew about our new venture.

When we opened, shortly before Christmas 1991, we held a press launch and over 120 journalists turned up, which created quite a buzz with lots of excellent publicity. The timing was good and the business prospered, so much so that by 1994 we were able to create a wholesale business for the Carluccio's range, too, and sell our branded products through other retail outlets. Although the Carluccio brand was a success more or less from the start, like I always say, it takes at least ten years to become an overnight sensation and behind ours lay years of experience and expertise and knowledge of both Italian food and how to market it, that came directly from the partnership established between Priscilla and myself.

Lepre al Barolo

~~~~~~~~~~~~~~~~~~~~~~~~~~~~~~~~~

Hare in red wine with grapefruit

In Italy, hunters are very keen to catch a hare, which is known as a very clever animal. The best preparation is to cook the meat with the king of wine, Barolo.

Serves 8
1 large hare weighted 2 kg (4½ lb), skinned, cleaned and cut into 16 pieces
seasoned plain flour for coating
8 tbsp olive oil
salt and pepper to taste

For the marinade
juice of 2 pink grapefruit
500ml (18 fl oz) red wine, preferably Barolo
55g (2 oz) raisins
5 cloves
grated peel of 1 orange
10 bay leaves
1 large spring fresh thyme
1 spring fresh rosemary
2 garlic cloves
1 tbsp honey
a bunch of celery leaves
1 large carrots, finely chopped
1 tbsp strong (English) mustard
25 g (1 oz) dried porcini

For the sauce
1 small onion, finely chopped
30 g (a good 1 oz) butter
55 g (1 oz) prosciutto crudo (Parma ham), sliced and cut into strips
40 g (1½ oz) plain bitter chocolate, broken into small pieces

Prepare the marinade by mixing everything together except of the dried porcini. Leave the hare to marinate in it for 24 hours.

Take the hare from the marinade and dry with a cloth. Dust with some seasoned flour and fry in the hot oil on all sides. Heat up the marinade. Remove the pieces of browned hare from the pan and deglaze the pan with a ladleful of the hot marinade.

Place the pieces of hare in a cast-iron casserole and pour over them the deglazed juices and enough marinade to cover, along with the aromatics.

Bring to the boil, turn down the heat and simmer gently for 2 hours until the hare is tender. After an hour of cooking, add the dried porcini, crumbled in your hand. (When not soaked first, they will add intense flavour.)

Meanwhile, to make the sauce, fry the onion in the butter until becomes transparent, then add the prosciutto strips. Take the pieces of hare from the casserole. Strain the liquid and add it to the onion and prosciutto, together with the chocolate. Stir well and simmer for a few minutes longer, seasoning to taste with salt and pepper. Pour the sauce over the hare and serve with a grilled or fried polenta.

CHAPTER THIRTEEN

Carluccio's Caffè

A s winter gave way to spring 1992, the Carluccio's shop and delicatessen were doing well. The initial selection of products and produce was carefully chosen, Priscilla's designs were really well received, and we were busy with customers from dawn to dusk. The Neal Street Restaurant's new Italian menus were a big hit with our customers and I was writing more books and making more TV appearances, and still managing to enjoy mushroom-foraging in what spare time I had! Even my car, with its personalised number plate (a Christmas gift from the boys at the restaurant), celebrated my interest in, and reputation for being, the 'mushroom man' – H19 CEP.

It was also around this time that Priscilla found another outlet for her talents – a country escape for us in Hampshire, hidden away down a wooded country lane, ablaze with wild garlic and cow parsley in late-spring, outside the village of Froxfield. The pair of seventeenth-century thatched cottages were Grade ll-listed but in dire need of renovation, and there were four acres of unruly garden, along with another four acres of fields to be brought to heel – but it was an idyllic spot, and ideal for us to take lots of quiet country walks, to entertain family and friends, and to go mushroom-hunting in the surrounding fields and woods. Priscilla soon created another wonderful home for us to complement the one in London, with an open-plan kitchen in which I loved to cook, since it was reminiscent of a Tuscan farmhouse. She also created a wonderful garden with the help of a young gardener, Dan Pearson, including a hazelnut copse (which was great for sourcing both hazelnuts and sticks for whittling), a vegetable and herb garden, and a soft fruit garden with raspberries, strawberries, black- and redcurrants in season – perfect for making English summer pudding. There were also bluebell woods, the scent from which was glorious in May and early-June, areas of rough grass and wild flowers to attract the bees and butterflies, and a field where a neighbour sometimes kept his sheep. In time an old barn was restored, creating a delightful large covered space, for entertaining or for the grandchildren to play in. It was a beautiful place and a wonderful way to spend time away from our working environments, somewhere really peaceful to relax in and enjoy.

Later that year I was asked by Emilie and Hugh van Cutsem, longstanding friends of Prince Charles, who is godfather to their eldest son Edward, to help them arrange a celebratory dinner party they wanted to host for his birthday at the Neal Street Restaurant. Arrangements were made for twelve people to come on 28 November, two weeks after his actual birthday, for dinner. This had to be very discreet, of course, but the menu was left up to me, with a request to make it vegetarian-friendly. On the day, Priscilla arranged the private dining room downstairs, complete with gold chairs displaying the Prince of Wales tartan in red and green, which she had chosen in his honour, and decorated beautifully with fresh flowers and candles, to make the event even more festive. She also spent the evening in the kitchen, ensuring all was well, while I managed the 'front of house' along with experienced waiters Bruno and Francesco, who felt very honoured to be working that night.

When the van Cutsens, the Prince of Wales, and other guests arrived, they were greeted with champagne and *hors d'oeuvres* of *vol au vents* filled with *fonduta con tartufo* – a fondue made from Fontina cheese from the Aosta valley and white truffles, a traditional dish from the Piedmont are. The menu was a mushroom feast and started with a *sauté* of wild mushrooms – ceps, chanterelles, milk caps and wood blewits – with a selection of antipasti for those who preferred otherwise. This was followed by *uova al tartufo,* truffled eggs – we had sourced some excellent white truffle from my friend Sandrino – one of the most elegant and refined of Piedmontese dishes, served with truffle crostini, all prepared by Gennaro. The main course was a *porcini risotto,* served with a timbale of courgettes. For dessert, there was a *panna cotta* served with a delicious *Moscato di Pantelleria*, a golden dessert wine made from the muscat grape. And then, with the coffee, the *pièce de résistance* – a wonderful, handmade cake representing a basket of mushrooms, fashioned out of coloured marzipan, made to order by Barbara Swiderska of the Extraordinary Cake Company. I was personally delighted, and have to say also relieved, that the evening had gone so well and everyone had had such a good time.

Another mycophile I met when he came to eat at the restaurant was Anatoli Danilitski, the Russian cultural attaché to London in the early 1990s. Like many of his countrymen, he knew about mushrooms and the pleasure of searching for, finding, cooking and eating them, and we had many an interesting conversation on this subject when he came to eat at the restaurant. He also told me of Mikhail Gorbachev's interest in mycology. So when I gave Anatoli a copy of my book *A Passion for Mushrooms* in 1992, I also gave him a copy to send to Gorbachev, with my best wishes. Some time later I received a totally unexpected thank-you note. In it Gorbachev wrote of how he, too, was a fan of what he described as '... quiet hunting, as we call the picking of mushrooms in our country . . .' His words stayed with me, they were so reminiscent of all those early, misty mornings I had experienced, first as a child in Piedmont and then all around the world, when the mushroom hunter sets forth into the quiet to look for this object of culinary desire. When I came to write a further book on this subject, *The Complete Mushroom Book,* which was published in 2003, it was sub-titled 'The Quiet Hunt' in recognition of this historic figure – the last head of state of the Soviet Union before its dissolution, the man responsible for *Perestroika* and *Glasnost*, ousted by a coup in 1991 and still finding time to write and thank me for my gift. It was the least I could do, to pay my respects from one mycophile to another.

Very sadly, this was also the year that I lost my mother. Maria Annunziatina Carluccio died unexpectedly on 27 August, while I was on holiday in Greece, and as I flew to Italy for her funeral I thought back over the life she'd lived while I grieved and came to terms with losing her. My *cara mamma* who always used to say, 'When God created Italy he looked down from above and said, "This is beautiful – I have to balance it," and he created the Italians.' She'd lived through two world wars, times of great difficulty and hardship, the loss of her youngest son, her husband, her eldest son, and in a way me, since by then I had lived far from home, first in Germany and then in Britain, for the last thirty years. I thought of the love she'd shown me, the squabbles we'd had, the successes she'd been proud of and the failures in my life that she'd witnessed and seldom commented on, trusting me to find my own way through. I realised then that however old you are, the loss of your parents is always a time of reckoning, the umbilical cord is cut for ever, and so it was for me. No one else ever loves you so unconditionally as your own mother, if you're lucky, and I knew that, in spite of everything, I'd had that love. I was also glad that she had been able to see me make something of my life, and be successful in an area I know she valued, because truth be told my first love of food and cooking came from her and it was a real gift she gave me, one on which I have built the whole of my professional life.

There were also, of course, many good and happy experiences during the early years of Carluccio's shop and deli but, combined with managing the Neal Street Restaurant, writing books and making TV programmes, I often found it hard to unwind or switch off. Time spent at 'the bothy', our country house in Hampshire, was a great solace, but it wasn't always possible to get away and enjoy the peace of the lovely gardens or take time to reflect while walking in the woods or whittling away a new design on my hazelwood sticks, planning a new book or cooking a meal for friends. There were times when I felt quite stressed and exhausted, when another board meeting about the accounts or a new aspect of the business felt like the last straw. I was now in my mid-fifties and could easily have considered taking life a little more easily. I enjoyed the creative side of my work very much, but the rest I found increasingly taxing. Although I didn't feel I could resent its success, it did feel at times as if Carluccio the man was being sacrificed to Carluccio's the brand and was, in some ways, being literally used to achieve this.

In 1993 I published *A Passion for Pasta*, and immediately began work on *An Italian Feast* which was published in 1996, by which time the wholesale arm of Carluccio's had been set up, going on to supply over 150 independent delis with Carluccio-branded regional foods from Italy. In 1997 *Carluccio's Complete Italian Food* followed publication of *An Italian Feast*, and then in 1998 a major BBC TV series *Antonio Carluccio's Southern Italian Feast* was aired, for which I also published a companion book of the same name.

Also in 1998, I received an enormous honour from my home country, when I was awarded the Commendatore OMRI (the equivalent of a British knighthood) by the President of Italy, Oscar Luigi Scalfaro. This is one of the highest-ranking honours awarded in Italy, and is given for 'merit acquired by the nation' in the fields of literature, the arts, economy, public service, social, philanthropic and humanitarian activities, and for long and conspicuous service in civilian and military careers. I received my award for services to Italian gastronomy. Luciano Pavarotti was another recipient of the same honour, for his services to music. I was so proud that my contribution to the appreciation of Italian food and culture had been recognised in this way. In addition, Carluccio's plc was granted a Royal Warrant as the Supplier of Italian Food and Truffles to HRH Prince Charles, the Prince of Wales, in the same year. All I had been doing, I felt, was sharing my great personal love for the simplicity and excellence of Italian food, my *minimum of fuss, maximum of flavour* ethos, in a way that the British had taken to their hearts through the restaurant, my books, the TV programmes, and Carluccio's itself – but to have this recognised and celebrated in this way by the Italian government itself was a great honour.

At this time also I was invited to join the Fondazione Altagamma, an association of Italian high-end companies that was originally founded in 1992 to strengthen the international presence of its member companies and support them in their growth. This was another major acknowledgement of my work, and Carluccio's remains to this day one of the ninety-eight members of the Altagamma International Honorary Council that contribute to promoting the highest values of the Italian lifestyle in their countries, sharing the criteria of the Italian Altagamma businesses: excellence of products, quality and customer service.

In contrast to these two accolades, in the same year I also received a personal blow when my longstanding collaborator, protégé and fellow mushroom enthusiast Gennaro Contaldo decided to leave the Neal Street Restaurant. To be fair, there is an inevitability about someone taking their hard-won experience and expertise, albeit gained by association with your own, and setting up their own restaurant –

which is what he did. But it is also true to say that I was hurt by the way it was done. In October 1998, Gennaro, my assistant Liz (who later became his wife and with whom he had a second family), and my head of service (also called Gennaro), all gave me letters of resignation on the same day! It came without warning or any prior discussion – three key people wanted to leave at the same time, in the run up to the extremely busy Christmas season, which had a huge impact on the immediate management of my business. I asked Liz to work her three months' notice, which she did. Then it became clear that they were leaving because Gennaro was setting up his own restaurant Passione in London's Charlotte Street. Because of this, he and I were estranged for a while.

By the time Gennaro left the Neal Street Restaurant in 1998, however, there were other plans afoot to which I also had to turn my attention. I was working on seven titles for the *Carluccio's Collection* series of books, Antipasti, Pasta, Baking, Mushrooms and Truffles, Fish and Shellfish, Vegetables and Salads, and Desserts, which were to be published in 1999 and sold in Carluccio's and other outlets, thus promoting the brand even further. At the same time, Priscilla was busy designing the concept for the first Carluccio's Caffè, and thinking about how to raise the necessary finance to launch it. In spite of our track record with the delicatessen and shop, and the successful wholesale business, the banks weren't then particularly keen to invest in us.

Simon Kossoff was actively looking for a new business proposition when he met Priscilla in 1997. Here was a man with exactly the right credentials and vision, with a degree in economics combined with his postgraduate studies in the hospitality business, and subsequent experience working for the Pizza Express restaurant chain and then with Bob Payton at My Kinda Town (famous for its Chicago Pizza Pie Factory restaurants of the late 1970s). He immediately got and ran with our idea about combining a deli and food shop with an informal, all-day café serving authentic Italian food to complement it. Initially there was no interest from venture capitalists who, at the time it would seem, were happier to invest in the dotcom boom rather than in the bricks and mortar of real ideas with a proven market. But it was a meeting Simon had with the Seattle Coffee Company founder Scott Svenson, who had recently sold the chain to Starbucks and was looking for other business opportunities, which turned things around. Svenson loved the whole concept, and came on-board to help realise Simon's plan to finance not one but three initial cafés. The result was that Priscilla and I went into partnership with three former directors of the My Kinda Town restaurant group, creating a team with Simon as managing director, and Peter Webber and Stephen Gee as non-executive directors. Priscilla and I retained a 20 per cent share of the company. My responsibility was to create the menus and train the chefs and general personnel, while Priscilla and Simon managed the running of the cafés.

The money was in the bank by July 1999 and in September financial director Frank Bandura joined the team, before the first Carluccio's Caffè, opened in November in Market Place, London W1 – just to the north of Oxford Street, about halfway between Oxford Circus and Tottenham Court Road tube stations. It was an excellent site, close to the busy shopping heartland but in a quiet street, where local workers, residents and shoppers could all find excellent coffee, delicious freshly made soups and *focaccia*, pasta dishes, salads, puddings . . . and a deli and shop as well. Customers would pop in for a coffee and then buy some olive oil or pasta to take home. They would come and pick up some antipasti to take back to the office for lunch, or would stay and eat a three-course meal with a glass of wine. Service was brisk and friendly, the selection of food suitable for every appetite, large or small. The concept really struck a chord and we were busy from the word go. The following November, the second café opened in the

Fenwick department store in New Bond Street. Then on Valentine's Day in 2001 we opened in St Christopher's Place, the third of the three cafés for which the initial investment had been secured. Because it was a Valentine's Day opening we used the opportunity to extend the opening hours for the cafés to the evenings too, allowing for a romantic, candlelit supper.

Then we opened in Canary Wharf, and the first café outside the capital in Kingston upon Thames, Surrey. In 2002, four more opened: in West Smithfield and Ealing in London, at the Bluewater shopping centre in Greenhithe, Kent and in St Albans in Hertfordshire. In 2003 we opened four new cafés in London's Brent Cross shopping centre, Islington, Tunbridge Wells and Bicester village shopping centre.

Also in March 2003 I set up a cookery school with Westminster's Kingsway College to train the chefs needed to work in the business. It was essential that the quality of our menus was consistent and reflected absolutely the Carluccio ethos of authentic Italian food. The focaccia bread, for example, is always baked every day in each of the cafés and delicatessens, and that's been the case since 1999, so it means that every chef who works at one of our cafés has to know how to make it to the Carluccio standard. And we don't skimp on the authenticity of the ingredients, either – which is why the mozzarella cheese is always made from buffalo milk. It just doesn't taste the same if it isn't. On one thing we have always been agreed, and that is that the cafés rise or fall on the basis of their reputation, and that reputation for excellence in Italian food has always been insisted upon and will remain so for as long as I am consulted about and responsible for the food and its delivery.

The rollercoaster ride of Carluccio's Caffè continued with the new millennium. In 2004, another five cafés opened: four in London (Fulham, Putney, Hampstead and South Kensington), and one in Windsor, Berkshire. The following year saw another two open, in

St John's Wood, London and also in Esher, Surrey. Twenty cafés in six years . . . and they were opening every day of the week for breakfast, lunch and dinner. All this was done alongside my continuing to run the Neal Street Restaurant, and increasingly heavy book-writing and filming schedules. Then, in December 2005, as per the original contract, the business was floated on the Alternative Investment Market, valued at £53.6 million and, finally, I could take more of a back seat while continuing to work as a part-time food consultant for, and face of the brand, Carluccio's.

Looking back, it's easy now to see where the holes started to appear in my personal life, and in my marriage too, but at the time I was so busy with it all, I didn't see the hairline cracks turn into gaping fissures. Vaguely, at the back of my mind, I knew I wasn't as happy as this success should have made me. I began to feel that I was merely a representation of the brand; that in promoting the authenticity of Italian cuisine, I was fast losing sight of the authenticity of myself. My artistic life, for example, came to a grinding halt. There was no time now to visit the Royal College of Art on a Sunday morning with my friend Eduardo Paolozzi when there was no one else around, sculpting with clay, which I loved to do. I still have the life-sized head of him that I modelled as we talked together of art, culture, and the Italy we loved.

Eduardo was an extremely kind and generous friend, renowned for donating his artwork to friends left, right and centre! He made a huge collage dedicated to me and my mushroom passion, with a cut-away section of the earth showing how the mycelia of the fungi sprout and grow into mushrooms. It was a beautiful piece of work, made up of off-cuts sourced from the Royal College of Art, which I displayed at the restaurant, as over the years I replaced various paintings and pictures of Terence's with my own collection of original art.

I was very proud to know Eduardo and missed him greatly when he died in 2005, especially his uncomplicated friendship. He never boasted about his amazing accomplishments even though he was one of the most influential British artists of the twentieth century. I pleaded on numerous occasions with many ambassadors of Italy for him to be recognised by them with some appropriate honour, even though he had been born in Scotland to Italian immigrant parents, but that recognition came from the British government, which awarded him a knighthood in 1988. Like me, he loved women, wine and food, and was blessed in his wife Freda and three lovely daughters – one of whom, Emma, is a silversmith and jewellery designer, and since her father's death calls me her 'father'.

By now, even mushroom-foraging had to be scheduled into a diary overflowing with meetings. I began to feel my life was spiralling out of control, and it concerned me. What worried me more, on reflection, was that I felt powerless to do anything about it. I just kept going with the workload, hoping it would sort itself out, but it didn't. It came as something of a shock, for example, to discover that on relinquishing full control of the business, in return for the financial rewards it yielded, I had signed over the rights to my name. Carluccio's, now a registered brand and transferable asset, was no longer a name I could use in any future business purpose. Not that I had any intention of effectively competing with myself, but it did seem odd that somehow my name was of more value now than I myself appeared to be. Certainly my concerns about all this were dismissed, and Priscilla was much more pragmatic about it than I could ever be, but still it niggled at me. Maybe because it had been her exceptional business and design acumen that had realised the Carluccio's business, she had probably always understood what it meant while I, in retrospect, was not sure that I had.

Now the company had been floated, we were financially very secure, but another move was in the offing. Priscilla decided that it made better sense to sell the Landridge Road house and buy somewhere else to live, a pied-à-terre in London rather than a full-sized house. That pied-à-terre turned out to be an apartment in Richard Rogers' newly designed Montevetro building on the banks of the Thames at Battersea, on the opposite side of the river from the Chelsea Embankment and Cheyne Walk, where I'd first lived when I came to London. The site Rogers built on had previously been a disused Rank Hovis flour mill. Work began in 1994 to convert it into the very modern, eye-catching building that opened to residents six years later. It seems to be made completely from glass, with each apartment's gleaming floor-to-ceiling windows reflecting the sunshine or cloud, the dawn sky or the city's lights, depending on the weather and time of day. I could see that it made a lot of sense to have a home with a twenty-four-hour concierge service, car parking and other facilities when we were both working, and it was not far from Battersea Park in which we could walk and enjoy a bit of greenery now that we were without a London garden.

The views from our new home on the sixth floor, overlooking the Thames, its bridges and Chelsea Harbour, were spectacular, but the modernity of the flat didn't appeal to me as much as it did to Priscilla, with all its steel and glass and nowhere to hang my pictures. For her, it was the perfect place to showcase examples of good design from the Conran Shop, but it never felt like my home. Along with the flat, Priscilla began work on her next project. This was to be her very own shop, for which she would source beautiful home furnishings and other items, from designers like her previous business partner Paola Navone, much as she had done for the Conran Group. Delighted to be back in a world she so obviously enjoyed, she embarked on her plans with relish, going on to open her shop Few and Far on the Brompton Road a few years later.

In 2007, however, recognition of my contribution to Britain came like a seventieth birthday present in the form of an honorary – because I am an Italian still – OBE, the Order of the British Empire. Or, as I like to say in deference to my passion for mushrooms, the *Order of the*

Boletus Edulis. The ceremony was held at the Italian Embassy, rather than the Palace, and my OBE was pinned to my jacket by Tessa Jowell, then Secretary of State for Culture in Tony Blair's Labour government, saying as she did so what great pleasure it gave her. The Embassy hosted a wonderful party to celebrate, with food supplied by Carluccio's, of course, for about 200 family and friends, organised by Priscilla who was there with Lucy and Granby and their children, too.

It was definitely a great honour to be recognised by the British public in this way but it was ironic that it came in the year that the Neal Street Restaurant was forced to close, when property developers in the area decided not to renew its lease. After running it for twenty-six years, the closure was to leave a huge gap in my working life, but for others who had enjoyed eating there over the thirty-six years since it had opened, it was possibly an even bigger loss. Either way, it represented a change in fortunes for Neal Street, which seemed to lose some of its old charm. Today the original site of the restaurant is a clothes shop, one of a ubiquitous American branded retail outfit. No doubt the street will soon look like every other, with no individuality left, as it becomes just another exercise in money-making. I was kept busy letting staff go, sorting out the final accounts, taking the pictures off the walls, getting rid of the furniture and fittings. Everything was put into an auction at Sotheby's. They produced a catalogue and made a wonderful exhibition of the contents, which realised far in excess of its estimated total – £166,740 against a pre-sale estimate of £77,000–111,000. I kept only one painting that I was particularly fond of. It was by Patrick Caulfield, a British artist and friend of mine who'd died in 2005. I wish now I had kept more but at the time I was so upset I just wanted to get the clearance over and done with. It was a sad day for me when the restaurant closed, and the end of a happy era.

It was at times like this that I found my distress relieved by an activity that, for a short time at least, cancelled out all other thoughts or considerations. What started out for me as a harmless and occasional social opportunity in order to forget my troubles became, in time, something of an addiction. I was not a drinker, although I enjoyed wine and a glass of Laphroaig to finish my day. I also smoked, in spite of the health warnings, but this wasn't the problem either. The thing that gave me some respite from my depressed and anxious feelings was gambling and, to be more specific, gambling in casinos. I have often thought about what it is that makes gambling so attractive because the reality is that, when you have lost a lot of money, it makes you feel foolish and angry with yourself, which in my case reinforced my depression. But going into the plush, darkened casinos, where people pander to your every whim in their desire to help relieve you of your money, is very soothing. It's also quite exciting to gamble and win, which often happens: there can be no addiction without some element of reward. There is a sense of ritual, anticipation and excitement to it, which momentarily replaces everything else that feels bad at that point. The rush of adrenalin gambling gave me made me feel alive again, in a life where I hardly seemed to matter any more. It was sheer, expensive escapism but for me it worked to alleviate – for a short time at least – an inaccessible, internalised sense of loss or resentment or pain.

There came a time, however, when I had to address this problem, so after another big financial loss and an ultimatum from Priscilla, I booked into an addiction centre in some distress. It was an interesting process, coming to terms with my 'addiction to gambling', but I felt entirely at odds with the rest of the people there who were, by and large, addicts of a different sort. Group therapy served to make me feel even more depressed as I heard others pouring out their woes, and only made me feel worse about my own inability to manage my emotional life. Resolving to do better, and with the support of my doctors, I discharged myself, having agreed to a course of antidepressants as I recognised that my gambling was a symptom of a deeper malaise. I also agreed to go with Priscilla for some marriage counselling and sat through a number of sessions listening to my faults writ large, with all the blame for everything that was wrong being heaped at my sorry door.

In the end I could stand it no longer. I wrote a suicide note and took an overdose, hoping this might be a way out of my deep depression, an alternative to the way I was feeling, however terminal. I didn't think beyond wanting to make it stop. I came round to find myself in a private psychiatric hospital, my stomach pumped, my heart empty. I stayed there for several weeks until finally, in spite of the dismal surroundings, I found a way to rekindle my motivation. I made the decision that I would seek the help I needed.

In spite of these difficult times, the year was not all bad, even though having to close the Neal Street Restaurant in particular was a great sadness and its loss had highlighted many aspects of my life that were problematic, precipitating my latest depression and spiral into self-destructive behaviour. But I had survived, and that year I made one of the TV documentaries of which I am most proud: *Carluccio and the Renaissance Cookbook*.

Commissioned by the BBC, and first broadcast in December 2007, the programme was about Bartolomeo Scappi, famed sixteenth-century chef to Pope Pius V. Scappi published his cookbook *Opera dell'arte del cucinare* in 1570, listing 1000 recipes and describing cooking techniques, preparation methods and the use of ingredients imported from the newly discovered Americas. It was a fantastic project to work on, travelling to Italy to film and reproducing some of his recipes for the programme: *porchetta* (roasted suckling pig), *riso alla Lombarda* (Lombardy-style rice), *sarde in saor* (Venetian-style sardines), *pomi sdegnosi* ('disdainful apples', a sixteenth-century recipe for baked aubergines) and, my personal favourite, of course, *torta di funghi* (wild mushroom tart). The following year, 2008, the University of Toronto Press published a beautifully produced translation of Scappi's masterpiece under the title *The Opera of Bartolomeo Scappi* edited by Terence Scully, which is an interesting book for anyone serious about Italian cooking. It is the one I myself turn to from time to time, to reinvigorate my passion for Italian cuisine and gastronomy. Bartolomeo Scappi, one of the world's first celebrity chefs! The rest of us can only follow in his esteemed footsteps.

Uova al tartufo

~~~~~~~~~~~~~~~~~~~~~~~~~~~~~~

Truffled eggs

This is by far the simplest way to enjoy fresh white truffle. You must always wait for them to be in season, from October to December, to use the real thing as truffle oil just isn't enough. Keep your truffle stored around raw eggs as the eggs will absorb the intense flavour of the mushroom.

Serves 4
butter, for greasing
8 eggs
8 tbsp double cream
salt
about 45 g (1½ oz) white truffle (more
    if you can afford it!)
bread, to serve

Preheat the oven to 180°C/355°F/gas 4. Grease four large ramekins with butter.

Break 2 eggs into each ramekin and pour over the cream. Season with salt and then place in the preheated oven. Start checking after 5 minutes to see if the whites have set. Remove from the oven when they have.

Cut the white truffle into slivers and scatter over the eggs. Serve immediately, with bread.

CHAPTER FOURTEEN

New Beginnings

he New Year dawned and 2008 initially felt like a clean sheet on which to draw. The film on Scappi that I had worked on the previous summer for the BBC had been broadcast in December 2007 and been really well received, and I was now working on another new book, *Antonio Carluccio's Simple Cooking*. My assistant of the last six years, Tanya, left to have a baby and I advertised for someone else to help me. There were over 200 applicants, who were whittled down to a handful I thought might be appropriate for the job. Anna-Louise was one of them and, when I first saw her smile, I thought we would work well together. She was my first choice and thankfully she agreed to come and work with me, proving herself invaluable over the subsequently very busy and often very difficult years.

One of the first things we had to do in February was move out of the old office in Neal Street and into new offices in Tavistock Street, which we shared with an old friend, Michael Palin, and his television production team. There was continuing training of the chefs and organising of the menus, and various promotional events for Carluccio Caffè to be done, too. Then in March Priscilla opened her new shop, Few and Far, in the Brompton Road and was kept extremely busy travelling to source products for that. Increasingly she and I, whether by design or default, were becoming like ships passing in the night.

On one visit to 'the bothy' in early May that year, I was driving down the lane to our house when I saw a neighbour who lived nearby. Neither Priscilla nor I really knew her except to wave a greeting and say the occasional hello. On this occasion, however, she gesticulated for me to stop and when I wound down the window she told me she had something for us. She had taken a lovely photo of our house after some exceptional snowfall some months previously, and thought we might like a copy. It was indeed a lovely photo, showing off 'the bothy' to its best advantage, looking very seasonal in the snow, the bright winter sunshine illuminating the dark, bare branches of the surrounding trees in attractive contrast. I thought it might make a nice Christmas card that Priscilla and I could use in the future.

Quite touched by her thoughtfulness and simple gesture of kindness, I thanked our neighbour effusively for her kindness and, wanting to give her something in return, in the Italian manner I gave her a kiss. After some years of distance between Priscilla and myself, this moment of brief affection lifted my spirits. I was pretty sure by this time that rekindling the warmth in my marriage was no longer possible, and losing the emotional and physical intimacy Priscilla and I had once shared was a great sadness in my life. This friendly gesture, for that was all it was, had been genuinely heart-warming while also highlighting what I was missing, and over time we became friends, but nothing more.

That summer, in between filming, writing, and innumerable meetings about, and appearances promoting, Carluccio's (the restaurants continued to open across the UK and today there are fifty-seven of them), amongst other broadcasts I had the pleasure of recording *Desert Island Discs* for BBC Radio 4, which was first broadcast on 6 July 2008. The series has been on air almost continuously since it was first conceived as a summer stop-gap of six programmes, devised by broadcaster Roy Plomley in 1942. There have only been four presenters in all that time. It is quite an accolade to be invited to take part, and it placed me in the diverse and esteemed company of politicians and playwrights, artists and athletes, business people and campaigners of every kind, to identify but a few of the thousand who've so far chosen their desert island discs.

It wasn't easy for a music lover like me to choose only eight tracks. Finally I chose five classical pieces from Tchaikovsky, Rossini, Prokofiev, Saint-Saëns and Smetana; the Beatles' song 'Yesterday' (which summed up my nostalgic mood at the time); the theme music from the movie *Il Postino* in recognition of my Italian heritage; and finally, an old Austrian folk song '*Es Steht Ein Alter Nussbaum*' ('There Stands an Old Nut Tree'), which was rather how I was feeling about myself! My luxury item was, of course, some white truffles, and my chosen book the *His Dark Materials* trilogy by Philip Pullman. Being interviewed by Kirsty Young, and having had to choose music that reflected something of my life, had made me think long and hard about things now that I had reached the ripe old age of seventy, and it was at about this time too that I resolved to write my memoirs, while I still could, though it would be some time before I actually got around to doing it.

Aside from that brief and pleasant interlude on a fantasy desert island, work continued apace as I started a new TV programme, *Carluccio and the Leopard,* to be shown on BBC4. I was thrilled to be doing this, travelling to Sicily to discover more about one of the most successful novels ever written in the Italian language, *Il Gattopardo,* or *The Leopard* by Giuseppe Tomasi di Lampedusa, originally published in 1958 and one of my favourite books. It is set during the years of Italian unification, the time of Garibaldi's struggle against the Bourbons, a hugely significant era in Italy's history. It is also the story of Fabrizio Corbera, Prince of Salina, modelled on Lampedusa's own great-grandfather in fact. The book features a vibrant and compelling description of a celebratory Sicilian dinner, which I attempted to recreate in the television programme. But this was *cucina baronale*, the cuisine of the aristocracy – not *cucina povera*, the cuisine of the poor – and was not entirely easy to reproduce!

The cuisine of Sicily is extraordinary, influenced as it has been by twenty-five centuries of invasion by the Greeks, Arabs, French and Spanish, and reproducing dishes described in a work of literature posed its own challenges. The recipes we replicated for the programme included a *zuppa di fave secche* (soup made from dried white broad beans, soaked overnight), a macaroni pie, or *timballo*, which is in fact one of the richest dishes I have ever cooked, with its combination of cooked pasta, fried chicken and chicken livers, cubes of ham, beef stock, wine, vegetables, the unborn eggs from the ovary of a chicken – a delicacy impossible to source in time for the filming schedule, so we used the hard-boiled yolks of quails' eggs – fried onions, truffles or porcini mushrooms, and wine, all wrapped up in pastry and cooked in the oven. To follow, I made Don Fabrizio's famous and favourite dessert, rum jelly served with a glass of Marsala wine. It was quite a feast and great fun to research and prepare while also exploring the wonderful history, culture and scenery of the island on which the novel is set.

Continuing difficulties in my marriage complicated this busy schedule. In August that year, Priscilla and I took a holiday in Majorca. It was not a success. I was unhappy and preoccupied, and Priscilla was exhausted from work. What should have been a reinvigorating break for both of us became a week of tense silences and accusatory conversations. Thinking back, the holiday was a mistake, but after twenty-seven years of marriage, I still somehow thought the difficulties between us might blow over and we could find a way forward, even if just as friends, based on what we'd built and achieved together over the years, even though I hadn't a clue how this might be done and was uncomfortable at the thought of more counselling.

On returning home, exasperated by my depressed mood no doubt, Priscilla challenged me on my commitment to her and our marriage. At this point, out of respect for the years we had shared and in the hope of future friendship, I should have taken the opportunity to say I was sorry but thought our marriage had run its course and we should find some gracious and amicable way to separate. As it was, I said nothing, and she asked me then, point blank, if there was someone else. Initially I refused to answer Priscilla's question because, in reality, there wasn't another woman on the scene, certainly not in the way she meant: I wasn't having an affair.

As the argument escalated, I lost my cool. More out of anger than with any proper thought for what I was doing, I capitulated and said yes, there was a woman . . . And the moment I said it, I knew there was no going back. It was over. But first there was a huge scene, and recriminations, and I retaliated, and we both said, as couples do at this point, terrible things to each other from which there seemed no way to return. At that point I couldn't begin to retrieve any good and happy memories of our time together on which to build any sort of future. It just seemed completely pointless, all of it, everything I had ever done in life. And yet again there seemed no way out as depression took hold of me.

In desperation I saw my doctor, and he increased my antidepressant medication. I tried to get on with things. We did the photography, already scheduled at 'the bothy', for the new book and Alastair Hendy's wonderful photographs belie the anguish I was in as we completed work on it. Then, at the beginning of September, I went off to attend an event at the Olympia exhibition halls in London for one of the charities I support in association with Carluccio's. Action Against Hunger is a hugely impressive charity that campaigns and fund raises to help those millions of children worldwide who suffer from the deadly effects of malnutrition. It is a cause to which I was, and remain, very committed. Before the event had even begun, however, a woman in the audience collapsed, and I reacted very badly. Already suffering from extreme exhaustion after the events of the last few weeks, late nights spent arguing, retreats to the casino to gamble, too much whisky and not enough sleep, I too was on the point of collapse.

Making my apologies, I abruptly left the venue and beat a retreat home: Priscilla was away in France, and I could be alone. I locked myself away and tried to deal with my rising anxieties in the only way I felt was open to me. The whisky bottle by my side, my depression, self-loathing and self-pity spiralled, and I started to write the first of several suicide notes. Anna-Louise, my personal assistant, alarmed to hear that I had abandoned the event for Action Against Hunger, felt that I was at risk and rang me, saying she was on her way. She came immediately, but when she arrived I refused to answer the door and let her in. There had been a previous incident, the week before, when I had been toying with a sharp knife and had frightened myself by deliberately cutting my hand, in an effort to obliterate the emotional pain with a physical one, resulting in a trip to the Accident and Emergency department for stitches. I had made excuses at the time, saying it was an accident while sharpening a knife in the kitchen. Since then Anna-Louise had become very concerned, keeping an eye on me as far as she could. Now she was really worried and took the only course of action open to her. She asked the concierge to let her in, explaining the urgency of the situation.

I don't really know what happened next because, in all honesty, I had had too much to drink combined with my medication so my recollection of events is hazy. All I do remember was the overwhelming feeling of sheer desperation and a need to find a way to make the emotional pain stop. If I had drunk myself to oblivion that might have prevented what happened next. As it was I was too keyed up with the adrenalin caused by the continuous distress of the last few weeks.

I remember Anna-Louise urgently telling me to calm down but, snatching up a pair of old scissors I used to use for cutting my hair, I locked myself in the bathroom, intending to find some way to stop this emotional turmoil and pain. Even I can see now how ludicrous this may seem, but anyone who has felt similar, extreme distress will understand how the feeling can spiral into the despair of self-destructive behaviour. I have met many people since who have shown me great charity and generosity in acknowledging how I felt, rather than belittling me further, for which I am truly appreciative. But at the time it was an instinctive reaction to the intolerable pressure under which I found myself. I placed the sharpened point of the scissors against my chest where I judged my heart to be and, using my body weight, pushed the blade of the scissor in with as much force as I could muster until I felt the tissues give. I was thinking of nothing at the time except preventing the terrible thoughts I was having from going round and round in my head. It was almost like having an out of body experience: I remember pushing the scissor's blade hard, and wondering what was stopping it – in fact, it was a rib. I continued to push.

Meanwhile Anna-Louise had been banging on the bathroom door, beseeching me to open it. When I continued to refuse, she rang the police for assistance. It was just as well. We didn't know it at the time, but the scissors had penetrated the pleural cavity close to my lung, and I was in considerable danger. The police arrived, with an ambulance in tow, and while the paramedics got to work, ensuring I was stable before transporting me to hospital, with towels holding the protruding scissors steady to avoid further damage, poor Anna-Louise was left once again to pick up the pieces.

I tell this story now to set the record straight. At the time, it was considered necessary to protect my professional reputation, not that I cared much about it then, but the press picked up on the incident immediately and something had to be said. A statement was issued that I had had an accident in the kitchen while sharpening a knife. That was how it was first reported, and I reiterated the story again and again when asked about it later by journalists and others. I'm not sure anyone bought it, though, especially when I checked into the Priory after being discharged from hospital. Priscilla was already on her way back from France via Eurostar when she was contacted about my 'accident', and came to see me in the hospital. I was then told that I would never again be able to return home, the marriage was over, and she was seeing a solicitor to arrange the divorce. I have not seen her since.

After recovering from the necessary surgery at the hospital, I spent the rest of September in the Priory. I don't think I have ever felt more abandoned or alone or angry. I spent long days and nights, wrestling with my past and considering my future, trying to make sense of both. The rest of the time I just slept. There was group therapy, which I couldn't bear, and one-to-one sessions with my psychiatrist, but I am not sure how much progress I had made by the time I left. In my heart I longed for restorative Italian sunshine, to be cooking in the old kitchen of a Piedmont farmhouse, walking on an Amalfi beach, sharing a bottle of wine with friends, happy and carefree, back in the days when Carluccio was just a man and not a brand. It seems churlish to look a gift horse in the mouth, but it was hard not to feel resentful of the impact the last few years had had on me.

Although I hated being in the Priory, my days there were made bearable by the love and support shown by many of my friends. Those who couldn't visit or call wrote to me, and I'm sure it helped my recovery.

I left the Priory to move into my new, rented home at the beginning of October. Anna-Louise had found me a house to live in on Bishop's Road in Fulham, not a million miles from where I had lived before in Landridge Road, so I knew and liked the area. She had also fielded the press, kept the business side of things going, and collected all my possessions from Montevetro. She transferred these to my temporary home, where I would spend a year while the divorce went through. Without Anna-Louise, I would have been completely lost and I bless the day she agreed to come and work with me.

Divorce proceedings between Priscilla and myself were conducted via a mediator. I agreed to the grounds of adultery, because although this wasn't strictly accurate, it facilitated what the press would call a 'quickie' divorce. Our business interests had been dealt with at the time of the original flotation of Carluccio's, so the only thing left to resolve was the financial interest in the two properties – the house in Hampshire, which was Priscilla's anyway, and the Montevetro apartment. Once this was done, things went through uncontested, and by May 2009, after twenty-eight years of marriage, I was free and able to start looking for a new home.

Luckily, I did have something to look forward to. Just before our divorce proceedings commenced, I had been invited to Australia, as a guest of the South Australia Tourism Commission, to participate in their week-long Tasting Australia event. Set up originally in 1997, this was designed to showcase all that was best about Australia's amazing food and drink, and the extraordinary mix of cuisines its inhabitants enjoy, from Greek, to Asian Pacific, to Italian, to straightforward barbecues. I was delighted to travel there to be inducted as a 2007 Melbourne Food and Wine Festival Legend, and to participate in a series of events promoting Italian food. Through my television programmes and books I had quite a following already in Australia so I enjoyed a very warm welcome when I arrived, which was delightful, and because they take food seriously and appreciate really good ingredients, it really was a wonderful visit and went some way to restoring my enthusiasm for life.

While I had been away, Anna-Louise had been busy house hunting for me. She had found several to have a look at, but there was one that she thought would work really well for me. It was an end-of-terrace house, in a cul-de-sac, so as well as being quiet it also benefited from a large garden with a garage at the front and additional parking space. Internally the house had been well organised, with a nice open-plan kitchen leading to a dining area and comfortable sitting room that extended on to a deck in the garden, with a small lawn and a walled area which would work really well for fruit trees. There was a study at the front, where I could work and store all my files and work-related books.

It was perfect, and I felt very happy about my new home. We even arranged to have the original mosaic of the Carluccio's brand name, which had been on the doorstep of the first shop in Neal Street, restored to its former glory as my new, front doorstep. First I had to go to France to do the food for a friend's wedding, but when I returned from this at the beginning of September, Anna-Louise had already moved me in, and organised a wonderful house-warming party for me with lots of my old friends there to wish me well. As 2009 drew to a close, and my new garden with its summerhouse, herb bed, quince and pear trees began to take shape, I began to feel that I might one day be happy again.

Christmas, however, was a difficult time for me. It always is. I find it exacerbates feelings of loneliness, seeing families getting ready to spend the festive season together, with all the celebratory foods in the shops and the playing of Christmas carols. I feel then nostalgic for happier times: Christmases spent with my family as a child in Italy; my first Christmas in Vienna, which had been so magical. I particularly miss the fact that I was not fortunate enough to have children and grandchildren of my own, and that I am now more or less estranged from some of my former stepchildren, with whom I was involved for nearly thirty years, and their children, my surrogate grandchildren, whose births I'd celebrated in the past. I began the second decade of the new millennium feeling a little morose, in spite of some bright prospects for the New Year.

One thing that did please me, however, was that I was once again collaborating with my old employee and fellow mushroom enthusiast Gennaro Contaldo. After many years of estrangement following his departure from the Neal Street Restaurant in 1998, we settled our differences and did some work together. First, Jamie Oliver's magazine editor Andy Harris commissioned us to write an article, which was published in the May/June issue of *Jamie* in 2009, and this led to discussion of a possible TV series, to be made by Jamie's TV production company, Fresh One Productions. Gennaro had published four cookbooks by this time, although his restaurant Passione had been forced to close in March 2009 in the recession that affected so many businesses, so he was keen to explore other opportunities. He had already made a few television appearances, first on Jamie Oliver's show *The Naked Chef* and also on the BBC's *Saturday Kitchen* show, where he set a record of 16.36 seconds for making a three-egg omelette. He had continued to mentor Jamie during his early career, and was very involved in his UK restaurant chain, Jamie's Italian. The provisional idea for a TV series was to do a food tour of different areas of Italy, and so the four-part series *Two Greedy Italians* was commissioned by BBC2.

The filming schedule was quite tough, since the series had to be ready for transmission the following May, but they were good programmes and I enjoyed making them. The first one focused on the changing face of the Italian family, and how meals had once been, as was my childhood experience, at the heart of family life. The second episode looked at the influence of *cucina povera* – poor man's food, and how this had actually made Italian cuisine easier to promote around the world. In the third programme we looked at the pride taken in Italian regional cuisine, and the competition for status between the different regions, which included returning to my hometown of Borgofranco to look at the specialities of Piedmont. Finally, in the fourth programme, we looked at the role of religion, how it might exploit or enhance or be linked to Italian cooking, and its continuing influence in a Catholic country. Along the way, we did of course cook, and these dishes included some of my personal favourites: *stufato con polenta* (slow-cooked family stew with polenta), *crostata di ricotta al limone* (lemon and ricotta tart), *tagliatelle con salsa di fegato di pollo* (pasta ribbons with chicken liver sauce) and *zuccotto* (bread and butter pudding made with panettone).

As well as being driven around by Gennaro in a rather cramped 1960s Alfa Romeo car throughout the filming (it has to be said, I no longer have the svelte figure of my youth, when you could have fitted me and three other adults into a Fiat 500), the programmes showed that we Italians were not just greedy for food, but also for life, music, culture and romance. While Gennaro is a Roman Catholic and I am an agnostic, we were both devout in our appreciation for and love of the best of Italian food, and for me never more so than when we visited San Patrignano in Rimini and ate a meal there.

San Patrignano is an extraordinary community of around 2000 recovering drug and other addicts, who live and work and cook and eat together. Vincenzo Muccioli set it up in 1978, and it was his vision to create a therapeutic community, free of charge, where young people could recover from their various addictions and be professionally trained for employment. It was to be somewhere they would be accepted without question, somewhere that they could make their home. The kitchen and dining room is one of their big successes, because as well as cooking for the whole community, chefs working there are trained for future employment, and food products are produced for sale, including wine, cheese, bread, cakes, salami, olive oil and honey, marketed worldwide under the San Patrignano label.

Muccioli, sadly now dead but whose visionary spirit lives on, said: 'The core of the problem is not drugs . . . it is the human being with his fears and the black holes that threaten to suck him in. Ours is a community for living, where you can restart in life after years spent as a social outcast.' It was a different sort of family life I found there, a very special one that people join when they stray off course and find themselves in a dark place. I saw such happiness, motivation and fulfilment there that, profoundly moved by the atmosphere of hope, I came home with a little piece of it in my heart. I saw how the young people there learnt to cook with patience, love and passion, which is truly a recipe for life itself. I had forgotten this for a while, but after visiting San Patrignano I was able to see some things more clearly. 'Welcome to the family,' I was told while I was there. 'The medicine here is love. You cannot buy it, it's free.'

Torta di ricotta e limone

Ricotta and lemon tart

This is a delicious, inter-regional lemon tart made with fresh ricotta cheese, typical of the south, and a little mascarpone, a cream cheese of the north. Try to get sheep's milk ricotta if you can as it is much tastier. When we filmed the making of this tart, I served it with pears in red wine (overleaf).

Serves 8
1 x 400 g (14 oz) packet ready-made
  puff pastry
plain flour, for dusting
finely grated zest of 1 lemon

For the filling:
300 g (10 oz) ricotta
200 g (7 oz) mascarpone
200 g (7 oz) candied peel (citron and
  orange)
120 g (4 oz) caster sugar
6 eggs, separated

Preheat the oven to 180°C/355°F/ gas 4.

Roll out the pastry on a lightly floured work surface until it is 2–3 mm thick. Lay over a 25-cm (10-in) loose-bottomed tart tin and gently push the pastry into the base and up and over the sides. There will quite a bit of overhang. Cover with a damp cloth while you make the filling.

In a large bowl, mix the ricotta, mascarpone and candied peel with 100 g (3½ oz) of the sugar and five of the egg yolks.

Put all six egg whites in another large, clean bowl and whisk until fluffy. Add the remaining sugar and continue whisking until stiff. Using a large metal spoon, fold the whites through the ricotta mixture then pour into the pastry-lined tart tin. Fold in the overhanging pastry and brush with the reserved beaten egg yolk.

Bake in the preheated oven for 30 minutes, until the pastry is risen and golden and the filling retains a slight wobble. Leave to cool for 2 hours, then sprinkle with lemon zest. Serve either on its own or with roasted pears in red wine.

Roasted pears in red wine

Tuck eight pears into a suitably sized dish with high sides and bake in the same temperature oven for half an hour until the skins start to bubble. Pour over enough good red wine to cover, sprinkle with caster sugar and bake for another half an hour, by which the wine will have reduced to a sweet syrup.

CHAPTER FIFTEEN

In Natura Veritas

he process of learning, I have found, never stops and I think I have never been more open to learning about life as I am now. As a young man I thought I knew it all; now I feel as if I am older and wiser but not so arrogant to realise that there is still much to learn and enjoy, and this realisation brings me great pleasure. It has been hard won. A few years ago I felt that there was not much left to live for. I felt burnt out and exhausted and as I struggled to find some sense and meaning in life, I started the inner conversation and contemplation that led to the writing of this book.

Today I am working as hard as ever, but I am more involved with the creative side of my life, through my cooking, the recent television series *Two Greedy Italians* and my books. I also have more time for other activities, which have helped rebuild my inner faith in people and the restorative power of connection, through my work with a number of charities. Not all of it is about food, although sometimes I find myself cooking a meal or providing a cookery lesson for someone who has won me in a fundraising auction, or hosting a coffee morning for Macmillan Cancer Support.

Sometimes I have been asked by friends to contribute my time, as Stephen Fry asked me to support the Terence Higgins Trust which has done such amazing work for people with AIDS over the years; or my dear friend Katrine Boorman asked me to support the Warrior Programme, which runs programmes to successfully rehabilitate traumatised ex-servicemen. It is a privilege to support them, as I also do as an Ambassador to the Prince's Trust. Carluccio's Caffès have long supported Action Against Hunger, and I have also worked with Alberto Crisci and his inspirational Clink charity, which runs a top-class restaurant inside a prison enabling inmates to train and learn the skills and self-esteem that can create work opportunities for them in the hospitality industry once they've served their time. I am never happier than meeting all the good people who make these things happen, and the people they happen for.

I often think that if I had followed a more academic path in life, I might have studied anthropology such is my lifelong and continuing interest in people, young and old. This abiding interest is what makes any interaction in life, whether through business or pleasure, at a party or in an airport departure lounge, an interesting one. It is the people you meet along the way, the conversations you have and the love you share that are important, and it is true to say that the food business has afforded me opportunities to make the widest connections possible, all over the world in all walks of life. As a boy I could never have imagined that I, a stationmaster's son from Italy, would one day dine with the future king of England. It seems incredible.

I love England and living here, it is absolutely my home, but sometimes I have felt an observer on my own life, a foreigner and perennial outsider: the English way has often felt very alien to me. This business of the 'stiff upper lip', the passive-aggressive way of not saying but subtly telegraphing displeasure through body language, is something I have found difficult, and never more so than when I have unexpectedly found myself the focus of media attention at personally very difficult times. I cannot complain about the publicity that comes from promoting my passion for Italian food, but it is true to say that I have sometimes found it very difficult at times of personal distress.

This attitude is not just reserved for those of us perceived as foreigners, of course. I can remember when the Conservative party MP Cecil Parkinson came with his family for dinner at the Neal Street Restaurant, one evening in 1983 shortly after the news broke of his 12-year relationship with his secretary Sara Keys and the imminent birth of their child, forcing him to resign as Secretary of State for Trade and Industry. As he and his wife and daughters arrived, all the other diners stopped talking and stared at them. Feeling upset on their behalf by this censorious behaviour, I greeted them warmly and showed them to their table, discreetly instructing my staff to pay them every attention to compensate for the hostility exuded by the other guests. It is not for us to judge, I felt – this man and his family were entitled to enjoy their meal.

For me, being able to relax and enjoy a meal, whatever the circumstances, lies at the heart of a restaurant's hospitality. Sometimes, however, it's not always possible to keep negative news from its door, and never more so that on 11 September 2001, when the terrible events of that day clashed with a special, thirtieth anniversary celebration of the Neal Street Restaurant. Great effort had gone into the planning of this private event, with a carefully designed menu and selected wine list, its extensive invites to the great and the good who had supported us over the years. We went ahead as the impact and implication of this shocking news filtered through, and I addressed the diners in a sombre voice, expressing grief for the assault on New York and its people, and echoing everyone's thoughts that although we could no longer celebrate, as such, we could take comfort from each other's company. It was a very sad and moving occasion. I'll never forget it, or seeing Terence Conran with tears in his eyes, on a rare occasion allowing us to see the man behind the business entrepreneur.

When I come back to the question, why does anyone write their memoirs, I think I wrote mine because I wanted to leave a record, rather than just a bald CV, of what matters to me. Maybe if I had had children of my own (and as far as I know, there are none!) I would have felt less inclined to write my own story, but over the last few months I have found the experience both cathartic and comforting in equal measure, creating as it has an opportunity to reflect on my past, my present and my future.

In doing so, I am reminded of the fable of the butterfly that inadvertently fell into a bowl of milk. In order to survive, it starts flapping its wings furiously and, over time, turns the milk into butter on which it can safely stand. After years of frantic activity, I feel I can now stop for a while, take stock and peacefully contemplate my next steps. Writing this memoir has been part of this process.

At my recent seventy-fifth birthday, which I celebrated surrounded by the love of many good friends and especially Sabine, I felt very content. One special gift, from my friend, the extremely talented artist Fabrice Moireau, is my own coat of arms. It is a beautiful depiction of the many things that reflect my interests and enjoyment in life – porcini, the grape, my dog, the whittled walking sticks, a plate of pasta – surrounding the inscription *In Natura Veritas*.

I started my new future by establishing a small rockery, about one square metre in size, in my back garden. Inspired by the wonderful walks I used to take in the Alps, I collected about thirty Alpine flowers from various garden centres and planted them amongst the rocks. These tiny, perfectly formed flowers of unbelievable beauty and smell give me immense satisfaction, and remind me everyday that nature provides perfection that is often taken for granted. These flowers are in bloom for just a few months, only to be dormant – but not dead – under a blanket of snow for the rest of the year.

In Natura Veritas – in nature, truth – I feel these words are such an accurate reflection of my appreciation of nature and life itself. I have no religious belief, but it is this truth that has run like a seam through my life, to which I have always looked in times of both pleasure and distress, and on which I now reflect with real contentment and in anticipation of my future years, whatever they may bring.

Acknowledgements

Many people have contributed to my life's story, and many are mentioned by name within these pages. I would like to thank them, and those whose names don't appear, for the many and varied contributions they have all made to my personal journey over the last seventy-five years.

Although I have written many cookery books, writing a memoir is a different proposition and for her help with this I would especially like to thank Harriet Griffey. Thank you also to my publishers, Kate Pollard and Stephen King at Hardie Grant, for their commitment to producing a book to which I am proud to put my name.

Huge gratitude is due to my friend Raymond Blanc for his very touching foreword. Particular thanks are also due to my wonderful personal assistant Anna-Louise Naylor Leyland, without whom my life over the last few years would have been much more difficult if not impossible!

List of Recipes

Index

NB: page numbers in italic indicate illustrations